Defending
Israel

Also by Alan M. Dershowitz

Defending Israel

Israel

The Story of My Relationship with
My Most Challenging Client

Alan M. Dershowitz

ALL
POINTS
BOOKS
New York

First published in the United States by All Points Books, an imprint of
St. Martin's Publishing Group.

DEFENDING ISRAEL. Copyright © 2019 by Alan M. Dershowitz. All rights
reserved. Printed in the United States of America. For information, address
St. Martin's Publishing Group, 120 Broadway, New York, NY 10271.

www.allpointsbooks.com

Designed by Steven Seighman

Library of Congress Cataloging-in-Publication Data

Names: Dershowitz, Alan M., author.
Title: Defending Israel : the story of my relationship with my most
challenging client / Alan M. Dershowitz.
Description: First edition. | New York : All Points Books, 2019 |
Includes bibliographical references and index.
Identifiers: LCCN 2019021477 | ISBN 9781250179968 (hardcover) |
ISBN 9781250179975 (ebook)
Subjects: LCSH: Dershowitz, Alan M. | Zionists—United States—
Biography. | Propaganda, Anti-Israeli—United States. | Propaganda,
Zionist—United States. | Israel—Politics and government.
Classification: LCC DS151 .D47 2019 | DDC 320.54095694092—dc23
LC record available at https://lccn.loc.gov/2019021477

Our books may be purchased in bulk for promotional, educational, or business use.
Please contact your local bookseller or the Macmillan Corporate and
Premium Sales Department at 1-800-221-7945, extension 5442, or by email
at MacmillanSpecialMarkets@macmillan.com.

First Edition: September 2019

10 9 8 7 6 5 4 3 2 1

*This book is dedicated to an endangered species:
liberal supporters of Israel—"ken yirbu"*

Contents

Defending Israel

Introduction

The Endless Battle

Anti-Zionism and Anti-Semitism on the Rise

FOR LIFELONG SUPPORTERS of Israel, like me, this is the best of times. The nation-state of the Jewish people has never been stronger—militarily, economically, scientifically, diplomatically.

But Israel's future is at grave risk because of diminishing support from young people—soon to be our leaders—especially on the left.

Anti-Semitism, often disguised as anti-Zionism, is on the rise throughout the world. A recent *New York Times* headline read "Anti-Semitism Is Back, from the Left, Right, and Islamist Extremes. Why?" Its answer, in large part, focused on the Israeli government as "a point of divergence from the different strands of contemporary anti-Semitism."[1]

The sources of this bigotry vary—from newly elected members of Congress to rioters in Charlottesville, Yellow Vests in Paris, feminists in Chicago, gay rights activists in San Francisco, violent Muslim extremists in Sweden, radical university professors, supporters of boycotting Israeli products, academics and artists, and students taken with identity politics and "intersectionality." But its effect is the same: a growing opposition to the legitimacy of Israel as the nation-state of the Jewish people and a diminution of its bipartisan support. For many supporters of Israel, that is the core of "the second great mutation of antisemitism in modern times."[2]

In much of Europe, where anti-Semitism on both the hard left and hard right is increasing, Israel has become a wedge issue, sharply dividing left from right. It is possible, indeed likely, that unless current trends can be changed, this dynamic will cross the Atlantic and infect our body politic, even more virulently than it has today. The refusal of leading Democratic presidential candidates to accept invitations to speak at the American Israel Public Affairs Committee (AIPAC), the leading lobby group for Israel, which followed by several years the absence of several prominent Democratic legislative leaders at Prime Minister Benjamin Netanyahu's speech on Iran before a joint session of Congress, reflects a troubling movement within the Democratic Party away from support for Israel. At the same time, Republican support for Israel, especially among evangelical Christians, has strengthened. Israel is thus becoming a wedge in the United States as well—dividing many Democrats from Republicans and dividing Democrats among themselves.

This change has created new conflicts over party allegiances for many supporters of Israel, especially among liberal Jews who have historically voted for Democrats. They continue to favor the social policies of the Democrats—a woman's right to choose, gay rights, gun control, environmental protection, separation of church and state, a liberal Supreme Court—but they feel discomfort over the movement of some Democrats, especially among the young and radical elements of the party, away from support for Israel. This growing discomfort has not yet resulted in a discernable shift in party affiliation among most Jews—in part because the leader of the Republican Party is the very controversial President Donald Trump—but it is causing deep concern about the future of bipartisan support for Israel.

If the drift away from bipartisan support for Israel is not reversed, it will pose real dangers to Israel's security. Today Israel remains capable of defending itself from all external threats, with or without material support from the United States. But it is impossible to assess the impact on Israel's security in the event that an American government hostile to Israel came to power.

It is a goal of this book to try to influence, in a positive direction, this discernable drift away from bipartisan support for the Middle East's only democracy and America's most reliable ally. It is a daunting task, but a crucial one to help secure Israel's future.

I begin this task by telling the great adventure story of Israel's establishment—really, re-establishment—as the nation-state of the Jewish people, and of my long, sometimes challenging, relationship with this ever-changing democracy.

The nation-state of the Jewish people traces its origins to antiquity, but its modern history begins with a tiny, militarily weak, economically impoverished new state that was populated largely by Holocaust survivors, refugees from Muslim countries and long-time residents of Jewish Palestine. It was beloved throughout the world, except by its Arab neighbors. But now that it has become an economic, scientific and military superpower, it is regarded by many as a pariah. Like the Jewish people themselves throughout the ages, the nation-state of the Jewish people has become the victim of its own success. From the Book of Exodus,[3] to the Megillah of Esther,[4] through the "golden age" of Muslim–Jewish relations, to Weimar Germany, to revolutionary Russia, Jewish self-empowerment and success have resulted in reaction, enmity and sometimes catastrophe.

As Israel grows stronger, we are seeing it treated in many quarters as a colonial, imperialist, hegemonic occupier and bully. David has become Goliath as Israel's military arsenal has developed from "slingshots" (literally weapons contrived from surplus parts) into nuclear weapons and high-tech cyber measures and countermeasures, and its intelligence agency is considered among the most respected and feared in the world. It is as if much of the world loves weak and persecuted Jews but is fearful and jealous of strong and successful Jews who defy some old stereotypes (the Jew as nebbish and victim) while reifying others (the Jews as all-powerful controllers of the world and victors). Israel has become the Jew among nations—the object of disproportionate attention, excessive criticism and sometimes excessive praise. More is expected of the Jewish nation, just as more has always been expected of the Jewish people. British rabbi Lionel Blue once quipped that "Jews are just like everyone else, only more so."[5] Bishop Desmond Tutu put it more seriously and critically: "Whether Jews like it or not, they are a peculiar people. They can't hope to be judged by the same standards which are used for other people."[6] The same can be said of the nation of the Jewish people, which is subjected to a discriminatory double standard of judgment by Tutu and so many others.

Israel today is the most condemned nation in world. It is also more criticized now than ever before in its history. Some of this criticism is warranted, and it even comes from Israelis and American Jews who love Israel. I myself have taken issue with some of Israel's policies.[7] But the degree of condemnation and demonization is all out of proportion to what is warranted. Strong as it has become, Israel faces continuing threats to its security and very existence—from Iran, which has vowed its destruction; to Hezbollah, which has tens of thousands of sophisticated rockets aimed at its cities; to Hamas, which fires primitive rockets and firebombs across the border; to the United Nations, which condemns Israel more than all the other nations of the world combined; to campuses, which target only Israel with BDS (boycott, divestment and sanctions) and false claims of "apartheid" and even "genocide." No country faced with comparable threats can boast a better record of human rights, a higher regard for the rule of law or greater efforts to reduce civilian casualties.[8] Nor has any country in history contributed so much to humankind—medically, scientifically, environmentally, academically, culturally—in so short a time as has Israel in its relatively brief existence as an independent state. Yet, it is tiny Israel—with a land mass the size of New Jersey and a population similar to that of Papua, New Guinea—that is the focus of most of the world's protests.

Throughout my life, I have been defending Israel against demonization, delegitimization and double standards. In the beginning, it was against some of my Orthodox elementary school rabbis who did not believe in the religious justification for a Jewish state until the Messiah arrived, and certainly not in the legitimacy of the secular socialist state that David Ben-Gurion declared in 1948. In Zionist summer camp, it was against hard-left zealots like Noam Chomsky, who believed in a single secular state. Later in high school, it was against right-wing extremists, such as Meir Kahane, who believed that the Jewish state must encompass all of biblical Israel.

After the 1967 war, it was against the likes of Daniel Berrigan, who described Israel as a racist criminal entity. Then it was against right-wingers who supported annexing the entire West Bank and opposed the two-state solution. After that, it was against Jimmy Carter, who characterized Israel's control over the West Bank as "apartheid."[9] Then it was against Cornel West, who has accused Israel of being a colonialist state.[10] Now it is against the boycott, divestments and sanctions (BDS) tactic, the intersectionality movement[11] and efforts by hard-left professors and students to demonize and isolate Israel and treat it the way apartheid South Africa was treated.[12]

Although I have no actual lawyer/client relationship with Israel, I have been called "Israel's single most visible defender" and "the Jewish state's lead attorney in the court of public opinion."[13] I take this role seriously, but because I have no formal legal relationship with Israel, I am free to criticize its policies when I disagree with them. Notwithstanding such occasional criticism, I still defend Israel's right to be wrong about specific issues, as all democracies have that right, without delegitimizing it as the nation-state of the Jewish people. Israel is the only country whose very existence is challenged because of disagreements with particular policies it pursues.

In this book, I tell the story of my lifelong relationship with my self-appointed "client." To say that defending Israel in the court of public opinion has become increasingly challenging is to understate the reality. I try to explain—without in any way justifying—this change.

Because the story of my own passionate, if sometimes stormy, relationship with Israel also began in 1948, and because it is reactive to Israel's story, I combine both in this narrative.

The intensity of my own role in defending Israel has varied inversely with Israel's popularity around the world, and especially on university campuses, where I have spent nearly all of my life—more than 60 years. As disproportionate and undeserved demonization of Israel has increased exponentially, so too have my time and efforts—to the point that I now devote a majority of my professional priorities to defending Israel and its supporters. This will continue as long as Israel is unjustly attacked and I have the energy to respond to false accusations with credible defenses. In this book, I defend Israel, though not all of its policies, by truthfully telling its story: its successes, its failures, its virtues, its vices. I have lived by the principle that the best response to falsehood is truth, not censorship. I apply that principle to my defense of Israel in every forum in which it is unjustly attacked. I also tell my story: my defenses; the attacks against me; my changing views and tactics. Our stories are closely related.

The story of Israel can be told in numerous ways. It can be seen through the eyes of its pioneers, chalutzim, some of whom were my relatives, who left Europe in the late nineteenth and early twentieth centuries and made aliya to the promised land; through the eyes of European Jews who escaped or survived the Holocaust and found a new home in Israel; through the eyes of Sephardic Jews who were forced to leave Muslim countries in which their ancestors had lived for millennia; through the eyes of young Israelis who defend their country against wars and terrorism, often at the cost of their lives and limbs—as was the case with two of my cousins, one of whom was killed and the other left as a paraplegic; through the eyes of Israel's prime ministers, most of whom I have known, some more intimately than others; through the eyes of American presidents, several of whom have sought my advice over the years with regard to the Middle East; through the eyes of Israel's raucous political system, its frenzied media competition and its harsh ideological divisions, as manifested by two elections in close proximity in 2019. It can also be seen through the eyes of its current Arab population, many of whose relatives and friends were displaced—others of whom were left on their own—by the numerous wars waged against the Jewish population; through the eyes of Palestinian political and religious leaders, several of whom I have met over the years; through the eyes of its most virulent critics, many of whom I have debated and confronted.

I myself have seen Israel, through my own eyes as an American liberal Zionist, who was brought up as a modern Orthodox Jew and came of age as a more secular, but still traditional, agnostic who questions everything and everyone, even himself.

In this book, I narrate the challenging relationship between the nation-state of the Jewish people and myself, one of its most zealous, if sometimes critical, defenders. It is not a straightforward narrative, because the history of modern Israel is anything but straightforward, but I will try my best to present a coherent and objective account, as seen through my own eyes. I begin with my memories of the establishment of Israel as the nation-state of the Jewish people when I was a 10-year-old child in Brooklyn.

1

From Palestine to Israel

My Earliest Memories of Zionism

THERE WAS NEVER a time that Israel was not a part of my consciousness. But in 1948, when David Ben-Gurion declared the reestablishment of a nation-state for the Jewish people in Eretz Yisrael (the Ancient land of Israel), it became my passion. I was turning 10, and my parents sent me to a Hebrew-speaking Zionist summer camp, called Camp Massad, in the Pocono Mountains of Pennsylvania, where we followed, with deep concern and interest, the news of the War of Independence in which all the surrounding Arab nations attacked the new state. That was more than 70 years ago, and my passion—and concern—has never abated, though the nature and degree of my involvement have changed dramatically over these many decades.

I grew up in a religious Zionist home, attended religious Zionist schools and summer camps, sang Zionist songs, and recited Zionist prayers. Every home in our modern Orthodox Jewish Brooklyn neighborhood of Boro Park had a JNF (Jewish National Fund) "pushka" (charity box) with a map of Jewish Palestine on its blue-and-white metal surface. In the early years, before Israel became a nation, the charity was for purchasing and developing land for Jewish communities in what was to become Israel.[1] (I even have a collection of JNF boxes going back well before the establishment of the state. They show the increasing purchases of land over time.) Much of the land was bought from distant land speculators in Syria and other locations and from local Arab landowners seeking to profit from the high prices offered by the JNF.[2]

David Ben-Gurion, then the head of the Jewish Agency (the prestate "government"), was sensitive with regard to maintaining good relations with local Arabs.[3]

In elementary school—Yeshiva Etz Chaim (Tree of Life)—we sang "Hatikvah," which was the Zionist anthem of hope, before it became Israel's national anthem. I can still remember the original words, "L'shuv L'Eretz Avoseinu" (to return to the land of our fathers), which we sang until Israel declared statehood. These words of longing and hope were then changed to words of aspiration and determination: "Li' Yot am chofshi b'artzeinu" (to be a free nation in our land).

The lyric was different but the music was the same.

Even our social athletic clubs (they were called SACs), in which we played street games like stickball, punch ball, stoop ball and ringalevio, had Zionist names. Mine was the Palmach, which was the forward strike force of the Haganah, which became the Israel Defense Forces (IDF) after the establishment of Israel. Our club "song" was the battle hymn of the Palmach, which we sang in Hebrew: "rishonim Tamid anachnu Tamid, anu anu Hapalmach" ("We are always the first; we are the Palmach"). (Years later, at a charity event in Los Angeles, I learned that Vidal Sassoon had been a Palmach fighter, and so we regaled the crowed with an off-tune duet of the battle hymn.) The very idea of a Jewish army capable of protecting Jews was thrilling to young Jews in a neighborhood that included many Holocaust survivors who had lacked any protection.

Several months before Israel's establishment, we had watched the vote of the United Nations to partition British Mandatory Palestine into two states for two people: one for the Jews, one for the Arabs. The Jews immediately, if reluctantly, accepted the partition. The Arabs rejected it. (I own an original edition of the newspaper *Haaretz* that contains a report on the partition as the crucial step to statehood, as well as an original of the newspaper *Hamashkif* announcing the establishment of the state.) There was dancing in the streets. A school assembly celebrated the prelude to statehood by dancing the hora and offering prayers. Among the people I knew, there was no dissent or even doubt.[4] We were all overjoyed.

But joy soon turned to concern, fear and distress when the surrounding armies attacked Israel immediately upon its establishment. Distress turned to tragedy when the son of one of my mother's friends was killed. Moshe Perlstein had been studying at Hebrew University under the G.I. Bill of Rights when the fighting broke out, and he volunteered to join the Haganah. His death brought the war to our neighborhood. Our group of 10-year-old Zionists all imagined ourselves volunteering to fight for Israel's survival when we came of age. Our school raised money to buy a jeep that was shipped to Israel. Before being sent abroad, it was proudly displayed in the driveway of our school.

I attended Camp Massad during the summer of 1948, while the War of Independence was raging (we played sports there using Hebrew words; a "strike" was a "shkia"—literally, a mistake). The Zionists had resurrected the Hebrew language of the Bible and prayer into a vibrant, modern language suitable to the new nation. We were eager to learn Israeli Hebrew, and we did at Camp Massad. Our bunks and divisions were named after areas of Israel (Degania, Emek, Galil). All the counselors were fervent Zionists, even our division head, a 20-year-old student named Noam Chomsky, who was active in Hashomer Hatzair, the "guardians of the young," a left-wing Zionist group. Though Chomsky supported, in theory, a binational secular state, he was not opposed in practice to the state declared by Ben-Gurion. Every day during mealtimes, we heard reports in Hebrew of the progress of the war, and several Israeli counselors left camp to return home to defend their newly born country.

After the long, bitter war, where Israel prevailed, an armistice was declared under which Israel gained additional territory.[5] But victory came with a heavy price. The new nation lost 1 percent of its population, including many civilians who were murdered in cold blood.[6] Among the dead were young men and women who had survived the Holocaust, some volunteers from Europe and America—including Colonel Mickey Marcus, a World War II hero, who became Israel's first modern general and was the subject of the film *Cast a Giant Shadow* starring Kirk Douglas—and many chalutzim.

My uncle Albert (whose nickname was "Itchie"), my father's second youngest brother, stowed away on a ship to Israel in order to help defend the new nation. (He paid the fare several years later when he could afford to.) He eventually became an ultra-Orthodox head of a yeshiva in Bnei Brak and a religious opponent of political Zionism, though he continued to love the people of Israel. His youngest brother, Zecharia, a doctor of psychology, was to follow him several years later, changing his name from the Europeanized Dershowitz (originally Derschovitz) to the Hebraized Dor Shav (the generation that returned). At this writing, he is still living in Jerusalem and remains active in Israeli and Jewish causes.

Another one of my father's brothers had been a captain in the U.S. Army, and he proudly collected guns from his military colleagues to send to Israel. I remember my uncle showing me a Luger confiscated from a German POW that would now be used to protect Jews rather than kill them.

Both my father's and my mother's families had strong connections to Israel. In the early 1930s, my mother's father, Naftuli Ringel, traveled to Palestine to see if he could make a living and bring his family there. He bought a small piece of land on which he hoped to build a home near what is now Ben Gurion Airport. He returned to Brooklyn several months later, brokenhearted, with the realization that he could not make aliya with his wife and six children. He brought back several small sacks of earth from Rachel's Tomb, which he wanted to be buried with. I have one of these sacks in my home as a remembrance of my grandfather's visit to Eretz Yisrael before it was the State of Israel. (When I told this story to a leading political figure in Israel, he generously replied, "If your grandfather had made aliya, you would probably have my job today.")

My father's father was active in rescuing Jews from the Holocaust, some of whom settled in Israel. He obtained false affidavits from neighbors, promising "jobs"—including rabbis, cantors and other religious functionary positions—to unqualified people for nonexistent synagogues. The last such refugee to leave boarded the ship shortly before Hitler invaded Poland. One relative was trapped and couldn't leave, so my grandfather sent my unmarried uncle with his American passport to find her, "marry" her and bring her to safety in America. He did, and then he fell in love with her on the boat and they married in a real wedding upon their arrival in New York. Many of these refugees became prominent Americans, including one who served as chairman of the Columbia University Engineering Department; another became a rabbi in a large Los Angeles synagogue. Hence my natural sympathy for opening our gates to refugees—even illegal ones in extreme situations. (One of my favorite comic shticks was by the Russian-Jewish comedian Yakov Smirnoff, who would stand by the Statue of Liberty thanking her for rescuing him and his family from Soviet tyranny. Then, as he leaves, he turns to Ms. Liberty and shouts, "Now please keep the rest of those damn immigrants out!")

My parents and grandparents belonged to organizations that supported Israel—such as Mizrachi and Hadassah—and they contributed to Israeli charities despite their limited means. Everyone I knew did. My grandmother Ringel had a JNF pushka next to the party-line telephone; everyone who made a call was required to deposit a nickel into it for tzedakah (charity) for the poor Jews of Eretz Yisrael.

I grew up with an uncomplicated love of Israel, and support for its success, as a given. No one questioned it. No one had any doubts or qualms about the righteousness of our cause. To us, Israel was always in the right, and its Arab enemies were always in the wrong. The

Arab war against the Jews of Palestine and then Israel was a continuation of the Nazi war against the Jews of Europe. In fact, several notorious Nazi war criminals had received asylum in Egypt and other Arab countries and were helping them develop weapons systems with which to destroy Israel.

We all believed that if there had been an Israel in the 1930s and early 1940s, millions of Jews—who were trapped in Europe by Britain's immoral policy of strictly limiting Jewish immigration into its mandate and America's bigoted policies that denied visas to Jews seeking refuge from the Holocaust—could have been saved from the Holocaust.

David Ben-Gurion, who personified the new Israel, was the hero (although some, particularly the rabbis, didn't approve of his secularism and socialism). The Arab leaders—from Haj Amin al-Husseini to Gamal Abdel Nasser—were the villains. They were easy to hate because of their association with Nazism, communism, anti-Semitism and other despised ideologies.

They were calling for genocide against the Jewish population of Israel: "Drive the Jews into the sea." The issues were black and white: good versus evil, democracy pitted against tyranny, religious tolerance instead of intolerance, life versus death. The Bible commands, "I have set before you life and death . . . therefore choose life" (Deuteronomy 30:19, KJV). We chose life. It was an easy choice, especially in the shadow of the six million deaths during the Holocaust.

It was also easy to choose Israel because of who else was supporting the new nation-state of the Jewish people—and who was opposing it. Israel was a liberal cause, a leftist cause, a progressive cause, a Democratic cause, a labor union cause, a woman's cause, an academic cause, an African American cause—a cause that all good people, as we defined good, were supporting. Pete Seeger included Israeli folk songs in his popular repertory of working-class music. Left-wing Hollywood types raised funds for the embattled nation. Frank Sinatra helped to smuggle arms to the newly emerging state. Liberal college students spent their summer vacations volunteering in kibbutzim. Later, Martin Luther King and Robert Kennedy would champion Israel.

No one accused Israel of being a "colonialist" project, as some absurdly do today. Whose "colony" could it be? Certainly not that of the British, against whom they had fought for independence, or the Poles, Ukrainians or Russians, whose pogroms they had escaped from. Moreover, unlike the majority populations of America, New Zealand and Australia, Jews were among the aboriginal people of what became Israel. They were returning to their ancient homeland from which they had been forcibly exiled, not colonizing new lands in which they had no roots. The Jews of Palestine and then Israel were the vanguards of the national liberation movement of the Jewish people—a bulwark against colonialism, a liberal oasis amid a reactionary desert.[7] The Israelis were the heroes. Those who would destroy the new state were the villains.

No one questioned Israel's legitimacy. Its birth certificate was based on legal rules and documents: The Balfour Declaration of 1917, the San Remo Resolution of 1920, the League of Nations' Mandate for Palestine of 1922, the Anglo-American Treaty of 1924, and the UN Partition Plan of 1947. Israel was created by the pen, though it had to defend itself by the sword. This was no accident, since most of Israel's founders—Theodor Herzl, David Ben-Gurion, Menachem Begin, Ze'ev Jabotinsky and Yitzhak Shamir—had been trained as lawyers.

Nor did anyone—even Israel's most strident enemies—ever characterize the new nation with words such as "genocidal" or "apartheid," or hold it guilty of "ethnic cleansing" or "colonialism." Genocide is what happened *to* the Jews, not what the Jews had done to others. Apartheid was the denial of all rights to the black population of South Africa, not the equal rights guaranteed to Arab citizens of Israel. Ethnic cleansing was what the Soviet Union did to Konigsberg or the Allies did in Sudetenland, not the complex population exchange that occurred when Jewish residents of Muslim countries were forced to leave places they had lived for thousands of years, and when some Arab residents of the new Israel fled during the Arab-initiated fighting and were not allowed to return. Only bad people engaged in genocide, apartheid and ethnic cleansing, and Israelis were good people.

My family was both liberal and Zionist. Our political heroes were FDR, Harry Truman, Adlai Stevenson, Hubert Humphrey, Robert Wagner, Jacob Javits and Fiorello La Guardia. They were also modern Orthodox Jews who saw no conflict between their religious orthodoxy and their political liberalism, or between their Zionism and their progressive values.

We were centrist liberals who hated Joseph McCarthy and Roy Cohn, but we also despised Stalin and the American Communist Party. No "red diaper babies" in our family. We were taught that Jews were often caught between the black and the red—the black of fascism and the red of communism. We suffered under extremism and thrived under centrist liberalism, hence our centrist liberalism. We supported desegregation, opposed capital punishment, and contributed to the ACLU and NAACP, as well as to the Jewish National Fund. We knew that certain colleges, corporations and neighborhoods didn't welcome Jews, blacks, Catholics and other non-WASPs, but we also understood that these forms of "polite" bigotry were the last gasp of a dying WASP aristocracy. We were not particularly sensitive to discrimination against gays or women, but neither would we have consciously engaged in overt discrimination against any group.

We generally voted for Democrats, but sometimes we backed liberal Republicans (especially if they were Jewish) like Jacob Javits. We were proud to be called "liberals," the ones who cared about others and about preserving liberties. The Conservatives, on the other hand, were selfish, ungenerous and unconcerned about the rights of others.

We marched for civil rights, against blacklists and against the death penalty. We signed petitions against executing Julius and Ethel Rosenberg, though my parents feared that my name on such petitions would give me a "permanent record" as a communist sympathizer. We had doubts about the Korean War, and when we got a bit older, we opposed the Vietnam War. We saw no contradiction between our opposition to America's unjustified foreign military adventures and Israel's need to defend itself against violent neighbors dedicated to its destruction.

Our heroes all supported the establishment of a nation-state for the Jewish people, especially since the Holocaust (a term we didn't yet know) had seen the murder and relocation of so many European Jews, survivors of which were living in displaced persons camps with no country—until Israel was established—willing to take them in. We applauded the law of return by which Israel opened its doors to every Jew in need of asylum. We watched with pride as David Ben-Gurion, Chaim Weitzmann and later Abba Eban made the liberal case for a national homeland for the Jews.

Those who opposed the creation of Israel—the Arab and Muslim countries, some American State Department officials, segments of the British establishment, and European neo-Nazis—were perceived, quite correctly, as reactionary and anti-Jewish. The leaders of the new nation-state of the Jewish people were perceived, also correctly, as progressive and heroic. Still, they had to make the case for Israel against those—including the popular George Marshall, who was secretary of state when the United States recognized Israel—who were arguing that the new Western-oriented nation would destabilize the Middle East. The pro-Israel side prevailed in the court of public opinion—at least for the moment.

There were right-wing elements within Israel, but we took no positions on the internal disagreements between the left and right in Israeli politics. The Israeli right—personified by Menachem Begin—was relatively powerless. The Israeli left—personified by David Ben-Gurion—was in power. All Israeli leaders, regardless of their politics, were our heroes. To be sure, there were a few young right-wing zealots who hated Ben-Gurion and adored Begin and his late mentor, Ze'ev Jabotinsky, but they were on the margin. Among them was a young Zionist—a few years my senior—named Meir Kahane, who attended the same high school I did, where we both served on the debating team. We were later to become ideological opponents, though I also defended his right to express his contrarian—some would say anti-Muslim—views. (I had an Israeli cousin who had served in the Irgun with Menachem Begin and was on the Irgun ship *Altalena* when Ben-Gurion's forces opened fire on it. Till the day he died, he referred to Israel's first prime minister as "David F—ing Ben-Gurion.")

There were also some zealots on the left who considered Begin and Jabotinsky to be fascists and who wanted Israel to be closer to the Soviet Union. Among those was Noam Chomsky, who I first met in summer camp. We, too, became ideological opponents, though I defended his right to oppose—sometimes by questionable means—the Vietnam War.

For most of us, who stood near the center, there was no conflict between our domestic political views and our Zionism. Zionism was seen as a liberal program—the national liberation movement of the Jewish people. Some of the other "countries" in the region—such as Jordan, Iraq, Saudi Arabia and the Gulf states—had been artificially constructed by colonial powers, such as France and Great Britain. These colonial powers selected the artificial kings, princes and dictators to rule their colonies. Other countries such as Egypt and Iran were surrogates of the Soviet Union or the United States—pawns in the Cold War. Israel was an independent democracy, struggling for its survival in a hostile geographic location in which Jews had lived for thousands of years. In its modern incarnation, it had been built by hard-working chalutzim, many of whom lived on kibbutzim and moshavim (agricultural collectives). Young men and women from all over the world—Jews and non-Jews—volunteered to work on the collectives to make the deserts bloom. We praised the draining of the swamps and the destruction of habitats where malaria-carrying mosquitoes thrived, unaware that anti-Israel environmentalists would complain decades later that Israel had tampered with "natural wet-lands."

The leading American proponents of the nation-state of the Jewish people—such as Supreme Court justices Louis Brandeis and Felix Frankfurter, Rabbi Stephen S. Wise, Emma Lazarus and Henrietta Szold—were paragons of centrist liberalism. My generation of "religious "Zionists" forgave the secular bent of Israel's leaders. We supported the compromise Ben-Gurion struck with the rabbis, whereby the chief rabbinate assumed control over religious issues, such as marriage, divorce and conversion. (The number of Chassidic and ultra-Orthodox Jews was very small back then, and few expected it to increase so dramatically—and with it the power of the chief rabbinate over all Israelis and even non-Israeli Jews, a development now threatening Israel's democracy and its relationship with diaspora Jews.)

Even the hard left, including many communists, supported Zionism and the establishment of Israel, which they saw as a democratic-socialist island amid a sea of repressive Arab monarchies and tyrannies. Both the United States and the Soviet Union immediately recognized Israel, and Czechoslovakia (then under the control of the Soviet Union) provided arms for the Israeli army. The screenplay for the popular film *Exodus*—based on the equally popular book by Leon Uris—was written by Dalton Trumbo, a writer who had been blacklisted for his alleged membership in the Communist Party. It glorified the establishment of Israel and demonized Israel's Arab enemies.

In the post–World War II period, many new nations emerged from colonialism, basing themselves on national liberation movements. Transfers of populations predicated on ethnicity and religion were accepted as a reasonable price to be paid for stability and homogeneity.[8] For example, the partition of India and Pakistan following the end of Great Britain's colonial rule over a united India resulted in a massive transfer of populations and the creation of millions of refugees.[9]

Israel, established as the national liberation movement of the Jewish people, was accepted by the left, by anticolonialists and by most of the world.[10]

Israel's American opponents were reactionary, often anti-Semitic State Department bureaucrats (some of whom were the same ones who stopped Jews from entering the United States during the Holocaust), oil barons, political isolationists and some "establishment" German Jews. The "good guys" supported Israel; the "bad guys" opposed it. There was no cognitive dissonance between, or discomfort over, our liberal American values and our Jewish nationalistic aspirations.

Electoral choices were easy for liberal Zionists: vote for liberal Democrats like Adlai Stevenson who supported Israel, and vote against Republicans like Dwight Eisenhower who did not. In general, the left and the Democratic Party were more supportive of Israel than the right and the Republicans.

Oh, how things have changed over the past half century! Today, Israel's most fervent enemies are on the hard left, including many Jews. For them "Zionism" is a dirty word, often equated with "fascism," "colonialism," "imperialism," "apartheid," "genocide," even "Nazism." Many on the "soft left"—the kind of centrist liberals with whom I grew up—now also have a disdain for Israel. They cloak that general disdain with claims of opposition to specific Israeli policies or politicians, but polls show that their negative attitude toward the nation-state of the Jewish people often transcends specific policies or particular leaders.[11] This is especially true of younger liberals who were not alive when Israel struggled for its survival in the 1940s, 1950s, 1960s and the early part of the 1970s. It is now Conservatives and Republicans—including many on the Christian right—who are Israel's most fervent supporters. Some on the hard right—such as Pat Buchanan, Richard Spencer and David Duke—are as anti-Zionist as they are anti-Semitic, but they represent a far smaller proportion of the right than the growing proportion of anti-Israel extremists of the left. This shift does create cognitive dissonance for many liberal

Zionists, who support the Democratic Party's domestic agenda but tend to agree more with Republican policies toward Israel.

I will tell the story of this change in the chapters to come, as well as how it impacted my advocacy for Israel. It is sufficient here to note the contrast between my coming of age during a period of near universal support for Israel, and the coming of age of my grandchildren at a more challenging time.

Part of the reason why attitudes toward Israel have changed is the word "Palestine." When I was growing up, the "Palestine" was synonymous with the "Eretz Yisrael." The Jews who lived there were called Palestinian Jews. Immanuel Kant referred to European Jews as "Palestinians living among us."[12] The Jewish newspaper published in Jerusalem was called the *Palestine Post* (now the *Jerusalem Post*). The support group for the Hebrew University was called Palestine Friends of the Hebrew University. When Frank Sinatra performed a concert in the Hollywood Bowl in support of a Jewish state, it was called the "Action for Palestine" rally. I have an old record of "Palestinian Folk Songs" from before the establishment of Israel. They are of course Zionist songs about *Eretz Yisrael*. The Jewish National Fund raised money for Palestine. I own an old JNF charity box that says, "Made in Eretz-Israel (Palestine)." I also own an even older German tzedakah box for "Juden in Palestina." We contributed to the Jews of Palestine. Palestine was a positive name—a Jewish name—among American Zionists.

The area that was named Palestina by the Romans and was, before 1948, the British Mandatory territory of Palestine, belonged as much to its Jewish population as to its Arab one. To Jews, it was always Eretz Yisrael (the land of Israel) or Tziyon (Zion). No one, least of all the Arabs who lived in Palestine, called the local Arab population "Palestinians." Palestine was a geographic concept, not an ethnic or nationalistic one. Indeed, it was a somewhat artificial geographic area, whose boundaries were determined as much by political as by topographic considerations. The ethnic makeup of the geographic areas that came to be known as Palestine consisted of Arabs—both Muslim and Christian—and Jews, along with some Armenians, Druze, Baha'i, German colonists and assorted others. The Arab residents of this area were no more "Palestinian" than were the Jewish residents who lived in Eretz Yisrael. My friend Tzvi Groner's father—who was born in Hebron on the West Bank—referred to himself as "Palestinian" and had a Jordanian passport. Of course, he and all other Jewish Palestinians—some of whose ancestors had lived in Hebron and other Jewish areas of Yehuda and Shomron for generations—were ethnically cleansed from the Jordanian West Bank as soon as Israel became a state.

When the leader of the local Arabs, the Grand Mufti of Jerusalem Haj Amin al-Husseini, testified before the Peel Commission in 1937, he complained about the "detachment of Palestine from the body of other Arab territories," suggesting that the Arabs who lived in Palestine had no distinct national or ethnic character—they were part of the great Arab nation. He didn't want a separate Palestinian state for the Arabs. He simply did not want there to be a state or homeland for Jews anywhere in the region.[13]

Recall, as well, that what is now the nation of Jordan was also part of the original British mandate over what was called Palestine. It was cut out of the mandate in 1920[14] and called Trans-Jordan. It comprises a majority of the original Palestine Mandate and its population was composed largely of Palestinian Arabs. Jordan was truly a "colonial" project, as were the artificial nations of Iraq, Syria, Saudi Arabia and the Gulf states, which were created in the aftermath of the First World War by colonial cartographers sitting in Europe with drafting pens.

Jordan's population still consists of a majority of Palestinian Arabs who have been ruled by the Hashemite clan, a ruling royal family originally from Saudi Arabia.[15]

Many now call themselves Palestinians. The Jews of what is now Israel also referred to themselves as Palestinians—Palestinian Jews who lived in Eretz Yisrael to be sure, in contrast to Palestinian Arabs or just Arabs.

The point is that the local Arabs have now—beginning in the mid-1960s—coopted the word "Palestinian," so as to suggest that *they* are the only rightful residents of Palestine and that the Jewish residents of what is now Israel and has always been Eretz Yisrael are interlopers—or colonialists, imperialists or conquerors. Most ironically, the Jews of what was part of Palestine and is now Israel are sometimes even called "crusaders," out of historical ignorance of the tragic reality that Jews were among those brutally murdered by Christian crusaders in the eleventh and twelfth centuries.[16]

When the United Nations voted to partition Palestine into "independent Arab and Jewish states"—two states for two peoples—the name Israel was never mentioned, nor was the word "Palestinians."[17] Each group could choose to name its state as it pleased. Had the new nation-state of the Jewish people called itself "Jewish Palestine," instead of Israel, the optics would be quite different. But now, the newly named Palestinians—who used to be called Palestinian Arabs, or just Arabs—have laid claim to the name "Palestinian," and to the sympathy that comes with it, for having been displaced from their homeland, Palestine, by the interloping Jews.

The reality is that both Jews and Arabs lived in Roman-named Palestine—Eretz Yisrael—when the United Nations divided it into two areas in order to facilitate the establishment of two states for two peoples: the Jews of Palestine and the Arabs of Palestine. The area allocated to the Jewish state contained a majority of Jews, and there were hundreds of thousands of additional Jews waiting in displaced person camps in Europe and detention centers on Cyprus to be allowed to join family members the moment Israel declared statehood and opened its gates to Jewish survivors. There were also Jews who had lived—some for generations—in the part of mandatory Palestine that was allocated by the United Nations to become an Arab state. These Jews were forced to leave their homes and move to the Jewish state, while Arab residents of the Jewish area were welcome to remain—until Israel was attacked from both within and without. If the Arab states had not attempted to destroy the nation-state of the Jewish people at its birth, the Arab residents of Israel would have been allowed to remain in their homes, where many did remain. Indeed, today there are more Arab citizens of Israel than the total population of Arabs who lived in Palestine-Israel at the time of the partition.[18] So much for ethnic cleansing.

To this day, the leaders of the Palestinian authority refuse to recognize the concept of two states for two peoples, both of whom are indigenous to Palestine. They adamantly refuse to recognize Israel as the nation-state of one of these people: namely, the Jewish people. I know because I have put this question—Will you recognize Israel as the nation-state of the Jewish people?—personally to Mohammad Abbas. He has said no. As we will see, this refusal lies at the core of the ongoing conflict.

The anti-Israel Arab argument is as simple as it is simplistic and ahistorical: we are *the* Palestinians; Palestine is a geographic entity that extends from the (Jordan) river to the (Mediterranean) sea; the Palestinian Arab people rightfully own *all* of Palestine; therefore, there is no room for a Jewish State in any of historic and geographic Palestine. The fallacy is clear, if one substitutes history for labels: the geographic area was Eretz Yisrael before the Romans renamed it Palestina; it has always been populated by both Jews and Arabs who can both lay claim to being called Palestinians; it was only after the United Nations recommended a partition of Palestine into two states for two peoples that local Arab leaders began calling their people Palestinians; this change of labels did not change history or morality; it did not suddenly entitle the local population to *all* of Palestine, in violation of the United Nations Partition Plan, just because they now call themselves *The* Palestinians. The Jewish residents of Palestine—many of whom can trace their roots in the area further back in time than local Arabs—are as Palestinian as the Arab residents are. The geographic area rightfully belongs to both peoples; hence the case for the two-state solution, based on the United Nations partition of Palestine—Eretz Yisrael—into two states for two peoples.[19]

Had the Arab residents of Palestine—and their leaders—accepted the UN proposal of two states for two peoples, today's Palestinians would have a much larger state than any they can realistically hope to get. There would be no refugee problem, no occupation, no Israeli settlements and no continuous warfare. Tens of thousands of lives would have been saved, terrorism would not have become a primary tactic of asymmetrical warfare, and the economic situation of Palestinian Arabs would be far better than it currently is. To be sure, there might still have been conflicts between the Jewish and Arab states, but these conflicts would not have been over whether there should be a state of Israel and a state of Palestine. The entire fault for these continuing problems lies squarely at the feet of the Palestinian leadership, which wanted not to have a Jewish state at all more than they wanted a state of their own. Many moderate Palestinians and academics today recognize this reality and blame their past leaders for refusing to accept the UN partition.[20]

Even after the Palestinian Arabs—and other Arab countries—rejected the UN proposal and waged war against Israel, there was still an opportunity for the Palestinian Arabs to have a state of their own. The war of 1948 ended with an armistice and agreed-upon boundaries. These boundaries gave the Palestinian Arabs control over the entire West Bank and the Gaza Strip (now known as the pre-1967 armistice lines). Nothing, least of all Israel, would have stopped the Palestinians from declaring statehood in their territory. But they did not, and the Jordanian government occupied the West Bank, while the Egyptian government occupied the Gaza Strip. It was these governments, not the Israeli government, that prevented the Palestinian Arabs from establishing a Palestinian state in these large areas.

Nor were these occupations benign. During this period, many Palestinians left the occupied West Bank and Gaza Strip and became part of the "Palestinian diaspora." They were subjected to mistreat-ment and a double standard in many Arab countries. But the interna-tional community didn't care that Arabs were occupying the lands of other Arabs and denying them basic liberties. There were no campus demonstrations, no boycotts, no UN resolutions. These began only after Jews and their nation-state took over the preexisting occupation in a defensive war. The focus of these protests was not on *how* the Palestinians were being mistreated but on *who* was mistreating them.

The Palestinian Arabs were left in a terrible situation, not so much as a result of Israeli actions but largely because of actions and inactions by their own leaders and the leaders of other Arab countries. They could have been integrated into the populations of the West Bank and Gaza instead of being corralled into refugee camps as a way to keep hatred festering.

Many leading Palestinian intellectuals—such as Sari Nusseibeh—have criticized the Palestinian Arab leaders who rejected statehood for the Arabs of Palestine just because they didn't want statehood for the Jews of Palestine.[21] As Abba Eban once put it, "The Arabs never miss an opportunity to miss an opportunity." This quip, made in 1973, proved prescient, as Palestinian leaders missed opportunities for state-hood in 2000–2001 and 2008, as we will see in subsequent chapters.

But let's return to my youth, when Israel was first established. Back then, there were no subtle issues with regard to the precise terms of Palestinian or Arab recognition of Israel. The Arab position was clear from the outset. As all the Arab nations unambiguously put it in 1967, "No recognition, no negotiation, no peace." That was the grand mufti's position in 1937 as well—before he became a col-laborator with Hitler and an advocate of a different "final solution" to the "Jewish problem." The goal of the Arab leaders was the mili-tary destruction of Israel by Arab armies and/or terrorists. The Israeli position was clear as well: defend itself bravely against Hitler's suc-cessors. We were not aware of Israel's imperfections or questionable military actions. These only became public years later, when Israel's

"New Historians" took a hard look at what Israel had done to win its War of Independence.[22]

On the basis of what we knew back then, it was easy to choose sides in this conflict between good and evil. All good people chose the side of Israel.

It's fair to say that in 1948, we took Israel's side for granted. Israel had enemies, but they were external. We worried about Israel's survival—militarily and economically. But we didn't worry about defending Israel against delegitimization or demonization by political or ideological enemies. We did not obsess over Israel. It was in our consciousness, but as youngsters coming of age in postwar Brooklyn, we were more concerned with the fate of our beloved Dodgers (who regularly lost to the hated Yankees), with the success of our high school basketball teams (I was a substitute on mine, and once guarded Ralph Lipschitz—later Ralph Lauren—in Madison Square Garden) and with the girls who wouldn't go out with us unless we told them we were planning to become doctors (or at least dentists).

We were ordinary lower-middle-class kids, looking forward to doing better than our hardworking parents and immigrant grandparents. Our Zionism was an uncontroversial part of our psychic and ideological makeup. Life was easy. Conflicts were rare, and what few there were didn't involve Israel.

In subsequent chapters, I tell the story of how all this changed over the next 70 years, as much of the world (especially many on the left and in academia, of which I was a part) turned against Israel and uncritically adopted as a litmus test for progressivism the Palestinian cause—or more precisely the anti-Israel cause because no one seemed to care about the Palestinians when they were denied statehood and oppressed by non-Israelis, namely Jordan and Egypt. This development poses an existential, if not immediate, threat to Israel. It is not immediate because those at the forefront of this change are still a minority of our nation as a whole, but they may represent the future of the Democratic Party and thus challenge the long tradition for bipartisan support for Israel. American support for Israel, regardless of which party is in power, is essential to the continuous success of the nation-state of the Jewish people.

The challenge to bipartisan support for Israel has been gradual, with some dramatic moments, such as the Six-Day War, the Yom Kippur War, the rescue at Entebbe, the election of Menachem Begin, the Camp David Accords with Egypt, the destruction of Iraq's nuclear reactor, Israel's invasion of Lebanon, the Palestinian intifadas, the rejected peace offers by Israel, the boycott tactic against Israel, the election of Benjamin Netanyahu, President Barack Obama's Iran Deal, and President Donald Trump's recognition of Jerusalem as Israel's capital and the Golan Heights as Israeli sovereign territory. These events had a considerable impact on attitudes toward Israel, and on the nature of my defense of that ever-embattled country.

2

Israel's Quiet Period— and Mine

THE NEARLY TWO decades between Israel's War of Independence and its next war of survival in June 1967 were relatively quiet. The new nation was busy absorbing Jewish immigrants from the displaced person camps of Europe and from Muslim nations that were making it impossible for their Jewish residents—many of whom could trace their ancestry in these areas back thousands of years—to remain in the lands of their birth.[1] The Jewish refugees were part of what amounted to an exchange of populations, not so different from the one that occurred when Pakistan separated from India and millions of Indian Muslims were relocated to Pakistan while millions of Hindus and Sikhs were forced to leave Pakistan and move to India.[2] There were other massive population exchanges following World War II in addition to the one in the Middle East.[3] Approximately three-quarters of a million Jews left Muslim countries—many without a choice—and a roughly equal number of Arabs left Israel, some voluntarily, others by force. The Palestinians call the events that led to this transfer the "nakba," or catastrophe, but it was largely a self-inflicted wound, resulting from the decision to wage war against the new nation-state of the Jewish people. Had the leaders of the Arabs in Palestine accepted the UN partition, there would have been no refugee problem, as some Palestinian leaders have recently acknowledged.[4]

The European and Sephardic refugees came to Israel with few material possessions. The survivors of the Holocaust had lost everything, in terms of both family and fortune. The Sephardic refugees from Muslim countries were forced to leave their fortunes—and there were some who left considerable wealth behind—to the nations from which they were being evicted.

Despite the fact that these immigrants were all Jews, and therefore entitled to become Israeli citizens under the Law of Return, they had little in common. They spoke different languages, followed somewhat different religious rituals, and had enormous disparity in educational, cultural and economic backgrounds. They came from nearly every country in Europe and the Middle East, ranging from Germany to Yemen, Russia to Iraq, Romania to Egypt, France to Turkey, Lithuania to Morocco, Hungary to Tunisia, and Poland to Algeria.

They all had to learn Hebrew, a language that had been revived by early Europeans who had made aliya in the late nineteenth century and who turned it from an ancient language of prayer and scripture into a vibrant modern language of day-to-day conversation and contemporary literature.[5] The Sephardic Jews of Palestine, who had lived in Jerusalem, Safed and other historically Jewish cities, already spoke Hebrew, but most of the other olim did not. They also had to learn how to make a living and grow the struggling agriculture-based local economy—few of these refugees had any experience in agriculture—into a gross national product that supported a population that had more than tripled in the years between the establishment of Israel and the Six-Day War.

The Law of Return[6]—one of the first laws enacted by the Knesset, Israel's parliament—was a response to the tragic reality that millions of Jews could have been saved if the nations of the world had opened their doors to Jews seeking to escape Hitler. But even the United States, Canada and other liberal democracies that had been founded by immigrants shut their doors and ports. Recall the tragic case of the *St. Louis*, the ship filled with refugees from Nazi Germany seeking asylum, which was turned away from every port in the Western

Hemisphere. The ship and its passengers were forced to return to Germany, where many of the asylum-seekers were eventually murdered. A prominent public figure—Lavra Delano Houghteling, a cousin of President Roosevelt—reflected the views of many American bigots when she opposed the admission of Jewish children, saying: "20,000 charming children would all too soon grow into 20,000 ugly adults." The Canadian minister of absorption said, in reference to Jewish immigration, that even "none is too many."[7] Under the Law of Return, there would always be one country that would never close its doors to Jews in need of rescue and relocation. There was little controversy back then regarding the Law of Return in the immediate aftermath of the Holocaust, but now there are those who see this law as racist. Many other countries, with no history of genocide and exclusion, have similar laws that are not subject to similar criticism. This is yet another example of the double standard applied to the nation-state of the Jewish people.

My family experienced firsthand the poverty of the new nation. We had relatives who were struggling to make a living in Tel Aviv, Jerusalem and B'nai Brak. My father and mother sent money, second-hand clothing and other necessities to our Israeli relatives, on both sides of our family, who were having a hard time. Our synagogue conducted appeals to support the olim chadashim—the new immigrants. And, of course, every Jewish home had at least one pushka for the Jewish National Fund, and for organisations that collected money for poor and sick Israelis, for yeshivot (Jewish religious schools) and for the Haganah (the Israeli Defense Forces, IDF). When my own children were young in the mid-1960s, they went trick-or-treating not for UNICEF (of which we were vaguely suspicious, even back then, because of its association with the biased United Nations) but for Israel. And neighbors—non-Jewish and Jewish alike—willingly gave to Israel because they admired the young new nation.

Indeed the entire world, with the exception of the Arab nations, seemed to admire plucky Israel. Non-Jewish teenagers from Scandinavia, Germany, France and other European countries volunteered to pick oranges on the kibbutzim, which were seen as cutting-edge socialist collectives. Academics studied this new approach to agriculture, family and living. Israel was the "Sara Lee" of nations. (Remember the cake commercial, "Nobody doesn't like Sara Lee.") Even Iran and Turkey, both non-Arab Muslim countries, worked with Israel, militarily and economically.

Israel was seen as weak, both militarily and economically, and it posed no danger to anyone. Sure, it had to defend its civilians against fedayeen terrorist attacks primarily from Jordan and Egypt, as well as from Syria and Lebanon. The fedayeen were Palestinian terrorists who crossed the borders into Israel to attack civilian targets. These attacks were encouraged and often facilitated by the Arab nations surrounding Israel. The fedayeen were later incorporated into the Egyptian and Jordanian armies, and then into the Palestine Liberation Organization (PLO), which was founded as a terrorist organization in 1964, years before Israel captured and occupied the West Bank and Gaza Strip.[8] The expressed goal of the PLO was the destruction of the Jewish state that existed within the pre-1967 armistice lines.[9] Few criticized Israel's self-defense tactics, though historians now report that some were quite brutal: Israel occasionally responded to terrorist attacks that targeted Israeli civilians with tit-for-tat reprisals against Jordanian and Egyptian civilian targets.

Israel was never more popular and never less controversial than in the eight years between 1948 and 1956. It was also never weaker and more vulnerable. Its economy was in shambles with rampant inflation. They told a joke back then—which in light of subsequent events isn't funny—that reflects the Israeli situation in the 1950s. There were very long lines at Israeli banks to withdraw money and spend it before inflation made it worthless. At one Tel Aviv bank, the line was so long that a furious customer shouted, "I'm sick of standing on line. I'm going to shoot Ben-Gurion." Two hours later, he came back and stood at the end of the line that had barely moved. The others asked why he had come back to this line, to which he replied: "The line to shoot Ben-Gurion was even longer."

During that period, I remained supportive of Israel. Everyone did. But I didn't have to prioritize my defense of the nation-state of the Jewish people, because no one we knew or cared much about was attacking or criticizing it. To be sure, there were controversies, but they were not about Israel's right to exist or its foreign policies. The controversies were largely domestic: Were the rabbis securing too much power in the increasingly secular nation? Were there downsides to the kibbutz movement? Was Ben-Gurion's utopic model of an agriculture-based economy (similar to the model Jefferson proposed and Hamilton opposed) viable in the second half of the twentieth century? (Israel, under prime ministers Shimon Peres and Benjamin Netanyahu, was to shift its economy from oranges to Apples—and other technological innovations.) Was there too much sexual freedom—we called it "promiscuity"—in Israel? (As teenage boys, we wanted to go there and see for ourselves, but we couldn't afford it.) Was Ben-Gurion becoming a tyrant, having served as Israel's only prime minister? Was Israel too close to the Soviet Union and not close enough to the United States? Should Menachem Begin and Yitzhak Shamir, who were both the heads of terrorist organizations during the pre-state period, be allowed to serve in the Knesset as members of the opposition, where, someday in the not too distant future, they hoped to become the leaders of the country?

This last question deeply divided my friends and family. There were some who idealized Jewish terrorists while condemning Arab terrorists. There were others who believed that all terrorism was wrong and that no one with a history of terrorism should be allowed to govern. I was in the latter category, but I also believed that the passage of time could turn a terrorist into a statesman. Obviously, a majority of Israelis agreed and elected both Begin and Shamir to the prime ministership several decades after the establishment of Israel and the creation of a united IDF.

These and other questions were interesting to us, as young Zionists, but the rest of the world didn't seem to care much about Israel, except to support its struggle for military and economic security.

During my high school and early college years, I was consumed with other passions: opposition to McCarthyism; support for racial equality; getting Adlai Stevenson elected president; the Brooklyn Dodgers' first ever World Series win in 1955 (I own Don Zimmer's ring from that series); and bringing football back to Brooklyn College.

I was always a contentious kid attracted to controversies—in school, in summer camp, in my neighborhood—and to defending the underdog. Israel was neither controversial nor perceived as the underdog. So I focused on other issues while still maintaining an interest in Israel. This interest led me to attend a thickly accented speech by David Ben-Gurion, several speeches by British-accented Abba Eban, and wrestling matches by Rafael Halperin, Israel's champion and a symbol of the new Israeli—bronze, ripped and athletic. In 1952, Abba Eban was elected vice president of the UN General Assembly—a feat no Israeli could come close to replicating today.

Hovering in the background was the constant military threat against Israel by those Arab countries committed to its destruction. The illegitimate leaders of those countries—illegitimate because they were either placed in their hereditary positions by colonial powers or attained them by bloody coups d'état—threatened to "throw the Jews into the sea," distracting from their own domestic difficulties. Chief among those who threatened Israel was Egypt under its young new leader Gamal Abdel Nasser, who had helped to overthrow King Farouk in 1952. Nasser's ambition was to rule over a United Arab Nation that would include all the Sunni Muslim countries in the region. These countries—which included Syria, Jordan and Iraq—had little in common beyond language, religion and a desire to rid the region of its "Jewish interlopers."

Egypt already had the strongest and largest army in the region. Now the Soviet Union was beginning to deliver massive supplies of modern weapons to Egypt—including state-of-the-art jets, tanks and munitions—that would guarantee them both qualitative and quantitative military superiority over Israel. The United States, at the time, was refusing to supply arms to Israel, which was getting its weapons primarily from France.[10]

The combination of Egyptian threats to destroy Israel and the increasing supply of Soviet arms that would make this threat viable caused the Israeli general staff to consider a preventive attack on the Egyptian army. The flow of Soviet arms was beginning but had not yet reached the point of no return—when an attack against Egypt would have been unsuccessful. The legality of a "preventive" as distinguished from a "preemptive" attack was questionable under international law.[11] The former occurs before there is an actual or planned attack from the other side. For example, had the British and French attacked the growing German military machine in the mid-1930s in order to prevent it from becoming the most powerful army in Europe (in violation of the Versailles Treaty at the close of World War I), that attack—which might have saved 50 million lives—would have been deemed "preventive" and thus of questionable legality. On the other hand, Israel's later attack against Egypt and Syria that began the Six-Day War in 1967 was deemed "preemptive" because Egyptian forces were massed near Israel's border in what looked like preparation for an imminent attack against Israel. The consensus of international law scholars—as reflected in law review articles, books and academic conferences—was that a preemptive attack was lawful, but a preventive attack was generally not.[12] (International law, in the early years of Israel's existence, generally was balanced when it came to the Arab–Israeli conflict. More recently, it has been weaponized by hard-left academics against Israel.)

In 1956, Israel did not fear an *imminent* attack, but it reasonably feared an *eventual* attack from an enemy that would be capable of destroying it if it were allowed to become massively armed with modern Soviet weaponry (the buildup of Germany's military power in the 1930s was clearly part of Israel's collective memory). Any attack on Egypt would be preventive, rather than preemptive, unless Egypt committed a casus belli—an act of war, as defined by international law—against Israel.

A casus belli need not include an actual military attack. It could include other acts of war, such as the blocking of international shipping lanes to the commercial vehicles of the enemy country. And this is precisely what Egypt did when it nationalized the Suez Canal and prevented Israel from using this vital waterway. It had also blocked the Straits of Tiran, thereby denying Israeli access to the Gulf of Aqaba and its port in Eilat.[13] These acts of economic warfare, backed by military power, constituted casus bellis and entitled Israel to respond militarily.[14]

Accordingly, any military action by Israel would be neither entirely preventive nor preemptive. It would be reactive and, therefore, lawful, even if the primary object was to prevent Egypt from attaining military superiority that would enable it, at a future time, to destroy the new state.

France and England, on the other hand, had not been the object of any casus belli. Their ships were free to sail through the canal and the straits. These colonial nations were fearful of losing their influence in the Middle East if the canal were to be successfully nationalized and wrested from their control by Egypt.

The three countries, for somewhat different reasons, decided to attack Egypt to regain control over the canal, to open the straits to Israeli shipping and to set back Egypt's growing military superiority. It is doubtful that these decisions were influenced, to any substantial degree, by international law; rather, they seemed motivated by self-interest. Historically, most such decisions are indeed based on self-interest, and international law, which is quite malleable, is employed as an after-the-fact justification for or defense of the decisions. What the late secretary of state Dean Acheson once said applied more to Israel than to France or Great Britain: "The survival of states is not a matter of law."[15]

On October 29, 1956, Israeli forces invaded the Sinai by air, land and sea, capturing key strategic positions, such as the Mitla Pass and Sharm el-Sheikh, as well as the Gaza Strip. Two days later, French and British forces joined the battle with a massive bombing campaign. Nasser responded by sinking 40 ships in the Suez Canal, blocking all shipping.[16]

By the end of the Suez Crisis, Egypt's entire air force had been destroyed, along with much of its tank and armored forces. Israel also captured one of its major naval vessels that was shelling Haifa. The Straits of Tiran were opened to Israeli shipping, while the Suez Canal remained closed to all shipping for months. Israel suffered many more casualties (172) than did the French (10) or British (16). Egyptian casualties were far greater though impossible to quantify, with estimates ranging from 1,000 to 3,000 soldiers and as many as 1,000 civilians, mostly from the British bombing campaign and street fighting.[17]

The war was unpopular in Britain and led to the downfall of the Anthony Eden Labour government and the weakening of the French government. President Eisenhower was widely praised around the world for helping to bring it to an end, though many supporters of Israel thought he acted too hastily, denying Israel the opportunity to degrade the Egyptian military further. His actions, which were perceived as one-sidedly against Israel, confirmed the view of my family and friends that they were right in supporting Adlai Stevenson and that the Democratic Party was the pro-Israel party—the Republicans not so much.

I was in my second year at Brooklyn College during the Suez Crisis and active in school politics, beginning my run to become president of the student body (on a platform that included bringing varsity football back and getting more free parking). I wrote op-eds and letters on a variety of subjects. I don't remember whether this Suez situation was among them, but I do remember debating a hard-left critic of Israel's invasion, which I supported, as did all my friends and colleagues. "If Israel decided they had to attack, there must have been good reason, because Israel is a good country that does the right thing." That was our mindset. It wasn't quite "Israel, right or wrong." It was, "Israel is always right, and its enemies are always wrong." This, it turns out, is closer to the truth than its opposite even today: if Israel does it, it must be wrong—which today's anti-Israel zealots espouse. (It is a striking parallel to an old Polish proverb: if there is something wrong in the world, the Jews must be behind it.) Consider, for example, "pinkwashing"—the bigoted term that espouses the absurd view that Israel is good to gays only to whitewash—pinkwash—how bad they are to Palestinians.[18] More on this in subsequent chapters.

We were not thoughtful or nuanced in our defense of Israel back in the mid-1950s and early 1960s because there was no need for thought or nuance. To us, and to most Americans, the issues were black and white, and no reasonable person believed that Israel was a bad country that did bad things.

Following the cease-fire that ended the Suez Crisis, things quieted down again for a period between 1956 and 1966, during which I completed college—having been elected president of the student body and captain of the debate team, which never debated any issue relating to Israel because there was no controversy. We debated capital punishment (I was against it), recognition of "Red China" (I was for it), whether 18-year-olds should have the right to vote (I was for it), and socialized medicine (I was for it).

I also completed Yale Law School, where I was first in my class and served as editor in chief of the *Yale Law Journal* (again, without editing any articles relating to noncontroversial Israel). Despite these accomplishments, I was turned down by all 32 Wall Street law firms to which I applied.

Near the end of my first year in law school, David Ben-Gurion announced the capture by Israeli Mossad agents of Adolf Eichmann, the Nazi fugitive who had overseen the "final solution" to the "Jewish Question." His abduction from Argentina clearly violated international law, and Israel was condemned by diplomats around the world.

But the daring escapade and the decision to put the mass murderer on trial in Israel was applauded by many Americans, Europeans and, of course, Israelis. I was thrilled to see this notorious Nazi being brought to justice in Israel, where he would be prosecuted by Jewish lawyers and tried by Jewish judges. He was defended by a German lawyer. Not only would Eichmann be on trial in the Jerusalem courtroom, but the Israeli judicial system would also be on trial in the court of public opinion.

I was offered my first opportunity to visit Israel to observe the Eichmann trial. One of my favorite law school professors was Telford Taylor, who had served as the chief prosecutor at the Nuremberg Trials, where he replaced Supreme Court justice Robert Jackson. One of the radio networks had asked Taylor to go to Jerusalem and offer ongoing commentary on the trial. Taylor asked me to go with him as his assistant. I was dying to go, but I had just been elected editor in chief of the *Yale Law Journal*, a great honor and responsibility—and also a path to a Supreme Court clerkship. Reluctantly, I had to decline Taylor's offer. Instead, I listened faithfully to his insightful observations about the remarkable trial. When he returned, we discussed it at length, including whether the death penalty was appropriate (I thought not). Among the things he told me was that Hannah Arendt, who became famous for *Eichmann in Jerusalem: A Report on the Banality of Evil*, her polemical account of the Eichmann trial, was hardly ever in the courtroom. She came to Jerusalem with her mind made up in an effort to prove her predetermined thesis regarding both the banality of evil—the bureaucratization of mass murder—and the evil of Zionist leaders during the Holocaust. The facts that the trial disclosed—that Adolf Eichmann was far from banal and that Nazism was supported by some of Germany's most brilliant and nonbanal minds, including Martin Heidegger, who had been Arendt's lover before the war and remained her friend even after the Holocaust—were not included in her book because they undercut her thesis.[19]

I remained close to Telford Taylor—we traveled to the Soviet

Union and Israel together a decade and a half later, when we worked on behalf of Soviet Jewish dissidents and refuseniks. But I've always had some regret about not accepting the opportunity to observe one of the most significant historical events of my lifetime.

In the summer between law school and my first clerkship, I went south to train as an NAACP legal observer during the civil rights movement. The training took place at Howard, a historically black university in Washington, DC. Following several days of training by experienced NAACP lawyers, we were sent south to observe and report on marches, demonstrations and other forms of protest. It was an eye-opening and distressing experience, as I saw firsthand the kind of racism I had only studied in school: segregated bathrooms, lunch counters and schools. This was several years before the brutal murders of three civil rights workers and others seeking justice, so I did not experience or see the violence that was to ensue, but I saw enough to assure a lifetime commitment to civil rights and equality.

Following law school, I was fortunate to clerk for two Jewish judges who were both ardent liberals and Zionists. The first was Chief Judge David Bazelon of the United States Court of Appeals for the District of Columbia. He counted among his closest friends the Israeli ambassador to the United States, Avraham Harman, as well as other Zionist leaders and Jewish legislators, such as Senators Abraham Ribicoff, Jacob Javits and Richard Neuberger. These important supporters of Israel, who voted for pro-Israel legislation and pressed the Kennedy administration to increase its support for the nation-state of the Jewish people, were frequent lunch guests in his chambers, and I was always invited to join (though not to speak unless spoken to).

The attorney general was Bobby Kennedy, with whom the law clerks had lunch in the courthouse. I was selected to pick him up at the Justice Department and walk him to the judges' dining room. He regaled us with fascinating stories of the months he spent in Israel as a journalist for a Boston newspaper during the War of Independence.[20] He loved Israel, Israelis and American Jews—who loved him in return, despite his father's somewhat questionable history during the run-up to World War II[21] and his early support for McCarthyism. During the walk back, the attorney general urged me to come work at the Justice Department after my clerkships.

My year with Judge Bazelon solidified my belief—if it even needed solidification—that one could be a liberal American patriot and a strong supporter of Israel, with no conflict. That belief was strengthened further by my second clerkship with Justice Arthur Goldberg, who had just replaced Felix Frankfurter (another fervent Zionist, though not a very good Jew, especially during the Holocaust).[22]

Goldberg and his wife Dorothy had grown up in Midwestern Zionist circles. They were active in both labor and Zionist causes, and their annual Seder combined labor songs, Zionist songs and a small amount of actual prayer. Among their close friends growing up was a Zionist from Milwaukee named Goldie Meyerson (nee, Mabovitch), who later changed her name to Golda Meir and became the first female leader of a nation who was not the wife or daughter of a male leader. (I would later meet and interview her.) Goldberg, too, had lunches with visiting Israeli dignitaries and leading American Zionists, to which I was always invited.

My two years of clerking strengthened both my liberalism and my Zionism and prepared me for my dual career as a Harvard professor and Israeli advocate. During those years there was little controversy regarding liberalism or Israel. All my friends were both liberals, which meant they supported racial equality, freedom of speech and other center-left positions, and Zionists, which meant they supported Israel's right to exist as the nation-state of the Jewish people. President John F. Kennedy was not as enthusiastic about Israel as his brother Bobby (or his other brother Teddy, with whom I later worked closely). But nor was he as critical of Israel as President Eisenhower, who strongly opposed Israel's military actions in Egypt during the Suez Crisis. Lyndon Johnson, who was then vice president, was among the most pro-Israel politicians in history. I recall Justice Goldberg telling me about a visit by liberal senator Hubert Humphrey to Israel, during which he could hear fighter jets in the distance. Humphrey asked his guide whether the jets "were ours or theirs." By "ours," he meant Israel's. Everyone in the early 1960s was on Israel's side in its never-ending battles with Arab countries that refused to accept a Jewish state.

This simplistic view was to prevail until Israel's victory in the 1967 Six-Day War, after which everything began to change.

3

Six-Day War

The Making of an Israel Defender

SOME CRITICS DIVIDE Jewish supporters of Israel into two groups: those who only began to love Israel after they could take pride in its dramatic victory in the Six-Day War, and those who actively supported Israel before that glorious victory. I fall into the latter category. I began my "second career"—as a defender of Israel in the court of public opinion—during the run-up to the June 1967 war, when it looked like Israel might be destroyed by the combined armed forces of Egypt, Syria, Jordan and other Arab nations.

The year 1967 was also one in which the Harvard Law School faculty would vote on whether to promote me from assistant professor without tenure to full professor with lifetime tenure. I had begun as an assistant professor in 1964, just before turning 26. I had been a popular and successful teacher and had written several articles on criminal law, and I also coauthored with Jay Katz and Joseph Goldstein a case book on *Psychoanalysis, Psychiatry and the Law*.[1] But I was only 28 years old, and no one so young had ever been granted tenure at Harvard Law School. My lack of legal experience—I had never really practiced law—was also a negative factor. Because the tenure process is so secretive and because the tradition at the time forbade any effort by a candidate to seek support or even to inquire whether a senior professor was for or against them, I was in the dark about my prospects, though I believed they were promising.

It was against this background that I began my so-called second career.

Tensions between Israel and its neighbors had increased between the end of 1966 and May 1967, during which time terrorists raided Israel from Egypt, Jordan and Syria. Israel's subsequent reprisals had generated support within the Arab world for a military attack against the Jewish state. Egypt's Gamal Abdel Nasser declared that the national goal of his country was "the eradication of Israel." His state-controlled media called for Israel to be "wiped off the map," and he demanded "Israel's death and annihilation." Syria's defense minister called for a "war of annihilation."[2] Yemen's foreign minister said, "We want war. War is the only way to settle the problem of Israel."[3] And the then chairman of the PLO—Ahmad Shukeiri—threatened to "destroy Israel and its inhabitants, and as for the survivors, if there are any, the boats are ready to deport them."[4] This was before Israel replaced Jordan and Egypt as occupiers of the West Bank and Gaza Strip. For these Arab leaders, *all* of Israel—Tel Aviv, West Jerusalem, Rishon Leziyon—was "occupied" by Jews. Their goal was to end these "occupations" and rid the entire "Zionist entity" of its Jewish population by military conquest.

Having grown up amid survivors of the Holocaust, we took those threats literally and seriously. We knew from the 1956 Suez Crisis that Israel had a good army, but we also knew that the Egyptian, Syrian and Jordanian armies had been strengthened over the years. As King Hussein of Jordan—later a peace partner with Israel, but at the time an implacable foe—put it in the run-up to the Six-Day War, "All of the Arab armies now surround Israel. The UAR [Egypt], Iraq, Syria, Jordan, Yemen, Lebanon, Algeria, Sudan and Kuwait. . . . There is no difference between one Arab army and another."

We were frightened for Israel. War seemed inevitable, especially after Nasser once again blocked the Straits of Tiran from Israeli shipping—an act of war that Israel could not accept—and demanded that the UN peacekeepers, who had been positioned in the Sinai as part of the cease-fire that ended the Suez Crisis, be removed. The removal of these peacekeepers meant that the massive Egyptian army could be positioned near Israel's border, ready to strike nearby civilian targets at any time. Not only was Israel's existence as the nation-state of the Jewish people at risk, but the lives of its citizens were also in danger. Arabs were threatening another Holocaust, just 22 years after the end of World War II.

I became energized. Now Israel was the underdog. It was time for me to become one of its public defenders, at least at Harvard, where I had some visibility. I helped to organize a group of faculty supporters for Israel, which eventually evolved into a permanent monthly lunch group of Jewish faculty who were willing to identify as Zionists. I was the only law school faculty member who regularly attended.

I organized students both at the law school and throughout the rest of the university, some of whom went to Israel to help when exams ended in May. I brought together Israeli visiting professors and scholars to help educate us about the realities on the ground. Among the scholars that I worked with were two who became lifelong friends: Aharon Barak and Yitzhak Zamir, who both became deans of the Hebrew University Law School, attorneys general and justices of the Israel Supreme Court. I solicited financial contributions for Israel from colleagues. Professor Livingston Hall, an elderly Brahmin, gave me $1,000 in cash and said, "Make sure this goes directly to the Israeli army." It did. I personally delivered it to an Israeli military attaché.

I also became acquainted with a young Canadian lawyer named Irwin Cotler, whom I met when he was a graduate student at Yale Law School. Irwin went on to become a distinguished law professor, a human rights activist and eventually the Canadian attorney general and minister of justice. We became lifelong friends and colleagues, later working together on freeing Soviet Jews from communist oppression. Our friendship began in earnest during the run-up to the Six-Day War.

When the war broke out, I actually thought about volunteering to go to Israel to help, but the Israeli counsel general wisely advised that I would be of more help remaining in Cambridge and garnering support for Israel.

Support for Israel was not controversial, even among the left-wing faculty (with the exception of Professor Roger Fisher, who was an early supporter of the Palestinian cause, and, of course, Noam Chomsky, now emiritus professor at MIT and an outspoken radical, who rarely, if ever, supported any Israeli action). I was active in the anti–Vietnam War movement and other liberal causes, but even many antiwar activists tended to support Israel's right to defend itself. It wasn't my principled support for Israel that raised any hackles. It was my very *public* advocacy for the Jewish state that caused concern. Professor Paul Bator cautioned me not to "wear my Jewishness on my sleeve." He meant well, being one of my supporters for tenure, but he honestly believed that being too openly Jewish could hurt my chances. I politely thanked him and told him that Harvard would have to accept or reject me for who I was and that I would remain a public supporter of Israel. This was not too courageous or foolhardy on my part, since I already had tenure offers from Stanford, Chicago, Columbia, Yale and New York University, though I preferred to remain in Cambridge, where my kids were in school.

In the end, I received tenure at Harvard and continued to be a very public supporter of Israel, even as that stance became more controversial and unpopular.

When the war began on June 5, 1967, I gathered with a group of my faculty friends and colleagues—including Marty Peretz, who was soon to become the publisher of the *New Republic*; Michael Walzer, an eminent political theorist; Robert Nozick, one of the world's most distinguished philosophers; and Dick Wurtman, an MIT scientist who pioneered research on melatonin—to watch and wait. Our main source of "inside information" was Professor Nadav Safran, an Egypt-born Israeli, who was teaching government at Harvard. Safran had fought for the Haganah in Israel's War of Independence and had sources in the Israeli military and intelligence community. (Unbeknown to us, Safran also worked with the CIA, receiving funding for conferences and books.) He provided us information before it had been made public.

By the second day of fighting, we knew that the Israeli air force had destroyed the Egyptian air force on the ground. Safran told us that Jordan would soon be attacking Israel, because King Hussein felt he would be humiliated among his peers and subjects if he stayed out of this fight. In the months before the war, he had criticized Nasser for not helping Jordan respond to Israeli cross-border attacks in retaliation for fedayeen terrorist raids against Israeli civilians. He had accused Nasser of hiding "behind the skirts" of the UN peacekeepers. So now he felt obliged to lend his powerful Jordanian legion to the fight. Safran told us that the battle with Jordan would cost many more Israeli lives than the attacks against Egypt and Syria. He was right. Because King Hussein later made peace with Israel, he received a pass from many contemporary historians on his early warmongering and support for terrorism, as well as for the killing of Palestinians during Black September.[5] I later met King Hussein in his palace in Amman. He could not have been friendlier or more anxious to maintain a peaceful relationship with Israel. But in 1967, the king was anything but friendly toward the nation-state of the Jewish people. Despite his subsequent peacemaking, he has the blood of many Israelis, Palestinians and Jordanians on his hands. He also bears considerable responsibility for Israel's half-century occupation of the West Bank, which Israel would not have captured if Hussein had not attacked.

Our Israeli colleagues rushed back to join their military units, arriving in time to participate in the final stages of the short but decisive war. When it was over, we celebrated the victory, joyously, joining many American Jews who had hitherto remained silent but who were now basking in the pride of the Israeli military victory. Nearly everyone—Jews and non-Jews—was overjoyed by the outcome. Even antiwar activists praised Israel for the tiny number of civilian deaths that resulted from the IDF's surgical precision in zeroing in on military targets. It was a time of great joy and pride for Israel, as tourists flocked to see the newly liberated areas—including the Western Wall, Jewish Quarter and Mount Scopus—that had been closed to Jews during Jordan's two-decade-long occupation of these historic religious historic and nationalistic sites.

A joke being told in the United States during these heady days reflected our positive attitude toward Israel and Israelis: A group of American-Jewish tourists is at a Tel Aviv nightclub. They applaud the acrobat and magician, but then an Israeli comedian begins to tell jokes in Hebrew. One of the tourists laughs loudly at his punch line. His friend says, "But you don't understand a word of Hebrew, so how do you know he's funny?" The laughing tourist replies, "He's an Israeli, so I trust him. He must be funny!" That was then.

Soon after the war ended, Justice Arthur Goldberg, who had left the Supreme Court to become the U.S. ambassador to the United Nations, asked for my help. The French (who had earlier been one of Israel's major weapons suppliers—as well as suppliers of components for their nuclear program—but who by then had turned against Israel under the leadership of Charles de Gaulle) and Russians (who broke diplomatic relations with Israel during the Six-Day War) were working on an important Security Council resolution that would, in effect, serve as a peace treaty and roadmap for the future of the Arab–Israeli conflict. Goldberg wanted to be sure it would be fair and not endanger Israel's future. He asked me to come to New York City to be a sounding board and help with his proposed wording.

The thrust of the resulting resolution—which famously became known as "Resolution 242"—was land for peace: Israel would return land captured from Arab countries in exchange for peace and recognition. There were, however, several sticking points on which Goldberg was working. The first was how much "land" for how much "peace." Israel was unwilling to return to the pre-1967 borders, which made it extremely vulnerable to attack—only 10 miles wide at its narrowest point, and its north and south could easily be cut off.[6] It also didn't want to see Syrian troops once again on the Golan Heights, from which they had fired munitions into the Israeli civilian areas below. The Arab states were unwilling to make peace in exchange for anything except Israel's complete destruction. From August 29 to September 1, 1967, eight Arab heads of state, along with Palestinian leaders, met in Khartoum and issued a joint statement declaring, "No peace with Israel, no recognition of Israel, no negotiations with it." Israeli leaders had been—in Moshe Dayan's words—"Waiting for a telephone call" from Arab leaders. Israel promised to be "unbelievably generous in working out peace terms," in Abba Eban's words. Instead of the phone call, they got "the three no's," as the Khartoum Declaration came to be called. As Eban later put it, this was the first war in history in which "the victors sued for peace and the vanquished called for unconditional surrender."[7]

Despite this categorical Arab rejection of the land-for-peace formula, the Security Council moved forward in its efforts to come up with a fair resolution that would be approved unanimously, especially by its permanent members, each of which is granted veto power.

Goldberg worked tirelessly to come up with a consensus formula, but the French and Russians insisted that Israel had to return *all* of the captured land in its lawful defense war. They claimed that no country should be allowed to hold on to land captured during a war, even a defensive war. But following World War II, as well as other wars, nations were not required to return land captured during wars. Territorial adjustments were the rule rather than the exception in postwar diplomacy.[8]

The United States, Great Britain and Israel (which is not a member of the Security Council) wanted a resolution that allowed Israel to maintain control over areas necessary to its security. They did not want to force Israel to return to its vulnerable borders, which Eban had characterized as "the Auschwitz lines." There was an impasse, but Goldberg—who had been a brilliant and successful labor negotiator and had settled many strikes—refused to give up. Finally, he and Hugh Foot, Lord Caradon and Great Britain's UN ambassador, came up with a compromise they hoped would be acceptable to the French and Russians: the French version of the resolution would call for Israel—in exchange for peace—to withdraw from "des territoires." This suggests, without expressly stating, that Israel was expected to withdraw from *all* the territories it captured. The English version calls for Israel to withdraw from "territories"—no *the*. All the negotiations were conducted in English, and the vote was on the English version. This led Goldberg to argue that the resolution left it open for Israel to make *some* border changes necessary to achieve "secure and recognized boundaries," as called for in other parts of the resolution.

I helped Goldberg draft a statement explaining the compromise: "The notable omissions in regard to withdrawal are the words 'the' or 'all' and [any reference to] 'the June 5, 1967 lines.' The Resolution speaks of withdrawal from occupied territories without defining the extent of withdrawal."

This issue has still not been resolved more than half a century after the compromise. One reason it hasn't is that the resolution does not require Israel to give up one inch of captured territories *unless* it receives in return "termination of all claims or states of belligerency and respect for and acknowledgement of the sovereignty, territorial integrity and political independence of every state in the area and their right to live in peace within secure and recognized boundaries free from threats or acts of force." The Arab states refused to comply with the quid pro quo set out in Resolution 242. When Egypt later agreed to these terms in 1979, Israel returned *all* the Egyptian areas captured during the war.[9] And when Jordan made peace in 1994, Israel gave back *all* the areas claimed by Jordan, but not the West Bank, which Jordan had ceded to the Palestinian Authority. Neither the Palestinians nor the PLO was referenced in the Security Council's resolution, which dealt only with states.

Although I worked alongside Goldberg in his efforts to achieve compromise, I can't take any credit for the outcome. I can take some credit for one aspect of Resolution 242, which calls for a "just settlement of the refugee problem." This was the resolution's only reference to Palestinians, though not by name. The Soviet ambassador tried to amend it to refer explicitly to Palestinian refugees, but that amendment was defeated, and Justice Goldberg later observed that "a notable omission in 242 is any reference to Palestinians. [The language of the Resolution] 'presumably refers both to Arab and Jewish refugees, for about an equal number of each abandoned their homes as a result of several wars . . .'"[10]

I helped persuade Goldberg to frame the refugee provision so that it could be interpreted to include the Jewish refugees from Muslim countries. Half a century later, neither refugee problem has been solved, but the wording of the resolution permits Jewish refugees to be included in any discussion or "just settlement of the refugee problem."

Following the acceptance of Security Council Resolution 242, I continued to work informally with Ambassador Goldberg, after he left the United Nations, on Israeli issues, legal cases (including the famous Curt Flood case, which led to the end of the notorious "reserve clause" in major league baseball, and the appeal in the Dr. Benjamin Spock anti-Vietnam case) and his unsuccessful campaign for governor of New York. (My colleague on that campaign was another former Goldberg law clerk, Stephen Breyer, now Justice Breyer.)

My support for Israel remained largely behind the scenes between 1967 and 1970, during which time I became a public media advocate for the nation-state of the Jewish people.

4

The PR War on Israel Begins

THE YEAR 1968 was the height of controversy surrounding the Vietnam War. Hundreds of thousands of American protestors gathered in New York's Central Park and on the Washington Mall. Faculty members canceled classes in some universities, while students in other universities walked out of classes. Early in the following year, President Lyndon Johnson would announce that he would not run for reelection. Although I supported the right of protestors to miss classes, I decided to take a more positive approach, organizing and teaching the first course on the legal issues surrounding the Vietnam War. The course received widespread media attention, with prominently featured stories in the *New York Times, Time* magazine and other media.[1] Antiwar lawyers, who were contemplating lawsuits against the war, sat in on the class. I was interviewed on radio and TV about the legal issues, including whether the Constitution authorized the president to wage war without congressional authorization and whether some of the means used to conduct the war—including napalm, fire bombings and assassinations—were lawful under international law.

At about the same time, I played a small consulting role in the defense of the alleged antiwar conspirators in the Dr. Benjamin Spock case. Justice Goldberg had agreed to argue the appeal for the

Reverend William Sloane Coffin Jr., who was convicted along with Dr. Spock, Mitchell Goodman and Michael Ferber of conspiring to counsel evasion of the Vietnam draft. I had met Reverend Coffin at Yale when I was a student, and I admired him. I recall that Noam Chomsky, who was an acquaintance at the time, was furious that he had been left out of the indictment, as he considered himself *the* leading antiwar activist. He complained to our mutual friend Leonard Boudin that he had been as radical as the indicted defendants were—as he had incited students to refuse to serve—and asked rhetorically, "What do I have to do to get arrested?" Although I personally disagreed with some of the tactics employed by war resisters, I believed that they were entitled to a zealous defense.

Goldberg won the appeal, and no one went to prison.

Shortly thereafter, I played a more significant role in the trial and appeal of the Chicago Seven, which grew out of antiwar demonstrations during the 1968 Democratic Convention in Chicago. The Chicago Seven case, with its wild shenanigans directed at Judge Julius Hoffman, had been a widely watched political trial involving some of the most prominent antiwar activists. The lead defense lawyer, William Kunstler—a radical lawyer who famously said that he only defended people he "loved"—had been held in contempt and sentenced to prison. He asked me to help write the appellate brief. I responded, "But I don't love you." He came back with, "I love you, so that's good enough." We won the appeal.[2]

One of the defendants at the trial was Abbie Hoffman, who reportedly made some crude remark about how his "Jew lawyers" cared more about Israel than about the United States. It wasn't clear whether he was referring to me or to another Jewish lawyer named Morton Stavis. (He certainly wasn't referring to Kunstler, who cared little for either Israel or the United States), but I called him out in a private letter, to which he responded with a two-page handwritten note that included the following:

*I never made a remark about my "Jewish Lawyers." I might
have spoken more positively about the PLO but I would never
make an anti-Semitic juxtaposition such as you think you heard.
If you read my current auto-biography you will see I flaunt my
"Jewishness" at every turn of the road.*

It was the first time I had heard a Jew speak positively about the
PLO, which, at the time, was an open and avowed terrorist organization that was hijacking airplanes, murdering Jewish children and
American diplomats, blowing up synagogues and urging the destruction of the Jewish state.

Israel had not yet built settlements in the territories it had captured
during the Six-Day War. The PLO regarded all of Israel as an illegal
settlement and called for its destruction by force and violence. Yet
Abbie Hoffman—and, as I would later learn, other radical leftists—
supported the PLO and opposed Israel's existence as a matter of
principle. I never dreamed at the time that this root-and-branch rejection of Israel's right to exist would soon spread from extremists on
the radical left to more mainstream academic leftists, and even to
some young liberals, in America and Europe.

At about the same time, I became active in the campaign to abol-
ish the death penalty. I had long opposed capital punishment, having written a letter to the editor of the *Washington Post* while in law
school opposing the execution of Adolf Eichmann by Israel.[3] I had
also drafted a dissent for Justice Goldberg while I was a law clerk,
suggesting that the death penalty violated the constitutional prohibition against cruel and unusual punishment.[4] The focus of the
campaign was on the racial disparity in the administration of capital punishment.[5] Justice Goldberg and I jointly authored an influential *Harvard Law Review* article titled "Declaring the Death Penalty
Unconstitutional."[6] I also litigated First Amendment cases involving
antiwar and anti-segregation demonstrators, as well as films such as

I Am Curious Yellow and *Deep Throat*, which were alleged to violate the obscenity laws.[7] *Newsweek* described me as America's "most peripatetic civil liberties lawyer and one of its most distinguished defenders of individual rights."[8]

It was against this background in liberal law and politics that I was asked in the spring of 1970 to make my debut as a public defender of Israel on national television. In 1970, Egypt and Israel were involved in a war of attrition, with many deaths on both sides. The conflict also became part of the Cold War between the Soviet Union and the United States. Proposals for an overarching resolution to the conflict were being offered around the world. One such proposal— which favored the Arab side—had been offered by the American Friends Service Committee, a Quaker group that had shown considerable bias against Israel. PBS was then running a program called *The Advocates* in a prime-time Sunday-evening slot, on which issues of the day were debated by lawyers, academics and public officials. Its founder and executive producer was my colleague, Roger Fisher, who was the only Harvard Law professor to my knowledge who supported the Arab side of the Israeli–Arab conflict. By today's standards, Fisher was a moderate supporter of the Palestinian cause—he did not believe that Israel was an illegitimate state—but in 1970 any support for the Palestinians was unusual.

Fisher supported the Quaker proposals and decided to do a two-part show—the first in the program's history—on the conflict. It would be a broad-based debate format and would be titled "The Middle-East: Where Do We Go from Here?" A specific question it raised was "whether the United States should give more or less military support to the State of Israel." The episode, which was widely watched, would win a Peabody Award.

I had previously been selected as an advocate or witness for the liberal side of several other questions—such as the death penalty and pretrial preventive detention—so it was natural for me to be asked to advocate for the liberal—that is Israeli—side of the questions presented for debate on this show. Fisher would advocate for the Arabs, which was then the conservative position.

My advocacy for Israel required that I travel there to interview Prime Minister Golda Meir, Defense Minister Moshe Dayan, Foreign Minister Abba Eban, General Yitzhak Rabin, Jerusalem mayor Teddy Kollek and other Israeli public officials and military leaders. I had never been to Israel because I couldn't afford the travel expenses, but PBS was paying for everything.

When I told Justice Goldberg that I would be seeing Prime Minister Meir, he said, "You have to bring Goldie a carton of Lucky Strikes unfiltered cigarettes as a gift from me and Dorothy. She loves them, but her security people don't let her have them." This was before I had any inkling of the carcinogenic effects of cigarettes, so I agreed to try to smuggle the contraband to the prime minister.

I was excited about my first visit to the Holy Land, and especially that, as a 31-year-old rookie "TV journalist," I would be getting to meet and interview the great women and men of Israel. This trip to Israel—my first of nearly 100—would be a transformative event in my life and in my defense of Israel.

The advocate against Israel, Roger Fisher, who was also the executive producer, was an admirer of the American Friends Services Committee, a political arm of the Quaker religion that had turned against Israel and had published a one-sided pro-Arab pamphlet. The Quakers had a significant religious presence in Arab countries and virtually none in Israel.

Fisher would get to sit in on my interviews, but I couldn't sit in on his interviews with Egypt's Nasser and Jordan's Hussein, since neither country would allow me to enter their territory because I was a Jew. This gave Fisher an unfair advantage, but there was nothing I could do other than register my protest, because he was running the show.

I flew to Israel with the director of my segment, a young lawyer named Mark Cohen (also excluded from entering the Arab countries), and we checked in to the American Colony Hotel, which was run by

Arabs in the recently captured East Jerusalem. (Fisher had selected the hotel because he felt more comfortable there than in Jewish Jerusalem.) It was an elegant place, pockmarked with bullet holes from the battles that had taken place three years earlier in and around its structures. The food was marvelous, especially the weekend buffets of dozens of locally made Arab dishes.

I was now ready to visit Prime Minister Golda Meir. I wore baggy pants, scotch taping the carton of Lucky Strikes to my calf, and made it through security to an informal, private meeting before we began taping. When I was alone with the prime minister, I produced the hidden treasure and silently handed it to her. She kissed me and immediately speculated, "From Art and Dotty?" I confirmed her suspicion and told her that I had worked with Goldberg as a law clerk and on the Security Council resolution. She replied, "God sent Arthur to the UN at the right time." I quipped, "I read that you were an atheist." She laughed and said, "Sometimes I believe that things are *bashert*"—the Hebrew Yiddish word for predestined. She invited me to her residence for homemade chicken soup. I was shocked to see the run-down state of the prime minister's residence. Israel was indeed a poor country in those days. (Although Israel has gotten richer, the condition of the prime minister's residence hasn't changed that much, except for enhanced security.)

When we began our formal recorded interview, with Fisher present, I asked the prime minister to make the case for American support of Israel, and she answered brilliantly, displaying her love for both of the countries she had lived in. (She had little love for the Ukraine, where she was born, and remembered her father boarding up the door to their home to protect it against a threatened pogrom.) Golda had been educated in the United States and made aliya when she was 23, after her marriage to Morris Meyerson, a sign painter and fervent socialist. They joined a kibbutz but shortly thereafter moved to Jerusalem, where she became active in labor politics.

Her love for both Israel and America came through in every answer. So did her legendary toughness. Ben-Gurion had once told his cabinet that only one of them had "balls," pointing to Golda. She insisted that Israel would never return to its insecure pre-1967 boundaries but that everything else was subject to negotiation. She also insisted that the Arab states had to acknowledge the legitimacy of "an independent Israel state" with which they were prepared to "live in peace."

Golda gave me a letter of introduction attesting to my love of Israel that opened doors with other government officials. Meanwhile, an Israeli-Arab lawyer, who represented accused terrorists, gave me a letter that attested to my support of the human rights of and due process for Palestinians. I worried about giving the wrong letter to the wrong people!

Following my interview with Prime Minister Meir, I met with Shimon Peres. Shimon, with whom I later formed a close friendship, was a young man on the way up. He had been a Ben-Gurion protégé and had held various posts in the Defense Ministry and other offices. Now, at age 46, he was about to be appointed minister of transportation and communications. But his expertise and experience were in arms acquisitions from European nations, including the components for nuclear weapons (which Israel still doesn't publicly acknowledge it possesses). He had just written a book titled *David's Sling: The Arming of Israel*.[9] The David referred, of course, to the biblical King David, who as a youth had defeated the giant Goliath with a slingshot. But it also paid homage to another brave David—Ben-Gurion—who had tasked Peres with acquiring arms for the new state.

Peres was cultured and charming. We talked about art, music, restaurants and films. He told me that he thought Picasso's Blue Period was his best and observed that French was the language of diplomacy because it was so vague. He recommended an Italian restaurant, whose atmosphere was elegant but whose food turned out to be mediocre. He boasted of being related to the American actress Lauren Bacall, who shared his original birth name, Perske (or Perski). He was also down-to-earth. He was a man of war and weapons who wanted nothing more than to turn the swords he had acquired into plowshares. His personal vision for Israel's future was different from his mentor's vision. Although he spent his early years—after making aliya at age 11—at a kibbutz working as a shepherd, he saw Israel's future not as a self-sufficient agricultural society but as a nation that would use its most important natural resource as the basis for world-class technological innovation. That resource was the creativity of its citizens. The second most important resource a nation must possess is water, he told me, bemoaning Israel's limited supply.

My interview with Peres focused mainly on the need for the United States to provide military assistance to Israel. He predicted renewed fighting with Egypt and the need to deter Arab aggression by increasing Israel's qualitative military superiority over the combined Arab armies. A strong Israel will not attack its neighbors, he argued, but a weak Israel will be attacked by those neighbors. The best assurance of peace in the region is an overwhelmingly strong Israel. He did not, of course, mention Israel's nuclear weapons, which he had helped to develop, but he talked proudly of its growing naval and air power and its reliance on technology and intelligence. He made a powerful case for our side of the debate question regarding American military support for Israel.

Peres had a real impact on my own thinking concerning Israel. I came away from our meeting with renewed confidence in my view that a militarily powerful Israel provided the best chance not just for Israel's own security but also for peace in the region. It is a position from which I have never deviated. Nor did I then, or do I now, believe that my support for a militarily powerful Israel is inconsistent with my opposition to the Vietnam or Iraq War. A militarily weak Israel would face immediate threats of annihilation, whereas neither Vietnam nor Iraq posed any comparable threats to American security. As Prime Minister Benjamin Netanyahu was later to put it, "If the Arabs put down their weapons today, there would be no more violence. If the Jews put down their weapons today, there would be no more Israel."

Abba Eban—who had been one of my heroes ever since my father and I watched him on television make the case for Israel—was his usual eloquent self. But in person, he was less charming than he was on TV or from the lectern. He rarely made eye contact with me, looking off into the distance as if he were lecturing to an audience. His remarks appeared scripted, as if he was repeating by rote what he had said many times. Nonetheless, he made brilliant arguments—in the broadest strokes—that we could and did use effectively to make our case during the live debate.

Yitzhak Rabin was the opposite of Abba Eban. He looked straight into your soul with his piercing eyes. His focus, as a military leader turned diplomat, was on assuring that Israel's new borders would prevent future attacks from being successful. While Eban was in the clouds discussing broad philosophical issues, Rabin was in the weeds focusing on practical problems Israel faced in the imminent future.

I interviewed several other Israeli generals who were stationed in the West Bank and police officials who were responsible for preventing domestic terrorism. I also visited several cities in the West Bank, which was quiet. Israel had not yet built civilian settlements in the captured territories, and we were able to sit at cafés in Hebron and other West Bank cities, including Jericho, Bethlehem and Ramallah, and drink delicious coffee with local Arabs. At the time, the West Bank—which most Israelis refer to by the biblical names Yehuda and Shomron—was sparsely populated, with primitive roads. It was beautiful and bucolic. Little did I suspect how contentious and bloody it would become.

I climbed Masada, the high desert fortress from which Jews in the first century held off the Roman legions until it was evident that they would be captured and enslaved. Choosing death over slavery, they committed mass suicide. One of Israel's slogans was, "Never again will Masada fall."

While in Israel, I renewed my friendship with the academics—now professors and soon to be attorneys general and justices—who I had met while they were visiting scholars at Harvard. I also met my Israeli relatives, nearly all of whom were Orthodox, ranging from ultra to modern. Several high school classmates had settled in Israel after completing their education in the United States, and I looked them up. One was a doctor, another a lawyer, a third a professor, and others were in business. The businessmen told me how to end up with a "small fortune" in Israel: "Come with a large fortune."

Although I was only making about $25,000 a year as a young full professor—a very decent salary in those days—my Israeli counterparts were making far less and needed to work at second jobs or receive assistance from abroad. In short, Israel was a "second world" economy whose citizens—many of them brilliant and highly educated—had "first world" aspirations and spending habits. It was a prescription for disaster unless Israel could change the direction of its economy. Nearly every Israeli I interviewed reaffirmed the need for economic change and growth. Part of the problem was the extraordinarily high percentage of the GNP needed to acquire weapons from abroad, which could only be bought with hard currency. Israel had a nascent arms industry, but it was mostly for domestic consumption. Its balance of trade, especially with regard to arms, was seriously out of whack. David Ben-Gurion had built an economy geared to an agrarian state with kibbutzim and moshavim. Its socialism and strong labor unions fed the many poor immigrants who flooded the country after the British barriers were eliminated. But a self-sufficient agrarian Israel could not support the military budget necessary to defend it, nor the lifestyles of those who might emigrate to the United States or Europe if the economy did not improve.

I also visited the Gaza Strip and dined in several excellent restaurants in Khan Yunis and Gaza City. The strip was crowded and bustling, and several of the Arabs I met expressed relief that it was no longer being occupied by the Egyptians. Israeli soldiers mingled with the local population without apparent conflict. I found myself sympathetic to the Arabs of the West Bank and Gaza and especially to the families separated by the creation of refugees during the 1948 and 1967 wars.

But the sad state of the economy—despite being enhanced by contributions from American and European Jews—was not Israel's biggest or most imminent problem. The prospect of renewed warfare consumed the attention of Israeli leaders. Although Peres had been prescient in predicting renewed fighting with Egypt, and although there were continuing military confrontations in the Sinai and other areas (an Israeli cousin of mine, a young poet and an only child of Holocaust survivors, was killed during this war of attrition while serving in the IDF), most Israelis were still giddy over their victory in the Six-Day War. A sense of invulnerability was omnipresent, and tourism and immigration increased.

I came back to America after several weeks with a renewed sense of pride, ready to take on Roger Fisher in the live *Advocates* debate, armed with excerpts from the video interviews I had conducted that we would use as virtual "witnesses" in making the case for Israel.

The two shows were broadcast from PBS studios in Los Angeles, with live audiences. The narrow topic—"Should the U.S. give less or more military support to the State of Israel?"—quickly broadened into "The case against and the case for Israel." It was the first time I really had a chance to formulate and present the case I would be making over the next half a century. I read widely, prepared carefully and practiced repeatedly for my debut as "Israel's lead lawyer in the court of public opinion,"[10] as I would later be dubbed.

Fisher began his argument against U.S. military support for Israel in an eminently reasonable fashion:

> *The case I want to put to you tonight is the United States should give less military support to Israel. As I put this case, I ask your tolerance. I ask you to listen to what I'm saying with an open*

mind. Many Americans, particularly American Jews, naturally feel a deep, emotional commitment to Israel and the defense of that place. In this state of mind, you're likely to hear criticism of present policies of Israel as justification of all past Arab actions. The American Friends Service Committee has just produced a report on the Middle East. I agree with two phrases: "There is blame enough for all," and "There are no devils and no angels in the Middle East."

The real question is not the past but where do we go from here? During this hour I will present four things which Israel ought to do and which I believe the United States ought to urge Israel to do and use such military leverage as we have in that direction.

Fisher then laid out his proposals:

With respect to the Palestinian refugees, Israel should begin admitting them to the West Bank and to Israel itself. With respect to the neighboring Arab states, Israel should make a firm commitment of its willingness to withdraw its forces as part of a package settlement. With respect to military matters, Israel should abandon the policy of escalatory retaliation—two eyes for an eye. With respect to negotiations, Israel should be prepared to sit down with indirect talks, not insisting that the first talks be face-to-face.

He called President Nasser and King Hussein as his key witnesses. Nasser began with a straight-out lie, ignoring the "three no's" at Khartoum:

All arrangements for peace which were included in the Security Council we agreed about. There was no agreement from Israel in principle about the word "withdrawal" from the Arab occupied territories. [Note that he didn't say "Palestinian" territories.] So we are sure that Israel doesn't want peace but wants expansions. So we want President Nixon to use his influence with Israel and get from them a promise or a word that they are ready to withdraw from all the occupied territories and they are ready to solve the problem of the refugees according to the United Nations resolution.

Hussein testified similarly:

If they continue to occupy the territory they have occupied since June of 1967; if they continue to attack the Arab homeland, giving them more Phantoms certainly it's not going to help the move toward resolution at all and, in fact, is encouraging the further deterioration of the situation toward a climax and could jeopardize world peace.

I would have loved to cross-examine both Nasser and Hussein, but neither was in the studio, so I had to be satisfied with cross-examining Fisher:

Mr. Fisher, aren't you aware that President Nasser and King Hussein speak in one language to their people and say one thing and speak very differently to the American public as they've been doing for years? For example, as recently as March 27, 1969, Nasser reiterated the Khartoum Resolution. "We have declared our principles. No negotiations, no peace, no relinquishing of one inch of Arab land, and no bargaining over Palestinian rights. These are our principles. We shall never give them up."

I then showed a clip of Hussein talking to his people in Arabic, with his words translated as follows:

Kill the Jews wherever you find them. Kill them with your hands,
with your nails, with your teeth.

The audience gasped. They had never before heard the suave, gentle, smiling king of Jordan speak in such genocidal terms.

After completing my virtual cross-examination of Fisher's witnesses, it was my turn to present my affirmative case. I adopted a multifaceted approach. On the narrow issue of U.S. military support for Israel, I argued along Peres's lines that a strong Israel is the best road to peace:

> *The United States should supply more military support to Israel,*
> *a country that merely wants to live in peace. The Arab belligerents,*
> *armed to the teeth by Soviet weapons, and now even pilots, are*
> *determined to destroy Israel as soon as they are strong enough*
> *to do so. They reject the UN cease-fire which Israel accepts. The*
> *interests of world peace and of the United States are best served*
> *by keeping the peace-seeking country—Israel—strong enough*
> *to discourage miscalculations by those who want war. For the*
> *United States now to impose a one-sided arms embargo against*
> *Israel would be for it to take sides against a small democracy*
> *threatened by external force.*

With regard to the issue of Palestinian refugees, although I sympathized with their plight, I placed the blame squarely where it belonged—at the feet of Arab leaders:

> *To understand this refugee problem, we must go back to 1947*
> *when the United Nations partitioned Palestine into two separate*
> *states. The Jews were given a small area in which they constituted*
> *a majority of the population. The remainder was to become a*
> *Palestinian state. Therefore, under the United Nations decision,*
> *every Palestinian could have lived either as a part of an Arab*

*majority in a Palestinian state or part of an Arab minority
in Israel—if the Arab countries had not attacked Israel, and
if Jordan had not annexed Arab Palestine. Moreover, on the
very day that the Arabs declared war against the new state, the
Grand Mufti of Jerusalem appealed to the Palestinians to leave
their homes. The secretary of the Palestine higher command
himself conceded that the refugees are a direct consequence of the
unanimous policy of the Arab states.*

*While the Arab leaders were telling their people to leave
their homes, what were Israeli authorities saying? They were
telling them to remain. In Haifa, for example, the Jewish Workers
Council issued the following plea: "Do not fear. Do not move
out. In this city, yours and ours, the gates are open for work for
life and peace." It is a tragedy that most of the Palestinians left.
But it must be understood that they were not seeking refuge
from oppression at the hands of Israel. They had a choice. They
could have stayed. They were not refugees in the same sense that the
survivors of Hitler's extermination camps were refugees. Those who
fled from Nazi Germany had no choice but to die or to seek refuge.*

I compared the plight of Jewish refugees from the Holocaust with
Palestinian refugees from Israel. I played film clips showing how
many countries in the world had turned away Jews fleeing the Holocaust, and then a clip showing Golda Meir describing what Israel had
done to Jewish refugees after the war: "We brought our people here."

I asked whether "the Arab states [can] say the same about their
people?" It was a rhetorical question, one that I proceeded to answer:

*The Arab countries put them in camps instead of taking them
into the numerous Arab homelands with a common culture,
language and religion. For example, Palestine had for years been
regarded as southern Syria. In 1951, Syria had wanted more
population. It arranged to have half a million Egyptians come*

*and settle. Yet when the United Nations asked Syria to accept
80,000 Palestinian refugees, they flatly refused. This and other
similar refusals led a research team in Europe to conclude that
the existence of the refugees were the fault of the inhuman policy of
the Arabs for the purpose of maintaining a menacing population
on the frontier with Israel.*

I argued that the "existence of a refugee becomes a refugee problem only if political considerations are permitted to outweigh human considerations." I pointed to post-partition Pakistan and postwar Germany as examples of countries that had resettled millions of refugees, from India and Sudetenland respectively. I then showed that more than 700,000 Jews were forced to leave Arab countries where their ancestors had been living for hundreds if not thousands of years. They, too, were resettled in Israel. Indeed, the number of Arabs that left Israel was approximately the same as the number of Jews who were expelled from Arab countries.

I had learned a great deal about the refugee issues—both Palestinian and Jewish—from my work with Justice Goldberg at the UN, and I made use of this knowledge in the debate, arguing that "what happened in the Mideast, therefore, can be understood as a legitimate exchange of land and population. There is, therefore, no moral imperative on Israel to take back large numbers of refugees 20 years after they left."

As to the broad question, "Where do we go from here?" I argued in favor of a two-state solution (being one of the first to do so). I was much criticized by both Israelis and American Jews for supporting a state for the Arab residents of Mandatory Palestine, but I was advocating nothing different from what the United Nations partition plan had proposed: two states for two peoples.

I called as a live hostile witness a leader of the Palestinian terrorist group Al Fatah to make the point that Palestinian leadership would rather there *not* be a Jewish state, and that they wanted this *more* than they wanted a Palestinian state living alongside Israel:

DERSHOWITZ: Didn't Jordan annex the Palestinian state? If not for Jordan's invasion against Israel, couldn't you have been living in Palestine? Could not [the Palestinians] have all gone to Palestine which was set aside by [the United] Nations, established a state and lived there?

. . .

OMAR: That was not their intention because they want to create a state in all of Palestine.

DERSHOWITZ: So what you're doing is you're fighting now, you're killing in order to get land.

OMAR: The Zionists are the only ones who impose this war on us by coming and colonizing our country, by using weapons of mass destruction . . .

DERSHOWITZ: They used the United Nations, is that a weapon of mass destruction?

We then had the following exchange:

DERSHOWITZ: Could I live in an Arab state today? I mean live, not be hanged in Baghdad.

OMAR: There are immigration laws which if you want to come and live in our countries should have to apply, immigration laws . . .

DERSHOWITZ: Immigration laws? They wouldn't even let me in to visit to interview Hussein or Nasser . . .

Following my cross-examination of Omar, I described my discussion with Abba Eban:

DERSHOWITZ: I asked the foreign minister if an independent Palestinian state on the West Bank would be consistent with Israel's security. He did not rule it out.

On the issue of borders, I relied on General Rabin:

YITZHAK RABIN: The Golan Heights topographically were in control over one-third of Israel. And Syria exploited their topographical advantage and opened fire whenever they wanted. The brutal attack on children exemplifies what's going on along the Lebanese border. If buses of children run now along the former Syrian border, there is no danger that such an eventuality would occur.

Rabin then turned to the West Bank:

On the morning of the fifth of June, 1967, when the Jordanians opened fire and moved their forces, we warned them twice but the Jordanians decided to go into the war. They were capable of shelling Tel Aviv because of the short distance from Jordan. 60 to 70 percent of the Israeli population were within the range of the Arab guns. I believe it's about 10 percent now. To give up at the present the cease-fire lines which gives us a military capacity to defend ourselves effectively without the need to mobilize our forces would be almost like committing suicide.

I then referred to a conversation I had with Ambassador Goldberg on Security Council Resolution 242:

I spoke personally to the United States ambassador to the United Nations who participated in the drafting of this—the Honorable Arthur Goldberg—he told me of the days of debate that went into this phraseology and that it means unequivocally that Israel is not committed to returning all the territories but is committed and the U.S. is committed to permitting it to make territorial adjustments necessary for its security. And that is Israel's position and that is the United States position.

Finally, I summed up my case:

The war in the Middle East will stop any time the Arabs want it to stop. Israel has reiterated its unconditional willingness to comply with the cease-fire if the Arabs will only stop shooting. Indeed, General Dayan recently said, "The government is ready to reestablish an unconditional and unlimited cease-fire even if this will enable Egypt to reorganize and put up SAM-3 missile sites." But the Arabs persist in seeking a military solution rather than a negotiated settlement. Mr. Fisher said that the initiative for peace lies with Israel. If only this were true. All objective people know that Israel will do almost anything for peace. The initiative lies as it has since 1948 with the Arabs in general and with Nasser in particular. The United States must not blackmail Israel into jeopardizing its security. Should Israel ever lose a war, we can understand what it would face by reading from the Jordanian military document captured during the 1967 war. The orders: destroy the agricultural village of Matzah and kill all its inhabitants.

Fisher was given the last word:

There's a very tough problem in the Middle East. It's not sure peace can be made. The sides as we have heard fell violently about the situation and are prepared to fight. Israel is prepared now to drop heavy bombs on Egypt, well beyond the Sinai, to reduce the possible risk that Russians might be able to get missiles there to help defend Egypt, which is undercutting their ability to inflict unlimited destruction on Egypt later. The Russians have put nothing there except defense equipment.

The problem is not should the United States rally to Israel's support in a hard-pressed fight. The question is, shall we take sides with an overwhelming military superiority now on the Israeli side, shall we take sides or shall we be the peacemakers?

The debate was now over and the viewing audience was asked to vote by mail. The tally was overwhelmingly in favor of Israel: 41,241 to 4,103—more than 10–1 in our favor. It was a sign of the times. The times would soon change, but many of the arguments would remain the same. Israel wanted a peace with secure borders. The Arab countries did not want a nation-state of the Jewish people anywhere in the Middle East. The facts would change, especially with regard to Israeli settlements in the West Bank, which would complicate the quest for a peaceful resolution. But Israel also evacuated settlements they built in the Gaza Strip in an effort to secure peace. So there were no insuperable barriers if the will for peace was present on all sides.

I was now ready to make the case for Israel to anyone who listened, having been energized and educated by my role in *The Advocates* debate.

Several years after this first *Advocates* program on Israel, there would be another one, in which a young Israeli named Ben Natai would reiterate some of the arguments I had made and add new ones. I had met "Ben" several years earlier, when he was an MIT student named Benjamin Netanyahu. We have remained friends since, despite our sometime political differences.

5

Chomsky Attacks Israel on Civil Liberties

In mid-1970, at the time of *The Advocates* debate, Israel was still supported by the vast majority of Americans and Europeans. Its annexation of Jerusalem and the Golan Heights and its occupation of the West Bank and Gaza Strip were viewed as necessary to secure Israel's security and reduce the likelihood of renewed warfare. Israel had not yet embarked on its policy of settling Israeli civilians in enclaves in the occupied territories. The occupations were military in nature, which were common when an enemy was defeated in a defensive war. (For example, the United States occupied Germany and Japan after World War II.)[1] The Arab leadership had a different view and resisted the occupation with terrorism, both from the occupied territories as well as from within Israel proper. This same Arab leadership had also resisted with violence the very existence of Israel within its pre-1967 borders, and indeed within its pre-1949 partition borders. Israel responded to Arab violence with harsh measures, including the employment of preventive detention against Israeli Arabs and Palestinians it suspected of terrorism but against whom it could not prove their suspicions in a court of law. This led to accusations that Israel was violating the civil liberties of Palestinians.

I decided to spend the summer of 1970 in Israel studying these accusations from the perspective of a pro-Israel advocate of civil liberties. I had written against the use of preventive detention in my own country, and I doubted I could be convinced that it was justified anywhere. I quickly applied for and received a small Ford Foundation grant, and I packed up my family and took off for Israel only a few weeks after I returned from my first trip.

To study this controversial issue, I traveled across Israel, the West Bank and the Gaza Strip, interviewing former and present detainees, lawyers, generals and politicians. Most left-wing Israelis favored preventive detention (or what they called "administrative detention") as a necessary evil in the war against terrorism.

The one political figure who strongly opposed it was Menachem Begin, the former head of the Irgun Zvai Leumi, a paramilitary group outlawed by the British as a terrorist gang during the pre-state period. When I met him in the lunchroom of the Knesset, he was the leader of the right-wing opposition, a hardliner. But he was also a fervent civil libertarian. Indeed, his party's name was Herut—liberty. Begin was a true libertarian philosophically, though a "hawk" when it came to defending Israel militarily. During our lengthy discussion, Begin—who was proud of his training as a lawyer—reminded me that the Knesset had never enacted a preventive detention law; the Israeli authorities were using British Mandatory law, which authorized the detention of any person whose confinement was "necessary" for "securing the public safety."

Begin told me that under this open-ended law, many of his Irgun colleagues had been detained for long periods of time with no due process or real opportunity to prove their innocence. "We should not be doing what they did to us," he insisted.

I spoke to other Israeli officials who believed Israel had no choice but to detain suspected terrorists. Meir Shamgar, who was then the attorney general of Israel, had previously served as advocate general of the Israel Defense Forces and would eventually serve with distinction as the president of the Supreme Court of Israel. He had seen the issue from all sides. As a young man, he had served in the Irgun and had himself been subjected to preventive detention for several years.

When we met, Shamgar explained to me how his emotions pushed him against the use of preventive detention, but his recent experience with Palestinian terrorism pushed him to differ with his former leaders' categorical rejection of its use in all cases. He explained why he believed it was sometimes necessary. He told me about cases in which reliable undercover sources planted within terrorist groups had informed the Shin Bet of impending terrorist attacks (the Shin Bet is the Israeli version of the FBI, whose job it was to ensure Israel's security from domestic danger, such as stopping the bombing of a local supermarket; the Mossad dealt with foreign threats). The suspected terrorist would be detained, but the only admissible evidence against him would be the testimony of the undercover source. If the source were called as a witness in an open trial, his cover would be blown and he could no longer provide lifesaving information. Also, he and his family might be killed. Nor could his information be provided to the court by the person to whom he relayed it; that would be hearsay, inadmissible in a criminal trial. But such hearsay, if deemed reliable and confirmed by other information, could form the basis for a detention order. It was a compromise with due process, but a necessary one according to Shamgar and other Israeli officials.

I visited several detention centers (the letter from Golda got me in), and I interviewed a number of Arab detainees (the other letter from the Arab lawyer got them to talk to me). They all claimed innocence, but I was later given the hearsay evidence against them that seemed convincing. One former detainee, however, a Palestinian lawyer named Sabri Jaris, made a strong case for his innocence. His brother was a Fatah terrorist in Lebanon, and Sabri was suspected of harboring him and a truckload of explosives and detonators that the Shin Bet had found. His brother had escaped, and Sabri was detained to prevent him from harboring or assisting his terrorist brother in committing future terrorist acts. I thought that was a stretch, and I told that to the authorities who had already released him but placed him under travel restrictions. Shortly after I interviewed him, Jaris escaped to Lebanon, where he became an official of Fatah but never himself engaged in any act of terrorism (as far as the Israelis know).

After studying the issue in detail—and comparing Israel's use of preventive detention to what British and Americans have done during wartime—I came to the following conclusion in a report that was published:

> *Having attempted to place the problem in context, I am, of course, entitled to my own personal views. I fully understand the arguments in favor of preventive detention as it is presently practiced in Israel; I am convinced that it is not being abused and that every effort in good faith is being made to apply it only to persons who have engaged in terroristic activities and are likely to continue to be so engaged. I am impressed with the tiny number of Israeli citizens actually detained. And I appreciate, of course, the danger that Israel faces from terrorism. Nonetheless, I personally favor repeal of the Emergency Defense Regulations and particularly of the preventive-detention provision. Nor is there any paradox in understanding the reasons behind a law in recognizing that it has been fairly applied, and yet, at the same time, in favoring its repeal. Although the potential for abuse has not materialized, abuse is inherent in the nature of detention laws of the kind now on the books in Israel. Such laws, in the words of Justice Robert Jackson, "lie about like a loaded weapon."*

I then proposed alternative ways of dealing with the prevention of terrorism:

> *If Israel feels that it cannot live with the normal rules of evidence in cases of suspected terrorists, then the Knesset should*

enact special rules of evidence for a narrowly circumscribed
category of cases during carefully defined periods of emergency.
All other safeguards should be provided, as in ordinary cases.
In the last analysis, such a system might result in the release of
some who are now detained. It is in the nature of any judicial
system that in order to prevent confinement of the innocent,
it might release the guilty. And those released might engage in
acts of terrorism. But risks to safety have always been the price
a society must pay for its liberty. Israel knows that well. By
detaining only 15 of its 300,000 Arab citizens, Israel today is
taking considerable risks. Indeed, what the world must come to
realize is that no country throughout recorded history has ever
exposed its wartime population to so much risk in the interest of
civil liberties.

My analysis of Israel's approach to preventive detention reflected
the approach I was taking toward the nation-state of the Jewish people:
I would try hard to understand the compromises it felt it had to make
with civil liberties—perhaps I would even give it the benefit of the
doubt—but I would not hold back from criticizing Israel when criticism was warranted.

My report, a version of which was published in *Commentary* magazine, elicited criticism from both sides. Some Israelis accused me of
not understanding the dangers they faced from terrorism and why it
was necessary to use every available tactic—preventive detention, enhanced interrogation, paid informers, targeted killings—to prevent
terrorism. Some civil libertarians, both in Israel and in the United
States, accused me of going easy on Israel and not being sufficiently
critical. Among the latter was Noam Chomsky, who challenged me
to a public debate on the issues of the Israeli–Palestinian conflict and
of civil liberties in Israel.

Today, Noam Chomsky is—and was even back then—one
of the most influential professors in the world, owing primarily to

his innovative, if controversial, theories of linguistics. He has been ranked as the most influential academic in the world. He proudly acknowledges that he "uses" his academic status to "make noise": "Since I was known professionally, I thought it was worth exploiting for a better purpose."[2] That "better" purpose has turned him into an all-knowing political guru, though his views on nonlinguistic issues tend to be more ideological than scholarly. His writing is opaque, often bordering on the incomprehensible. On several occasions when I have seen students carrying one of his political screeds, I have asked to look at it. Invariably the bookmark or bent page is near the beginning. I then inquire how much they have actually read and they admit, with embarrassment, that it's hard to get past the introductory pages. I suspect that Chomsky holds the world's record for the highest ratio of books bought to actually read from beginning to end.

Chomsky is a better speaker than he is a writer, but his speeches are polemical rather than analytic. They are sprinkled with phrases such as "there is no dispute about," or "everyone acknowledges," or "it is incontrovertible." These "argument stoppers" generally serve as preludes to both hotly disputed and flat-out false factual assertions. I recall him saying in one debate that it was "incontrovertible that Israel rejected Security Council Resolution 242, while the Arabs accepted it." When I read out loud the documentary evidence that proved that the exact opposite was true, he simply ignored the proof and repeated his "incontrovertible" assertion. That is his style, and his followers, of which there are many, regard him as a prophet who cannot be wrong.

Chomsky had emerged as a leading critic of American involvement in Vietnam, a war he regarded as one of imperialist aggression. We were introduced shortly after I arrived at Harvard in 1964 by Leonard Boudin, a great lawyer whose practice centered on representing people of the left, ranging from Fidel Castro to Dr. Benjamin Spock. I liked Noam, because he has a quick intellect and a strong passion. He is not fun to be with, however, because he has no sense of humor and little tolerance for opposing views, which he often characterizes as "unintelligent," "stupid" or "uninformed." He has called me "not very bright" and "strongly opposed to civil liberties." The first characterization is perhaps debatable. The second is flatly untrue.

His views on Israel in those days were typical of the Zionist left. He was affiliated with Hashomer Hatzair, near the extreme left of Israel's many ideological factions. He wished that the mandate had never been divided into two areas, one for the Jewish and the other for an Arab state. His preference was for a secular, binational, socialist state. But Israel had declared statehood, and the Jordanians and Egyptians had denied the Palestinians statehood by dividing the Arab portions of the mandate, with Jordan occupying the West Bank and Egypt occupying the Gaza Strip. That was the reality on the ground, and Chomsky had to deal with that messy reality. His support for the Palestinian cause had been quoted by Roger Fisher in his opening statement during *The Advocates* debate:

> *In America, there is little willingness to face the fact that Palestinians . . . have suffered a monstrous historical injustice. That worse injustice was done to Jews in the past is no reason for us to overlook the present plight of the Palestinians.*

His rabid hatred for the Jewish state was not yet manifest, and so when we were invited to debate in the early 1970s, I agreed, expecting a serious intellectual exchange of ideas with a fellow progressive. Our political views were quite far apart, even back then: I was a liberal Democrat and he was a radical socialist (or anarchist). Our views on Vietnam were somewhat similar—although his were more extreme—but our views on Israel, as I would learn during the debate, were quite far apart.

The debate—the first of several—was conducted in a large Boston church with a live audience of several hundred pro- and anti-Israel supporters. There were cheers and boos as well as a few shouted interruptions. But for the most part, the debate was civil.

Chomsky's basic position was that all of the British mandate over Palestine—what is now Israel and the West Bank—should be a single binational secular state. (No mention was made of the Gaza Strip.) He proposed two models for successful binational states: Yugoslavia and Lebanon. (He did not mention India-Pakistan before it was divided into two independent nations.) Yugoslavia, which was an assortment of ethnic and religious enclaves cobbled together and kept artificially unified by the charisma of Josip Broz Tito, was torn apart by bloody conflict after his death and ended up becoming several separate nations. Lebanon, which had managed for a time to divide political authority between its Muslim majority and Christian minority, also blew up in a bloody civil war that resulted in a mass exodus of its Christian population. It is now under the military control of Hezbollah, an Iranian-controlled terrorist group.

Neither Yugoslavia nor Lebanon—both failed states—is a positive model for Israel and the West Bank. Nor are there any other successful "one-state" solutions to comparable conflicts.

In my opening statement, I argued for a two-state solution with territorial border adjustments to strengthen Israel's security. Israel had not yet embarked on its controversial policy of building civilian settlements in the captured territories, so this issue did not arise. (When it did, in 1973, I strongly opposed that policy.) My plan called for Israel to annex a small percentage of the unpopulated or minimally populated areas of the West Bank and the Gaza Strip as buffers against future attacks. It should then gradually reduce and ultimately end its military presence in the West Bank and Gaza as soon as all hostilities and threats of hostilities ended and the Arab countries agreed to comply with the terms of Security Council Resolution 242. Implicit in my proposal was that Israel would not build civilian settlements in the areas it was prepared to return in exchange for peace.

My proposal was a variation on the Allon Plan, formulated by Israeli general Yigal Allon, which would have annexed parts of the Jordan Valley and other areas necessary for Israel's security and returned the remainder to Jordan in exchange for peace.

This is what I said about Chomsky's one-state scheme in our 1973 debate:

> *Putting aside the motivations behind such a proposal when it is made by the Palestinian organizations, why do not considerations of self-determination and community control favor two separate states: one Jewish and one Arab? Isn't it better for people of common background to control their own life, culture, and destiny (if they so choose), than to bring together in an artificial way people who have shown no ability to live united in peace.*

The audience overwhelmingly preferred my proposal to Chomsky's, although some thought both were too generous to the losing side of the Six-Day War. A small number of hard leftists favored Chomsky's proposal for a single state.

This was to be the first of several debates between Chomsky and me. This one ended in a friendly manner, with each of us respecting the other's perspective while agreeing to disagree about the optimal solution to the vexing problems. We continued to correspond by mail. In December 1970, I wrote to him complaining about a comparison one of his left-wing colleagues had made between Israel's wars of self-defense and America's war against North Vietnam. Here is his cordial response:

> *Dear Alan,*
> *I agree with you that comparisons between Israel and, say, North Vietnam are likely to be dubious, but not exactly for the reasons you give. North Vietnam was a backward peasant society, which has been under bitter attack and has received very little aid. Recall that in 1954, Bernard Fall predicted with "certainty" that North Vietnam would either suffer a disastrous*

famine or would become a Chinese colony if the US succeeded
in cutting it off from the south. I needn't comment on what
has happened in recent years. Israel, in contrast, was settled in
the first instance by educated Westerners and has received, by a
large margin, the greatest per capita aid of any country in the
world. It is the most advanced country in the region, by a vast
margin, and also the strongest military power. It does certainly
face potential dangers, but they can obviously not be compared
by those faced by North Vietnam.
Best, Noam

It was a perfectly reasonable and friendly response. Our subsequent interactions were not as friendly, as the hard left moved from the kind of criticism of Israel's policies leveled by Fisher on *The Advocates* and by Chomsky in our initial debate to delegitimation of Israel as the nation-state of the Jewish people.

My personal break with Chomsky came in 1973, when he supported a professor named Israel Shahak, who had characterized Israel as a "racist society," akin to Hitler's Germany. Shahak was a brilliant Israeli professor of chemistry, who, like Chomsky, was widely respected for his scientific accomplishments. But he was also widely reviled—except by Israel haters—for his comparisons of Israel to Nazi Germany. Recall that this was prior to Israel creating its controversial civilian settlements in the territories it had captured in the Six-Day War.

In an article in the *Boston Globe*, Chomsky called Shahak a civil libertarian. I wrote a letter to the editor disagreeing with him:

Let no one believe that Shahak is a civil libertarian. He is the
furthest thing from it. A civil libertarian defends the rights of
those with whom he disagrees as vehemently as those with whom
he agrees (consider, for example, the American Civil Liberties
Union's frequent defense of Nazis and right wingers). Shahak

*has never defended the rights of those with whom he disagrees
politically; nor has he ever attacked the practices of those with
whom he agrees politically. He is about as much of a civil
libertarian as are Communists who defend only the rights of
other Communists, or Ku Klux Klanners who only defend the
rights of other Klanners.[3]*

*The very best proof of Israel's commitment to liberty is that it
permits hate-mongers such as Shahak—and other Israeli-Arab
critics of Israel—to travel through the world on Israeli passports
spewing forth their venom. Can one think of any Arab country
that would permit a Jewish critic publicly to attack its regime?*

Chomsky responded that Shahak was a civil libertarian as well as
a "man of honor and principle who needs no lessons from Alan Dershowitz or anyone else on what it means to be a civil libertarian."

*Dershowitz has chosen to distort beyond recognition what
Shahak has said and done to vilify him as a "hate-monger" who
"spews forth (his) venom" against Israel. His resort to such tactics
and his refusal to consider the actual evidence that Shahak has
presented speaks for itself, I am afraid.*

I responded:

*I was not surprised at the belligerent tone of Noam Chomsky's
response to my letter regarding Israel Shahak. Though Chomsky
and I have been allies in numerous cases, I have seen over the
years that Chomsky will stop at nothing in attacking those who
support Israel or in defending those who attack it.*

*Chomsky disputes my statement that Shahak defends the civil
liberties only of those with whom he agrees politically. I again
challenge Chomsky to cite me instances where Shahak has ever
supported the rights of those who disagreed with his anti-Zionist*

*political views. . . . Why did [Shahak] refuse to condemn the
execution of Jews in Iraq or the oppression of Jews in the Soviet
Union? I am afraid that both Shahak and Chomsky do need
lessons on what it means to be a civil libertarian.*

Finally *The Globe* decided to end this unusual exchange of letters
on its editorial page and Chomsky got the last word:

*Dr. Shahak, acting with courage and honor, [has] produced
substantial evidence on violations of human and civil rights by
the Israeli government, avoiding no relevant instances to my
knowledge. Apparently unable to refute the facts, Dershowitz
has chosen to defame the man, in a manner which is as familiar
as it is deplorable.*[4]

From that point on my interactions with Chomsky became more
belligerent, as he and others pushed the hard left toward delegitimizing Israel. Our friendship would further deteriorate when, several years
later, he signed a petition in support of an anti-Semitic Holocaust denier named Robert Faurisson, who had published a book denying that
six million Jews had been murdered by gas, bullets and forced starva-
tion.[5] Faurisson claimed that *The Diary of Anne Frank* was a hoax.
He accused the Jews and Israel of exploiting the alleged Holocaust
for financial gain. Chomsky characterized Faurisson's lies as historical
"findings"—that there were no gas chambers or systematic killing of
Jews—based on "extensive historical research."[6] He described Faurisson as "a sort of relatively apolitical liberal." Chomsky also denied that
there were "anti-Semitic implications" in denying the Holocaust:

*I see no anti-Semitic implications in denial of the existence
of gas chambers or even denial of the Holocaust. Nor would
there be anti-Semitic implication, per se, in the claim that the
Holocaust (whether one believes it took place or not) is being*

exploited viciously so by apologists for Israeli repression and violence. I see no hint of anti-Semite implications in Faurisson's work. [Emphasis added][7]

I responded in a letter to the *Boston Globe*:

While some may regard Chomsky as an eminent linguist, he does not understand the most obvious implications in Faurisson's collective condemnation of the Jewish people as liars. . . . Failure to recognize the anti-Semitic implication of Holocaust denial is like saying there would be no racist implications in a claim that African-Americans enjoyed slavery, or no sexist implication in a statement that women wanted to be raped. The Holocaust is the central historical event of modern Jewish history. Efforts to deny or minimize it are the current tools of the anti-Semite and neo-Nazi. Not surprising both Faurisson and Chomsky are frequently quoted with approval by those hatemongers.

Chomsky's actions in defending the substance *of Faurisson's bigoted remarks against valid charges of anti-Semitism—as distinguished from defending Faurisson's* right *to publish such pernicious drivel—disqualify Chomsky from being considered an honorable defender of the "underdog" [as he had claimed]. The victims of the Holocaust, not its deniers, are the underdogs.*[8]

For me and many other liberal Jews, that was the last straw. At a time of increasing Holocaust denial or minimization—by Arab leaders, neo-Nazis and even some on the hard left—the idea that the most influential academic in the world would validate Faurisson's deliberate lies as "findings" based on "extensive historical research" was beyond comprehension. It was also beyond comprehension that Chomsky would allow Faurisson to use an essay he had written as an introduction to his anti-Semitic screed.[9] As a result of his getting in bed with this Holocaust denier, Chomsky became a pariah in the

Jewish community. This turned him even more ferociously against Israel. Indeed, it is likely that the nearly universal condemnation by the Jewish community of Chomsky for his role in helping to legitimate Holocaust denial pushed him over the edge when it came to Israel and its supporters. From that point on, it was hard to have a rational discussion with Chomsky on these issues.

Notwithstanding our growing animosity, I continued to debate Chomsky over the years,[10] even as his anti-Israel (and anti-American) views became more and more strident. Indeed, increasing extremism on both sides was squeezing the center and making nuanced discussion more difficult. The growth of the hard right and the settler movement in Israel contributed to this polarization. I was strongly opposed to the settler movement, believing it would make the two-state solutions more difficult. I must admit that I enjoyed sparring with Chomsky and others on both the hard left and hard right. I recall getting a call from Ted Kennedy before the Easter-Passover season in which he teased me:

"Al"—he was the only person who always called me Al—"you're enjoying kicking Chomsky's ass too much. You should cut it out for Lent."

Since Jews don't observe Lent, I kept up my criticism of Chomsky and others.

I also opposed turning the issue into a religious conflict over biblical claims to "Judea" and "Samaria." Both settler and biblical movements, which overlapped, tended to attract zealots for whom pragmatic compromise—so necessary to a two-state solution—was anathema.

Among the most extreme views on the biblical and settler hard right were those of Rabbi Meir Kahane, the leader of the Jewish Defense League, who I would later debate. But first, I was called on to serve as defense counsel for one of his followers.

Around the same time that I was becoming deeply committed to the defense of Israel—through my visits to Israel, appearances on

The Advocates, and debates with Chomsky—another transformative event was developing in my career and my life.

The Jewish Defense League was growing in popularity among some young Jews, especially in Brooklyn and Queens. Founded by Rabbi Kahane as a Jewish self-defense organization, it morphed into a confrontational group that threatened and employed violent means to secure its (often positive) ends. Its violent actions were universally condemned by traditional Jewish leaders—and by me and my friends. We supported the goals of the JDL, especially its advocacy for the oppressed Jews of the Soviet Union, but we despised its violent means.

A family friend and Boro Park neighbor was being accused of murdering a wealthy young woman who had been working as an assistant to the world-famous impresario Sol Hurok. The family friend, Sheldon Seigel, had been recruited by Rabbi Meir Kahane to join the Jewish Defense League.

I despised the violent means used by the JDL, but when a mutual friend asked me to defend Seigel—who was facing a possible death sentence—I felt I had no choice, based on my lifelong commitment to representing even the most despised people accused of crimes. I had represented non-Jews accused of violent crimes, so I saw no principle that would incline me to turn down a Jew—and someone whose family I know.

Seigel was accused of being the "engineer" who had made the smoke bomb that had been planted in Hurok's office, an action intended to be a protest against Hurok for bringing in talent from the Soviet Union as part of a cultural exchange program. "Bullets for ballerinas and bombs for balalaikas" was their slogan, along with "every Jew a 22 [caliber rifle]."

The smoke bomb was designed to frighten and cause panic, but not to kill. Tragically, its smoke in the enclosed area suffocated Iris Kones, a young Jewish woman from an extraordinarily wealthy family who were major contributors to Harvard, among other institutions. Seigel was charged with felony murder, because planting the smoke bomb, regardless of the lack of intent to kill, was a felony, and any death, even an accidental one, resulting from a felony is murder.

My pro bono representation of Seigel on constitutional grounds—the evidence against him came largely from an illegal wiretap—created difficulty for me at Harvard. The victim's relatives threatened to cut off all contributions to Harvard Law School unless I stopped representing Seigel or was fired by the law school. The dean called me in to tell me how "expensive" I was becoming, but that it was worth it. I persisted, and after months of litigation, the team I assembled won a total victory.[11] It was my first big win in a highly publicized case, and it helped establish my national reputation as a winning appellate lawyer at the age of 34.

My involvement in the JDL and Soviet Jewry cases brought me into close contact with the movement to help Soviet Jewry. I was convinced there were better ways to confront this important issue than through the violent means adopted by the JDL. I had read Elie Wiesel's book *The Jews of Silence*, which detailed the plight of the Soviet Jews who were being discriminated against and denied exit permits to Israel. I met with Elie, who urged me to travel to the Soviet Union to defend refuseniks—Jews who were refused exit permits—some of whom were facing imprisonment in the Gulag for protesting their unfair treatment. Two Jewish men were facing the death penalty for trying to steal a small airplane and fly several refuseniks to Sweden.

I helped assemble a team of international lawyers to go to the Soviet Union in an effort to save the lives and liberty of these brave refuseniks. I believe that there, but for the grace of God and the choices my great grandparents made to come to America in the nineteenth century, might go I.

The team was headed by my former professor Telford Taylor, who knew the Soviet chief prosecutor and chief justice from his days as a Nuremberg prosecutor. We traveled to the Soviet Union in 1974 to meet our clients and then to Israel to interview witnesses who had managed to emigrate. In the end, we helped to save the lives of the two refuseniks who had been sentenced to death and to secure the freedom of several who were facing imprisonment or were already in prison.[12]

I subsequently worked with Irwin Cotler to free the Soviet Union's most prominent refusenik prisoner, Anatoly Sharansky, who had been falsely accused of spying for the United States.[13] I helped persuade President Jimmy Carter to make an unprecedented and categorical denial that Sharansky had ever spied for the United States. This resulted in the death penalty being taken off the table, but Sharansky was sentenced to a long term of imprisonment. I then helped to arrange an exchange of prisoners, which resulted in Sharansky's release, after he had served eight years in the Gulag. We met shortly after he crossed the Glienicke Bridge to freedom, and he threw his arms around me and recited the Jewish Prayer, "Baruch Matir Asurim," blessed are those who help free the imprisoned. Despite the fact that I represented him without charge, that blessing was the most meaningful fee I ever earned. "Natan," as he is now called, made aliya upon his release from the Gulag and became one of Israel's most important moral and political leaders.[14]

My involvement in the JDL and Soviet Jewry cases was transformative in my career and my life. Now I was a full-time advocate for Israel, for Soviet Jewry and for the Jewish people—as well as for the liberal domestic causes to which I had devoted so much of my young life.

I also worked with Senator Ted Kennedy and other political leaders on broader diplomatic, legislative, economic and legal efforts to open the gates of the Soviet Union to the nearly two million Jews who were ultimately allowed to emigrate to Israel, the United States and Europe. It was one of the greatest human rights accomplishments in modern history, and the part of my career that I am most proud of.[15]

But these causes—or at least many of those who supported them—were coming into conflict, as it became more difficult to be a liberal supporter of Israel.

6

The Hard Left Denies
Israel's Right to Exist

ON THE MORNING of October 6, 1973—Yom Kippur—the Egyptian and Syrian armed forces attacked Israel. Although intelligence sources warned of an imminent attack, the Israeli military was caught off guard. Some Israeli generals had called for a preemptive attack against the enemy air forces, but Prime Minister Golda Meir refused, citing a warning from Henry Kissinger that if Israel once again preemptively attacked—as it had done in 1967—it would not receive any military support from the United States: "Not so much as a nail." At the time, Kissinger was effectively running American foreign and military policy because President Nixon was in the process of being removed from office.

The result of not preempting was an enormous casualty rate among Israeli soldiers in the first days of the war.

Many people around the world, not just Jews, were quite properly shocked that the attack had come on the holiest day of the Jewish calendar. Ironically, it would have been worse had the attack come on a busy weekday rather than on Yom Kippur, a day when the roads were empty and mobilization of reserves from synagogues and homes was facilitated.

Casualties were also high among Egyptian and Syrian soldiers. Before the war Anwar Sadat—who had replaced Nasser upon his death in 1970—had said he was willing to "sacrifice a million Egyptian soldiers" to recover the barren Sinai from Israel.

The fighting was ferocious, both in the Sinai and on the Golan Heights. The Syrian front was far more dangerous for Israel, because the Syrian army was in close proximity to Israeli civilian population centers—and the Syrians made no distinction between combatants and noncombatants.

On the second day of the war—when things were going very badly for Israel—Moshe Dayan reportedly said that "the Third Temple" was in danger because "the fight is over the entire land of Israel," as the Arabs intended "to conquer Israel, to eliminate the Jews." He reportedly suggested to the prime minister that Israel demonstrate its nuclear capacity by detonating an atomic bomb over an unpopulated area. Meir reportedly rejected the idea.[1] Although Israel has never publicly confirmed that it possesses a nuclear arsenal, everyone, especially the Arab countries, knew of its existence. They also knew that Israel had pledged never to be the first Middle East country to deploy a nuclear weapon (if it had one). Dayan wanted Syria and Egypt to see that Israel would break that pledge if its very survival was at stake. Meir wanted to maintain the pledge.

My Jewish friends and colleagues were at Harvard Hillel Yom Kippur services as the war unfolded. Our intelligence source, Professor Nadav Safran, provided a glum assessment. Everyone was shocked that the vaunted Israeli military could be caught so off guard. Prayers were offered for Israeli soldiers. Congregants hid transistor radios in their tallit (prayer shawl) bags. News reports were continually updated.

In the end, Israeli forces counterattacked and won the day. Only a United States–imposed cease-fire prevented Israel from destroying the Egyptian army, which its forces had encircled, with the help of a bold move by General Sharon. But the Israeli casualty rates were too high for a small country, and Golda Meir was soon replaced as prime minister by Yitzhak Rabin, a military hero–turned–peace advocate, who I had met three years earlier.

More importantly, Israel's self-confidence was shaken. This was not a clear military victory like the one six years earlier. Egypt and Syria celebrated the many casualties they had inflicted on Israel and the temporary regaining of captured land they had achieved in the first days of the war. When I subsequently visited Egypt in 1988, I was shown the museum that commemorated Egypt's "victory" over "the Zionist entity" during the "Ramadan war," so named by Egypt because their attack was during their holiest month. For Egypt, even small, symbolic victories are worthy of celebration, even if the ultimate result was a humiliating military defeat.

More than 2,500 Israeli soldiers were killed in the 19-day war, and more than 7,500 were injured. Total deaths among Arab soldiers amounted to more than 15,000, with as many as 35,000 wounded. Nearly 10,000 Arab soldiers were taken prisoner and quickly returned. Hundreds of Israeli POWs were tortured and murdered with their hands tied behind their backs. Documents discovered by Israeli troops during the war showed that Egyptian general Saad el-Shazly had distributed written orders to kill Israeli soldiers even after they surrendered. These deliberate and systematic violations of the Geneva Convention were ignored by the United Nations and the international community.

The biggest impact of the Yom Kippur War was that it demonstrated to Israelis and Arabs alike that Israel was not invincible. It had won this time, but it paid a high price. Next time, or the time after, it could actually lose. Everyone understood that no matter how many times Israel won, if it ever lost a single war, that would be the end of "the Third Temple."

It was against the background of this tragic war that the first major attack by a prominent American against the very legitimacy of Israel as the nation-state of the Jewish people took place. It came from an antiwar Catholic priest who I had once helped defend. His name was Daniel Berrigan, perhaps not a household name today, but back in the early 1970s he was one of the most prominent and charismatic figures in the antiwar movement. Left-wing attorney Leonard Boudin (whose daughter Kathy was convicted of murder after she joined the Weather Underground) had sought my advice when he defended Berrigan in 1971 against criminal charges growing out of his antiwar activities.

I had met Berrigan and been taken by his warmth and charm. Many Jewish, pro-Israel, antiwar liberals were similarly impressed by him. We were therefore shocked when, within weeks of the country's near annihilation at the hands of genocidal Arab armies, he published an anti-Israel screed, which many, including myself, thought crossed the line into anti-Semitism.

In a speech delivered on October 19, 1973, and published widely,[2] the Reverend Daniel Berrigan, S.J., described Israel as "a criminal Jewish community" that has committed "crimes against humanity," has "created slaves" and has espoused "racism . . . aimed at proving its racial superiority to the people it has crushed." It is logical, Berrigan declared, that "racist ideology, which brought the destruction of the Jewish communities at the hands of the Nazis, should now be employed by the state of Israel . . ."

Not content with attacking the Jewish state in these inflammatory terms, Reverend Berrigan also chastised the "Jewish people," who he described as "so proud" and so "endowed with intelligence," as being collectively guilty of numerous sins and crimes. American Jews were the special focus of Berrigan's attack, because they "have in the main given their acquiescence or their support to the Nixon ethos." The American Jewish community's leadership was "fervent in support of Nixon," who was thereby enabled "to mute the horrific facts of the Vietnam war in light of Jewish concern for Israel." This led to the supposed "fact" that "in Nixon's first term alone some six million Southeast Asians had been maimed, bombed, displaced, tortured, imprisoned or killed." Berrigan refers to the iconic figure of six million as "one of those peculiar facts which must be called free-floating; it was a statistic, it did not signify."

He concludes with a veiled threat both to American Jews and to Israel:

> *To put the matter brutally, many American Jewish leaders were capable of ignoring the Asian holocaust in favor of economic and military aid to Israel. Those of us who resisted the war had to live with that fact. The fate of the Vietnamese was as unimportant to the Zionists in our midst as was the state of the Palestinians. [Again collective guilt: I'm a Zionist who cared greatly about the fate of the Vietnamese as well as the Palestinians, as did many other Zionists.] But I venture to suggest that it is not merely we, nor the Vietnamese, who must live with that fact. So must Israel. So must the American Jews.*

I was outraged by Berrigan's bigoted and mendacious words, especially since they had come from an ally in the antiwar movement. These kinds of attacks from the hard left are common today, but they were unheard of back in 1973. I had no idea where this bigotry came from, since Berrigan had worked so closely over the years with so many Jewish lawyers, war resisters and civil rights activists. Some suggested that it reflected his theological views, but I saw no evidence of that. Whatever his motives, I feared that his words could have widespread influence among his many admirers on the left, so I felt I had to respond. I called my friend Leonard Boudin, who was his lawyer and friend. He had no idea that Berrigan felt that way or would publicly express such views. I told Leonard that I would be attacking his client. He said I should do what I had to do, but he couldn't become involved. I understood.

I then wrote and circulated the following public petition to the Harvard faculty and to every liberal I knew:

> *We are a group of Americans of all faiths and of diverse views on the Arab–Israeli conflict. Many of us have supported*

the Reverend Berrigan in his activities against the Vietnam War. Some of us have even defended the Reverend Berrigan and his colleagues before courts of law. We have different views on many issues of the day. But we are unanimous in our condemnation—indeed a strong word would be more appropriate—of the thoughts expressed in the Berrigan speech of October 19th. These irresponsible and blatantly inaccurate charges call for no substantive response. They speak for themselves as evidence of either the author's abysmal ignorance or his malice toward the Jewish people. The rhetoric—especially the suggestion of the collective guilt of the Jewish people for which Israel is to be made to pay—is tragically reminiscent of a bygone age. We call on all persons of good will—whatever their political views—to join us in condemning this bigoted attack on the Jewish people.

The response was overwhelming, with hundreds of people from every background signing on to my letter. Chomsky, of course, took Berrigan's side and attacked his critics for creating a "fabrication." Sadly, my old friend and client Bill Kunstler wrote a counter letter agreeing with Berrigan. But Kunstler's main lawyer Morton Stavis— who was far to the left of me and closer to Berrigan and Kunstler on most issues—joined my campaign to discredit Berrigan. He wrote his own heartfelt eight-page, single-spaced critique of his old friend and political ally, which included the following:

Firstly, moving as I do within New Left circles, I am quite accustomed to the fact that many of my colleagues and associates have views with respect to the State of Israel with which I strongly disagree. But some of the formulations which you employed are quite beyond moral disagreement and should not have been employed. I refer to language and rhetoric which is far from the truth and which has the effect of generating blind hostility rather than thoughtful consideration. I mention two examples:

"It is . . . logical, too, that racist ideology, which brought the destruction of the Jewish community at the hands of the Nazis, should now be employed by the State of Israel."

"American Jews—must live with the brutal fact that many American Jewish leaders were capable of ignoring the Asian Holocaust in favor of economic and military aid to Israel."

Aside from the factual inaccuracies of these statements [for example, the vast majority of Jews voted against Nixon and did not support the Vietnam War], the first of these formulations becomes the foundation for charging Israel with Hitlerism; the second can be the foundation for a far-ranging escalation of anti-Semitism in this country.

I suggest that a person of your sense of moral leadership ought to be making speeches to Arabs and Jews alike, telling them that they have to accept each other, that they have to live in peace.

Berrigan had crossed a line that even most hard-left critics of Israel would not cross—at least not yet. He did not back down. Instead he escalated his hateful and mendacious attacks on Israel and American Jews, becoming a full-fledged anti-Semite, repeatedly and collectively attacking "the Jews," "the Jewish Community," "Jewish Leaders" and "the Jewish People." (His language was subsequently emulated by another anti-Semitic cleric, Bishop Desmond Tutu.) Berrigan's bigotry did not stop some of his many followers—including hard-left Jews—from joining his campaign to demonize and delegitimize Israel. It was the beginning of an escalating war between liberal supporters of Israel (which included many who were critical of some Israeli policies) and hard-left delegitimizors of the nation-state of the Jewish people.

The Berrigan–Kunstler–Chomsky attacks were also the opening

salvo of my personal war with the hard left over Israel. My next target was the National Lawyers Guild.[3]

In the 1960s, I had worked closely with the Lawyers Guild on civil liberties issues, such as opposition to the death penalty, racial discrimination and criminal justice reform. But my collaboration with the Guild was to change rather quickly in the early 1970s when it was taken over by anti-American and anti-Israel extremists, most of them not lawyers.

The National Lawyers Guild was established in 1937 as an antidote to the American Bar Association, which was then fighting the New Deal, excluding black lawyers from membership and opposing the labor movement. The original Guild was an amalgam of Roosevelt liberals, CIO labor leaders, black civil rights lawyers and radicals of assorted affiliations and persuasions. Its membership over the years had included such distinguished lawyers as Thurgood Marshall, Ferdinand Pecora, Paul O'Dwyer, Louis Boudin (Leonard's uncle) and William Hastie. During its early years, splits developed between the anti-Communist liberals and the radicals. But the Guild survived and accomplished much good on the domestic front, which included an excellent record of providing legal assistance to the civil rights, labor and antiwar movements.

However, in the late 1960s and early 1970s, at the height of the antiwar movement, the Guild began to be taken over by younger, more militant lawyers from the New Left. Among their pet causes were Fidel Castro and the plight of Palestinians under what was called Zionist Occupation. As George Coak, an admiring Guild historian and a former editor of the monthly *Guild News*, described it, "At the Boulder (Colorado) Convention in 1971 the young veterans of the anti-war movement found they had the Guild in their own hands, and many older members withdrew from active membership. Legal workers [paraprofessionals and support staff] and jailhouse lawyers were admitted to membership." Law students were also admitted, thus strengthening the hold of the young radicals but replacing the percentage of actual lawyers in the Guild to less than half. The Guild no longer considered itself an alternative bar association but rather the prime organizer of "radical legal people" and the legal arm of "the American radical left."

Many of the longtime members of the Guild and even some of its founders, who sympathized with the sufferings of Palestinian refugees, were nonetheless outraged at the decision by the younger radicals to use the Guild as the legal propaganda arm of the Palestine Liberation Organization, which was then considered a terrorist organization. One founding member put it this way: "There is a group within the Guild which is absolutely determined to make the Guild a propaganda voice of the PLO. [T]hey are fostering splits and divisions within the Guild which threatens it very existence."

Earlier in its history, when it was a liberal organization, the Guild had supported the Jewish struggle for national liberation. It had opposed the American arms embargo against the new state. But after joining forces with the International Association of Democratic Lawyers, a communist front organization that, like the Soviet Union, refused to recognize the legitimacy of Israel, it turned more and more against the Jewish state and more and more in favor of Palestinian terrorism. As a long-term observer of the Guild put it,

> Basically, you had a situation where a bunch of Third World types wanted to ensure that the Jews in the Guild—and the Jews were almost certainly a majority—would be forced to eat crow, to choose sides. The guild changed dramatically in the 1960s and early 1970s when the veterans of the early days were displaced by the veterans of campus unrest who had gone from SDS to law schools around the country. They're angry, and rigid, and there's no better test of their control of the Guild than forcing the old timers to grovel, and there's no better evidence of their own militance—

if they're Jews—than toadying up to the PLO. Endorsing the
PLO has become a litmus test for Jewish radicals.

The Guild decided to send observers to the trials of accused Palestinian terrorists and to have them report back. One of the observers included in his report the following disclaimer: "I am opposed, on political as well as humanitarian grounds, to terrorism as means of achieving political change." But since the disclaimer expressly contradicted the approval of terrorism by the PLO and the International Association of Democratic Lawyers, the Guild leadership simply decided to excise it from the final report.

In the original report, the observer properly criticized Israel for "interrogating [the alleged terrorist] without the presence of counsel," but added the important caveat that he (the observer) was "personally familiar with this procedure in the socialist countries of Eastern Europe." Rather than risk the wrath of communist lawyers in these countries, the Guild leadership decided to delete this comparison.

The Guild's unwillingness to criticize "the socialist countries of Eastern Europe" was dramatically manifested in an exchange I had with Professor John Quigley, the national vice president of the Guild. After learning that the Guild had decided to send an observer to the trial in Israel, I telephoned Quigley and requested that the Guild also send an observer to the Soviet trial of Anatoly Sharansky. It was the belief of several experts on Soviet law that a request by the Guild to send an observer to the Sharansky trial could have a decided impact on Soviet actions, since the Soviet Union has a close relationship with the International Association of Democratic Lawyers and its constituent members. Professor Quigley was extremely candid in his response: he told me that he doubted the Guild would be willing to send an observer to a Soviet trial, since the "reality" of the situation was that a considerable number of the Guild members approved of the Soviet Union and would not want to criticize a Soviet judicial proceeding.

I wrote articles and made speeches exposing the hypocrisy and bias of the National Lawyers Guild. Many old members and some new ones resigned in protest. But the Guild persisted in its move away from its long-standing commitment to civil liberties and liberalism and toward following the Soviet line with regard to Israel, a line of increased nonrecognition and of no diplomatic relations. Even after the fall of the Soviet Union in 1989 and Russia's subsequent recognition of Israel, the Guild maintained its hard-left delegitimization of, and double standard toward, the Middle East's only democracy.

Members of the Guild also began to infiltrate the American Civil Liberties Union in an effort to turn it from a neutral defender of the civil liberties of all Americans to an advocate for agenda-driven left-wing causes. It succeeded in some areas of the country more than in others, to a point where today it has all but abandoned its original nonpartisan mission. More on this later—but now back to the mid-1970s.

On November 10, 1975, while Israel was still governed by the liberal Yitzhak Rabin and the Labor Party—and before it embarked on its controversial settlement policy—the General Assembly of the United Nations voted overwhelmingly to declare the national liberation movement of the Jewish people to be "a form of racism and racial discrimination." The vote was 72 in favor, 35 opposed and 32 abstaining. (This vote led Abba Eban to quip that if Algeria introduced a United Nations resolution declaring the world to be flat and accusing Israel of flattening it, it would win by a vote of 72 in favor, 35 opposed and 32 abstaining.)

The immediate effect of the vote was to encourage the banning and blacklisting of Israeli and other Zionist speakers on many university campuses, which had "antiracist" platform restrictions. But the significance of the vote went beyond its impact on campus speech. It was a reflection of a worldwide demonization of Israel, led by the Soviet Union, its hard-left followers throughout the West, and the Arab and Muslim world. It was now "legitimate" and "lawful" to single out the nation-state of the Jewish people for international condemnations as a pariah entity.[4] Israel was now in a category of only two nations: apartheid South Africa and the democratic nation-state of the Jewish people.

Matters only got worse when Menachem Begin became Israel's first conservative prime minister in 1977. Until then, David Ben-Gurion and his protégés in the left Labor Party had ruled Israel, while Begin and his right-wing party had been the opposition. The fact that Israel was governed by left-wing socialists and liberals did not stop hard left anti-Israel bigots like Berrigan from demonizing Israel as a fascist regime. Begin's surprise victory turned many American liberals and labor supporters against the Israeli government, and some even against the State of Israel. This significant change, which has endured to this day with several interstitial Labor governments, made the defense of Israel in left-wing circles increasingly difficult, despite the worldwide reality that many democracies have been governed in recent decades by conservative leaders, such as Margaret Thatcher, Ronald Reagan and Angela Merkel.

The election of Begin created some cognitive dissonance for many American Jews like myself and many of my friends and colleagues, who are both liberals and Zionists. We have had to confront this conflict over many years now, and it may well continue into the foreseeable future.

Likud and the Liberals

Israel Moves to the Right

I WAS IN Israel the night Menachem Begin was elected prime minister, watching the election returns at the house of my dear friend Yitzhak
Zamir, who was then the dean of the Hebrew University Law School.
(He would subsequently become attorney general and a justice of the
Supreme Court.) The other guests were all liberal academics, lawyers
and businesspeople who always voted for the Labor Party. They found
it hard to believe that the liberal socialist Israel with which they grew
up would now be led by a right-wing former leader of the Irgun, or
Etzel, as it was called in Israel. (Several years later, I was with some of
the same people when the uncompromising radical Meir Kahane was
elected to the Knesset. The shock was even greater.)

I, too, was surprised at the election of Begin, because as an American I thought that the dramatic rescue of the hostages at Entebbe the
previous year had solidified support for the Labor coalition, which
was in power at the time. Prime Minister Rabin had ordered the
operation—led by Yonatan Netanyahu, Benjamin's older brother, and
a student at Harvard, who was killed during the rescue—that captured
the imagination of the world. The daring raid did much to elevate Israel's prestige around the world. Several movies have been based on
it. But Rabin was forced to resign several months later when my old
friend Aharon Barak, who was then attorney general, charged his wife
with hiding an illegal bank account in the United States.

Rabin's forced resignation marked the beginning of a disturbing development wherein numerous elected Israeli officials have been serially investigated, prosecuted and removed from office. Some were guilty and deserved to be prosecuted, while the guilt of others has been questionable. More on this later.

Rabin was replaced by acting prime minister Shimon Peres, who was not nearly as popular as Rabin. Begin's party won more seats in the 1977 election than Labor and was able to form a hardline government. Continuing threats against Israel, both external (from Egypt, Syria and Iraq) and internal (terrorist attacks by the PLO and other even more radically violent groups) may have inclined some Israelis to give up on peace and demand more hawkish policies, such as annexing the West Bank. My friends watching the election returns believed that Begin's ascension to the prime ministership would set back efforts to achieve peace. Many American Jews agreed, and Begin's election began a period in which the Israeli right would frequently find itself in power, further alienating liberal American Jews.

It turned out, of course, that Begin was able to do what no other prime minister had done: make a peace treaty with Egypt. The credit for that achievement must be shared among several leaders, and there is still disagreement about how to allocate the credit. But Begin played an important role in this peace process. So did President Carter, who was the president least sympathetic to Israel since Eisenhower. But to his credit, he brought Begin and Anwar Sadat to the bargaining table, and the rest is history. Several books have told the story of Camp David, the best of which is *President Carter: The White House Years* by my former student and my friend Stuart Eizenstat, who was there, working side by side with President Carter.

Begin was also responsible for one of Israel's most courageous, if controversial, military actions: the bombing of Iraq's Osirak nuclear reactor in 1981. "Operation Opera," as it was called, ended Iraq's nuclear program. It was criticized by President Reagan, who was generally supportive of Israel, and it resulted in a unanimous condemnation by the Security Council. I supported the Israeli action, especially because it was accomplished with minimal casualties—10 Iraqi soldiers and one French civilian, who was not supposed to be at the reactor on that weekend afternoon.

Begin justified his decision to destroy the reactor before it became "hot" by stating that Israel could never bomb a populated Iraqi city in retaliation for a nuclear attack on Israel. As survivors of the Holocaust, Israelis could never "contemplate bombing [when] . . . tens of thousands of innocent residents would have been hurt."[1] Its only recourse was prevention, rather than retaliatory deterrence. I later wrote a legal analysis—contained in my book *Preemption: A Knife That Cuts Both Ways*—justifying the preventive attack.

Critics accused Israel, which has numerous nuclear weapons, of hypocrisy in attacking Iraq's nuclear weapons program. But Israel has said it would never use its nuclear arsenal aggressively, whereas if Iraq—and now Iran—were to develop a nuclear weapon, there would be every reason to worry that they would try to use it against Israel, despite the near certainty of nuclear reprisal by Israel with devastating consequences.

A decade later, when Iraq invaded Kuwait and then fired Scud missiles at Israeli cities, the world came to appreciate the necessity of destroying Saddam Hussein's nuclear facility, which by 1991 might well have been able to develop nuclear-tipped missiles to attack Israeli population centers. At the time, Dick Cheney, the American secretary of defense, commended the Israeli action as "outstanding" because it "made our job much easier in Desert Storm."[2] That assessment may well be an understatement: if Iraq had nuclear weapons when it invaded Kuwait, they might still be there! The United States would have been reluctant to send troops to a battle zone facing nuclear weapons. Witness the current North Korean standoff.

But not all of Prime Minister Begin's military actions have been vindicated by history. Israel's invasion of Lebanon in 1982 (called

"Operation Peace for Galilee") is now widely regarded as a strategic mistake.

In the eyes of many—not just myself—Israel was morally and legally justified in its initial foray into Lebanon in order to stop terrorist attacks against its civilians. The Palestinian Liberation Organization had moved its terrorist bases into southern Lebanon, from which they were crossing the border and murdering Israeli civilians. The immediate cause of the invasion, however, took place many miles away in London, where terrorists tried to kill, and succeeded in seriously wounding, Israel's ambassador to Great Britain, an act regarded by Prime Minister Begin as a casus belli, justifying a military response. The goal of the operation was to rid southern Lebanon of PLO terrorists, reduce the influence of Syria in Lebanon, and install a pro-Israel Christian government under the leadership of Bachir Gemayel.

In the end, after brutal battles with many casualties, Israel succeeded in its short-term goal of getting the PLO out of southern Lebanon—they were allowed to move en masse to Tripoli, where they remained until 1983. But over the longer term, the vacuum created by the departure of the Sunni PLO was filled by the new, more dangerous, Shia terrorist group Hezbollah (Army of God). It is more dangerous partly because it is motivated by unappeasable religious fanaticism as opposed to being a secular national liberation movement, and partly because it is a surrogate for Israel's strongest enemy, Iran, which funds, arms and directs it. Within a few years, Hezbollah would rule all of southern Lebanon as a virtual mini-state, bristling with Iranian-supplied missiles. This outcome must be counted as a strategic error on Begin's part.

In addition, Israel suffered enduring damage to its moral standing throughout the world—not to mention among Israelis themselves—for its role in the infamous Sabra and Shatila massacre of hundreds of Palestinian civilians by Phalangist militia members. The Phalangists were a Christian-Lebanese anti-PLO party, whose leader, Bachir

Gemayel, was willing to make peace with Israel. He had just been elected president of Lebanon when he was assassinated along with 26 others in a massive bombing at Phalange headquarters.[3] The assassins were believed to be Palestinian militants, since other Phalangist leaders had been similarly assassinated for their willingness to make peace with Israel. Among the victims were the family and fiancée of Elie Hobeika, a prominent Phalangist leader. Hobeika subsequently organized a gang of several hundred young Phalangists, called the "young men," to take revenge against Palestinians for the assassination of President Gemayel. This revenge took the form of a massacre of Palestinians—mostly civilians—in the Shatila refugee camp and the adjoining Sabra neighborhood.

Though no Israeli soldiers participated in the killings, the Kahan Commission—established by Israel to investigate the massacre—led by Yitzhak Kahan, the president of the Supreme Court, concluded that the Israeli military was "indirectly responsible for not stopping it" and that Defense Minister Ariel Sharon was personally responsible "for ignoring the danger of bloodshed and revenge."[4] Sharon was forced to resign as defense minister. His political career did not revive for several years. Meanwhile the Sabra and Shatila massacre became a black mark on Israel's moral standing in the world and a rallying cry for its enemies.

The Lebanon War itself, with its indecisive and morally costly outcome, was Israel's first unpopular war at home, generating massive protests. It was also unpopular among many of Israel's supporters around the world, because it did not seem as necessary to protect Israel's security as previous wars had been. Its controversial nature fueled harsh criticism across the international political spectrum and provided moral ammunition to Israel's enemies, coming as it did at a time of increasing efforts by the hard left to delegitimize the nation-state of the Jewish people.

I could not, and did not, defend all of Israel's actions in Lebanon, especially its role in the Sabra and Shatila massacre. But I did defend Israel against the disproportionate condemnation it was receiving from the international left, which refused to condemn the PLO for provoking Israel into invading Lebanon by its terrorist acts on foreign soil.

It was shortly after the Sabra and Shatila massacre that my own life was threatened by anti-Israel extremists. It was the first such threat I had received—but it would not be the last.

The establishment of the Kahan Commission stimulated me to write an op-ed for the *New York Times* in 1982 calling for the establishment of a second commission to investigate the role of the PLO in general, and its leader Yasser Arafat in particular, in the raft of synagogue shootings and bombings that were plaguing the Jews of Europe.[5] Synagogues and other Jewish institutions in Rome, Paris, Antwerp and Brussels had been attacked. The Rome attack killed a two-year-old child and injured 37 civilians. Dozens of men, women and children were killed and injured in other attacks, including a group of Jewish children waiting for a school bus to take them to a Jewish summer camp. The most lethal attack had been on an elementary school in Ma'alot, Israel, where Palestinian terrorists took 105 children hostage, 22 of whom were killed and 68 injured.

These attacks reminded me of the infamous 1963 bombing of the 16th Street Baptist Church in Birmingham, Alabama, by the Ku Klux Klan during the civil rights movement, resulting in four African American children killed and 22 others injured. The hard left justifiably condemned the KKK killings, but it was silent when the PLO killed innocent Jews in much greater numbers. To the contrary, more and more countries were beginning to "recognize" the PLO as a legitimate political organization, including its violent attacks on Israeli and Jewish civilians as a legitimate form of "resistance." For its part, the PLO and Arafat denied complicity in the murder of Jewish children and other civilians, despite their bloody fingerprints being all over these terrorist attacks.

The hard left, as usual, gave Arafat a pass on his personal involvement in the murder of innocent civilians as well as on his refusal to condemn terrorism. As is all too typical of the hard left, they tolerate all manner of human rights violations by anti-Israel and anti-American tyrants while railing against even the most minor deviations from perfection by Western democracies.

In my *Times* article, I pointed out that the world had demanded an investigation by Israel following Sabra and Shatila and asked, "Why is there no similar demand for an inquiry by the PLO into its own possible complicity in the recent spate of synagogue killings?" It was a rhetorical question, as my op-ed made clear:

> *Some will surely say that it is unrealistic to expect the PLO to conduct a full and open inquiry into possible responsibility for the synagogue killings. If the PLO refused, then its host countries—those who give it sanctuary, diplomatic status and other forms of recognition—should conduct their own inquiries. Countries such as Italy and France, where the atrocities occurred, should subpoena—indeed demand—relevant information from the P.L.O. If the P.L.O. refused to comply with the valid investigative laws of a host country, its office should be closed and its officials expelled.*
>
> *If, on the other hand, the P.L.O. cooperated with the investigation and was shown to have had no connection with the synagogue killings, it would establish the bona fides of its recent condemnation of terrorism directed against Jewish religious targets. This would certainly go a long way toward enhancing its claim to political recognition.*
>
> *The very fact that a call for a P.L.O. commission of inquiry seems unrealistic demonstrates the hypocrisy of those members of the international community who have been bestowing on the P.L.O.—and its leader—the benefits of recognition without demanding the responsibilities of recognition.*

Neither the PLO nor its host countries conducted any investigations. The PLO continued to kill innocent children, while more and more countries—as well as the Vatican and other religious groups—gave it recognition and treated its leader like a statesman rather than the mass murderer he was. This only incentivized the PLO and other terrorist organizations to increase their reliance on terrorism as the means to achieve their aims rather than on negotiation and compromise.

This perverse phenomenon led me to write a book titled *Why Terrorism Works*, which argued that the reason terrorism was increasing as a tactic of choice is *because* it works.[6] Because it worked for the PLO—gaining them more recognition—it was used more frequently and with more deadly results. In the *New York Times* op-ed, I called for putting Yasser Arafat on trial, documenting his personal role in ordering terrorist attacks against American, Israeli and European targets over a 30-year period.

The most immediate consequence of my initial op-ed was a serious threat on my life by PLO supporters. A Harvard graduate student from North Africa came to my office one afternoon, shaking with fear. He asked to close the door and he began to whisper: "They're planning to kill you."

I asked, "Who?"

"My two roommates," he answered. "You can't tell them I told you."

"Why do they want to kill me?"

"Because of what you wrote about Arafat."

"Are they serious?"

"Absolutely. They have a plan. They have been watching you. They know where you park your car and what time you leave the office. They are planning to stage a 'robbery,' and stab you to death. They have the knives."

"When?"

"This week."

"Did they tell you?"

"No, I overheard them from my bedroom."

"Is anyone else involved?"

"No, I don't think so. Just them."

I promised not to disclose his name, although it seemed clear the roommates would figure out who had betrayed their plot. As soon as he left, I called the Harvard police, who notified the FBI. The students were arrested and confessed to discussing my murder, but they denied having an actual plan or making a final decision. They were immediately deported, and I was told to report anything suspicious to the FBI.

Several years later, the FBI informed me that a neo-Nazi "lawyer" named Matthew Hale had put out a "hit" against me and that I required 24/7 FBI protection for at least a few weeks. To this day, I need police protection when I speak on university campuses.[7]

But it was not the threat of violence against me personally that caused me the greatest concern. It was the growing support for the PLO and the increasing efforts to delegitimize Israel. Both sides of the debate were becoming more extreme and more uncompromising.

Bipartisan support for Israel was still strong, but some on the hard right, led by hard-right political operative, columnist, TV commentator, and sometime presidential candidate Pat Buchanan, were turning against Israel, while some on the hard left, let by Berrigan and Chomsky, were solidifying their long-standing opposition to the nation-state of the Jewish people. In the years to come, the conflict between the Palestinians and Israel would play out less on the battlefield of the Middle East and more on the campuses and in the media of the United States and Europe.

8

Debating Extremists
Left and Right

Vanessa Redgrave and Meir Kahane

DURING THE 1980S, as extreme positions came to the fore on both sides of the Israel debate, I decided to engage with those who held these dangerous viewpoints, not only on behalf of Israel and Jewish interests but on behalf of liberalism itself. Even then, many on the anti-Israel hard left were challenging fundamental principles of free speech and civil liberties. At the same time, hard-right Israelis and their American supporters seemed more and more open to illiberal and even antidemocratic tendencies. As a liberal defender of Israel, but not of its illiberal policies, I felt a responsibility to make the centrist liberal case for Israel's right to exist as the nation-state of the Jewish people and to defend its citizens from both internal and external threats.

Of most immediate concern was the vociferous campaign by members of the international left to legitimate Palestinian terrorism and to delegitimize Israel in the minds of centrist liberals, especially among students. The most prominent leader of this effort was Vanessa Redgrave, the world-famous actor, who was also a member of the Workers Revolutionary Party, a radical British communist organization.[1]

Redgrave was not merely a "supporter of the PLO," like some other Western entertainment figures and celebrities; she was an active propagandist for the organization, which was then engaged in terrorism.

She attended training sessions at their camps, from which terrorist attacks were staged, and called for the total destruction of Israel ("I don't think there is room for a State of Israel."[2]) She was involved in the production of several short films—reminiscent of the ones made by Nazi film director Leni Riefenstahl—extolling the coming destruction of the Jewish state, and she was filmed at a PLO camp dancing while holding a Kalashnikov above her head, an image that was circulated around the world.

Redgrave herself described her role as "active in the struggle for the victory of the Palestinian Revolution," and she pledged to assist the PLO "in every possible way." She opposed the two-state solution to the Israel-Palestinian conflict, supporting instead a military solution under which the nation-state of the Jewish people would be destroyed.[3]

It was not surprising, therefore, that when the Boston Symphony Orchestra hired her in 1982 to narrate several performances of Stravinsky's opera-oratorio *Oedipus Rex*, many of the musicians protested that choice.[4] Some suggested that they would exercise their own freedom of association by refusing to perform with a PLO collaborator who justified the potential assassination of artists. Board members feared that the controversy might reduce contributions to the financially shaky orchestra. There was some concern about disruptions of the performances by the Jewish Defense League or other protestors.

In the end, the orchestra decided to cancel the performances. They offered to pay Ms. Redgrave the $31,000 she would have received if the show had gone on. Ms. Redgrave declined the offer and sued the orchestra for breach of contract and violation of her civil rights. She sought $5 million in damages, claiming that she had been effectively "blacklisted" and that she could no longer find appropriate work as a result of the cancellation.

The orchestra responded that Ms. Redgrave had, in fact, earned more money since the cancellation than before it, and that if anyone had refused to hire her, it was because she had used her art to serve the political ends of terrorism.

They also proved that Ms. Redgrave herself had turned down roles—such as the wife of Soviet dissident Andrei Sakharov in an HBO production—because she believed the film might hurt the cause of communism.

Despite my strong opposition to everything Redgrave stood for, I condemned the decision to cancel her performance. In doing so, I was joined by Lillian Hellman, the Screen Actors Guild and other artists and organizations. But, in addition to supporting her right to perform, I also supported the right of musicians to refuse to perform with her. I wrote that if I were a member of the Boston Symphony Orchestra, I would refuse to be associated in any way with her, "not because of her beliefs, but because of her collaboration with and participation in" the murderous activities of a terrorist group that targeted Jewish men, women and children. I cited the case of the great Metropolitan Opera tenor Richard Tucker, who refused to perform under the baton of conductors who had been Nazi collaborators. Tucker was applauded for his principled stand, and so should the Boston Symphony players who did not want to perform with a collaborator and supporter of terrorism. I took the position that the "musicians should have been allowed not to play, but the concert should still have gone on," with substitute musicians or a smaller orchestra.

Redgrave, of course, used the lawsuit as an opportunity to rail against "blacklisting" and "McCarthyism." I turned her complaints against her by pointing out that she herself had advocated the blacklisting of Israeli musicians. Several years earlier, she had offered a resolution to the British Actors Union demanding that they blacklist Israeli artists and boycott Israeli audiences. The resolution included an ultimatum that "all members working in Israel (must) terminate their contracts and refuse all work in Israel." (So much for the sanctity of contracts!) Several years later, she justified as "entirely correct" the blacklisting of Zionist speakers at British universities. And she praised the proposed assassination of Israeli artists, because they "may well have been enlisted to do the work" of the Zionists.

In the American context, Redgrave cloaked herself in the First Amendment and decried the return of McCarthyism. But in England, she was very much at the forefront of preventing those with whom she disagreed from speaking. She also supported the PLO policy of assassinating West Bank Arabs who expressed views contrary to the PLO. If assassination is the ultimate form of censorship—as George Bernard Shaw once wrote—then Redgrave supported a brand of deadly blacklisting that even Joseph McCarthy never practiced. Were her pernicious political party to come to power, it would make Mc-Carthyism seem mild.

Vanessa Redgrave does not believe in the right of free speech for everyone—only for those with whom she agrees. But I believe in the right of free speech for everyone—even hypocrites who collaborate with murderers. By my principles and those of many civil libertarians who share them, I believe that the Boston Symphony Orchestra was wrong to cancel Redgrave's performance. By Redgrave's "principles," the symphony was absolutely correct in its actions.[5]

Accordingly, at a press conference on April 29, 1982, I issued a challenge to Redgrave to debate me on the issues of blacklisting, as well as on the merits and demerits of her views and activities with regard to terrorism. I believed strongly not only in the right for people like Redgrave to hold and express their odious opinions but also in their duty to defend them publicly. She responded that she could not debate me because the Workers Revolutionary Party does not allow her to say anything that has not been approved in advance by its central committee.

What occurred next was reported in the *Christian Science Monitor*:

> *Alan Dershowitz—the Harvard law professor and noted "devil's advocate" who champions the unpopular and unfriendly in court—was sitting in a restaurant with his*

children recently when he saw a flier headlined, "Boston Against Blacklisting."

"I immediately wanted to attend this benefit. I'm against blacklisting," Professor Dershowitz commented later. "Then I saw who it was for. It was for Vanessa Redgrave."

So Dershowitz stood outside the theater, handing out fliers of his own, alleging that Miss Redgrave supports blacklists in England.

I then wrote an op-ed for a Boston newspaper explaining why I leafleted the event:

I've been preaching about the First Amendment for most of my adult life. So, I went out on the street and practiced what I'd been preaching. There I stood, at the entrance of the Boston Shakespeare Company, handing out leaflets I had printed up at my house and reproduced on my small home copying machine. The event was a fundraiser for an organization called the Anti-Blacklisting Defense Fund.

Now why in the world would I be leafleting an anti-blacklisting fundraiser? My own views on blacklisting have always been unequivocal: I'm against it. The reason I was there is because the event was a thinly disguised fundraiser for Vanessa Redgrave—who is suing the Boston Symphony orchestra for blacklisting her, but who is herself in favor of blacklisting and has proposed her own blacklist of certain artists. I thought that it was important for the public to know the facts about Ms. Redgrave's own attitude toward blacklisting artists whose politics differ from her own.

My leaflet provided these facts to those attending the anti-blacklisting fund-raiser and urged them to ask Ms. Redgrave to "explain her hypocrisy." Several members of the audience were surprised to learn of her views on blacklisting Israeli artists. Others said they knew of Ms. Redgrave's selective condemnation of blacklisting but didn't care, because—as one woman put it—"anything is fair in the war against Zionism."

Redgrave won her contractual suit against the Boston Symphony Orchestra, receiving minimal damages, but lost her suit alleging violation of her civil rights. She also lost big in the court of public opinion, as her hypocrisy regarding blacklisting and her active support for terrorist violence were exposed for all to see.

Unfortunately, what was then a fringe position of the extreme left regarding the boycotting of Israeli artists and academics has since become a mainstream view among many on the left. As I will show in subsequent chapters, the BDS (boycott, divest, sanction) tactic has become pervasive on campuses, along with efforts to silence opponents of this and other anti-Israel activities, such as anti-apartheid week.

Vanessa Redgrave refused to debate our fundamental disagreements over Israel and blacklisting, but Rabbi Meir Kahane—with whom I also had deep, but very different, disagreements regarding Israel—was eager to debate me.

Kahane had founded the Jewish Defense League in the United States, but its violence—even in the service of good causes, such as Soviet Jewry and protection of vulnerable Jews against anti-Semitic violence—alienated mainstream American Jews. The violent acts committed by his followers included bombings and shootings, though none had proved fatal until the accidental death of Iris Kones in the Sol Hurok office. Because of the distain of most American Jews for his methods, Kahane felt he and his organization had no future here. So he and some followers moved to the West Bank, where he formed a right-wing political party named Kach, which was accused of racism for its anti-Arab policies and actions, including violence. He traveled often to the United States to raise money and to preach his extremist views.

Kahane was eager for a mainstream platform because (unlike Vanessa Redgrave) he was in fact being blacklisted by Jewish organizations, universities and other institutions. These institutions refused to give him a platform because they regarded his views as racist, anti-peace and pro-violence. They did not want mainstream Jewish organizations to be in any way associated with his views or those of the JDL. Even Israel had banned his political party from running for the Knesset on the grounds that it was a racist party.

In my speeches and columns, I opposed this ban, and the Supreme Court of Israel overturned it because it was not authorized by law. The Knesset subsequently passed a law prohibiting racist parties from running, and Kahane's party was denied a place on the ballot.

Kahane, though he had support among some hard-right Jews, was a pariah to mainstream Jews, none of whom would engage or debate him. So when Avi Weiss, the liberal Orthodox rabbi of the Hebrew Institute of Riverdale, New York, proposed a debate between us, there was enormous pressure on me from mainstream Jewish leaders to decline.

But having challenged Vanessa Redgrave—whose views and actions were by any standard far more despicable than Kahane's—I decided that I could not turn down the challenge to debate him. (Both Redgrave and Kahane would of course reject any comparison between their views and actions.)

Here is how the *New York Times* reported on the event:

> *Nearly 1,000 people crowded into the Hebrew Institute of Riverdale, in the Bronx, to hear the three-hour debate. There were some mild hisses and boos, but the audience was generally polite. Outside in the rain, a handful of pickets carried signs calling Rabbi Kahane a racist.*

I began my presentation with an explanation of why I was willing to debate Rabbi Kahane:[6]

I am debating Rabbi Meir Kahane because too few blacks debated and responded to Reverend Jackson and Louis Farrakhan. I am debating Rabbi Kahane because virtually no Arabs are willing to debate Yasser Arafat. I think it is imperative that the world understand not only that the vast majority of Jews repudiate Rabbi Kahane's views but also WHY we repudiate those views. I am here as well to demonstrate my unalterable opposition to those Jews—Israeli and American—who seek to silence Rabbi Kahane. I recall, very vividly, spending election night in Israel with a group of some of Israel's most distinguished lawyers and judges. As soon as the ballots were counted and Rabbi Kahane's seat in the Knesset was announced, these distinguished, well-educated people, sat around that room deciding how to silence Rabbi Kahane who had been democratically elected to one of the most democratic Houses of Parliament in the world. Some said let's make it a crime to say what he believes, and such legislation has been drafted. Others said do not let him take his seat in the Knesset. Some said take away his immunity. Others said strip him of his Israeli and his American citizenship. Deport him. Blacklist him.

The democratic response to Rabbi Kahane is to answer him, to compete with him in the marketplace of ideas, to persuade people to reject his ideas on their merits and demerits. The democratic answer to bad speech and offensive speech is not censorship or blacklisting but rather more speech, more debate, better ideas.

I just finished, this weekend, trying to resolve my ambivalences about the speech of a terrible enemy of Israel, a woman named Vanessa Redgrave, who has been blacklisted by several organizations and who was not allowed to perform by the Boston Symphony Orchestra. My response to that was both to support her right to speak but then to challenge her to a debate on the merits of her abominable views toward Israel. She declined that debate because her party forbids her to debate. I am debating Rabbi Kahane because I want to upgrade the quality of the debate, to stop the kind of name-calling and personalization that has characterized so much of the attack on Rabbi Kahane. I am here because I disapprove of guilt by analogy, because I disapprove of efforts to show that he is just like Nazis who deported Jews, and who professed racial purity laws and conducted Kristallnachts. These analogies constitute an insult to the memory of the six million.

There is enough wrong with Rabbi Kahane's views without confusing them with the views of others who are also wrong. I want to find out here precisely what Rabbi Kahane's views are, and I want to try to answer them on their merits.

Kahane was not impressed by my free-speech argument. He insisted, "The greatest of tragedies is not that there are those who call me names, but there are those who would grant me the right to speak because they would also grant the right of speech to Yasser Arafat. That is the greatest tragedy—that Jews are unable to understand the difference between a Farrakhan and an Arafat and a Redgrave on one hand and Rabbi Meir Kahane on the other hand."

I understood the difference, but the First Amendment doesn't accept such distinctions.

Following these preliminary remarks, we moved to the substance of our disagreements. The first question put to us by Rabbi Weiss focused on Kahane's plan to evict, expel and transfer every Arab citizen of Israel. Kahane tried to defend his illegal idea:

First, no Arab in Israel wants to live in a Jewish state. And anyone who thinks so has contempt for the Arabs. The State of Israel was created as the Jewish state and so it is declared in the Declaration of Independence. What Arab wants to live in a Jewish state? The fact that Arabs don't rise up now is only because they're afraid.

Secondly, the question arises: assuming that the Arabs have become saints. Say, I accept that they all become saints. And they sit down, democratically, and they reproduce saints. I don't want to live under a majority of Arab saints. I didn't leave this country to live in Israel to live as a minority under anyone, saint or devil, whatever. So the question that I ask of people who are upset at the things that I say is: What is your answer to the voting question? Do the Arabs have a right to become a majority, democratically, peacefully, in the State of Israel? And when they do, you can bet that the Law of Return, which today applies only to Jews, will not apply to Jews but to Arabs. Do the Arabs have the right, yes or no? If the answer is yes, that's fine, you're democrats, not Zionists. If the answer is no, then you're Kahane.

I replied:

It's dangerous enough when Rabbi Kahane purports to speak on behalf of Jews, but when he also purports to know what is on the minds of the Arabs, we really do have a problem. If Arabs choose, for whatever reasons—economic reasons, political reasons, reasons of geography, reasons of convenience—to remain Israeli citizens, that's what they will remain. And Meir Kahane will not be able to and should not be able to expel or deport valid citizens of Israel.

When Israel was established, those who established it—from Theodor Herzl to Weizmann to Ben-Gurion—realized Zionism was a challenge. It is a great challenge to keep the Jewish state Jewish and democratic. Rabbi Kahane would throw up his hands and say there is no room for democracy. There is nothing Jewish about democracy. I beg to differ. The vast majority of Jews in this world support both Zionism and democracy. The false dichotomy that Rabbi Kahane is seeking to impose on us is not correct, and the ultimate implications of his dangerous views are, once the Arabs are expelled from Israel, then Jews who do not fit Rabbi Kahane's particularistic definition of his kind of

*Jew will also be expelled. And I further challenge Meir Kahane
with this question: The vast majority of Jews in Israel today are
not Orthodox Jews, and yet Israel is a Jewish State. What would
you do under your principles to the vast majority of Jews who
dispute your approach?*

Kahane did not respond. Rabbi Weiss then asked me the obvious
follow-up question: "Are you, Professor Dershowitz, prepared to accept the workings of democracy if those workings result in a state
that is no longer a Jewish State?"

I replied:

*You have just stated the challenge of twenty-first-century
Zionism. I do not shrink from that challenge. I do not think
most Israelis shrink from that challenge. To say that we
understand the challenge is not to say that we can anticipate
all the factors that will eventually lead to a solution to the
problem. I can only repeat what David Ben-Gurion's answer
was, what Golda Meir's answer was, what Chaim Weizmann's
and Theodor Herzl's answer was: "We must struggle to preserve
the Jewish character of the State of Israel." We must encourage
aliya [emigration to Israel]. We must open the doors of Soviet
Jewry and of Syrian Jewry and of Ethiopian Jewry. We must do
things to encourage demographic changes that will insure that
Israel remains a Jewish state.*

*Under no circumstances may we accept the false choice being
put to us. The choice about being a Jewish undemocratic state
where the minority prevails or a non-Jewish democratic state
where the majority prevails. We will not, we must not, allow
that false dichotomy ever to face us. If and when the time comes,
if through all efforts by Israelis there is no way of resolving the
issue, it will not be resolved by the rhetoric of Meir Kahane. It
will not be resolved by the answers of Alan Dershowitz. It will*

be resolved by the people of Israel through the processes which
they have chosen, through the processes which elected Meir Kahane
to the Knesset, through the processes which allow Meir Kahane
to speak freely in Israel where he would not be allowed to speak
in almost every other country in the world. The democratic
processes, the civil libertarian processes, the freedom processes, the
very legal processes that Rabbi Kahane both uses and condemns.

Rabbi Weiss then asked me about Judea and Samaria: "How important are our biblical and religious-legal rights to Judea and Samaria? Isn't the retention of the area critical to Israeli security? . . . If Israel has a biblical, legal and security right to Judea and Samaria, why not exercise that right immediately?"

I responded:

I do think that Israel has a biblical claim to the West Bank.
I also think the Arabs have a biblical claim to the West Bank.
I also think there are Christian biblical claims to Jerusalem. I
do not believe that in the modern world we should try to resolve
disputes over conflicting biblical claims by warfare. I do not
want to see the world, once again, in a war over conflicting
biblical claims, because there is no room for compromise when
one invokes the name of the Bible [and says] not only am I right,
but I alone am right.

What I believe is that Israel should not, under any
circumstances, compromise its security needs and its need to keep
Arab enemies away from its large cities. I do not favor the return
to the pre-1967 borders. I generally agree with the Allon Plan.
I generally agree with what I think the vast majority of Israelis
agree with and that is the willingness to make some territorial
compromise in exchange for assurances of peace.

I know this will not be a popular position. The wise,
thoughtful, reasoning compromise position almost never is. But

it is a position which, deep in my heart, I am convinced will strengthen Israel, will secure Israel, will make Israel able to cope with the twenty-first century in both a democratic way and a Jewish way.

We then turned to the divisive issue of the role of religion in Israel. Rabbi Weiss asked Kahane whether he "envisions Israel as a theocratic state governed by the Laws of the Torah." In responding, Kahane purported to speak for all Orthodox Jews:

Clearly there should not be one Orthodox Jew in the world that would not want a theocratic state. Putting it better, there should not be one religious Jew who would not want a state which is mandated by the Torah. . . . The Torah mandates a coercion because that is what God wants. . . . Is there one Orthodox rabbi that would not [want a theocracy]? Our ultimate aim must be to create a Torah state. If Israel will not be a Torah state, then God forbid, the Almighty will bring down upon us the punishment that he warned about in a Bible that is as applicable in 1984 as it was in the year 84.

I replied:

I believe in Zionism as a principle of choice, of opportunity, of challenge. Rabbi Kahane sees Zionism as a principle of compulsion, of separatism, of exclusion. There is no way of debating or arguing with someone who thinks all that is right is on his side and he speaks in the name of God. Until God speaks to us in much clearer ways, we, as human beings, will have to resolve these disputes among ourselves.

We were then asked to summarize our views of what it means to be a Jew and a Zionist. I presented not only my own view but also what I believed were the views of the vast majority of American Jews who rejected Kahane's false choice between Judaism and liberals.

I have the right to tell you, Rabbi Kahane, there is another Judaism that rejects your negative values. There is a Judaism which is positive. There is a Judaism which is embracing. There is Judaism of Rabbi Hillel that reaches out and gives the best of what we stand for to our children. There is a Judaism that does not require our kids to choose between a neo-fascist philosophy and a democratic philosophy in order to be a Jew. I want my children to revere the memory of Martin Luther King. I want my children to cry bitter tears if again we experience Japanese Americans being placed in concentration camps. To discriminate against anyone is to discriminate against everyone. The moral choice is also the pragmatic choice. To choose to defend the rights of others is to choose to have others defend our rights.

You'll remember the German theologian who said, "When they came for the Jews, I didn't say anything because I wasn't a Jew; when they came for the Communists, I didn't say anything because I wasn't a Communist; when they came for the gays I didn't say anything because I wasn't a gay; and then when they came for me and there was no one left to speak."

Rabbi Kahane did not agree: "I don't know what is Judaism and what is Dershowitzism. If one decides for himself what is Judaism, that is not Judaism."

Rabbi Weiss then asked us both to comment on our backgrounds:

In many ways you share backgrounds. Both of you attended Yeshiva University High School. Since that time, you have diverged so remarkably in your paths. Today you personify different views within the Jewish spectrum. What motivated you and who motivated you most to travel the paths you did?

I replied first:

I grew up in a household where my father, of blessed memory, always talked about defending the underdog, always talked about standing up for those who were least able to stand up for themselves. He always drew from the deepest Jewish values. My grandparents before them, my mother who is here tonight, has always seen much more clearly and with much greater Jewish vision than Rabbi Kahane. The rejection of simpleminded solutions, the necessity of obeying the commandments that when you live in a country, you obey the laws of that country, that you be a good patriotic American citizen and at the same time accept the best of Jewish tradition. . . .

The challenge of life is to define one's own goals, one's own needs. I offer my program to you. I offer it to you as a choice. I didn't tell you to accept my program in the name of anybody else or anything else. I ask you to consider it. I ask you to consider Rabbi Kahane's programs. I ask you to consider seriously the good parts of what he has to offer, because I think Rabbi Kahane has, certainly early in his life, made remarkable contributions to Jewish self-defense. The defending of Jews by walkie-talkies, by billy clubs, by phoning the police, by recourse to all appropriate needs. I only wish it hadn't sunk into the day that a bomb was planted in Sol Hurok's office causing the meaningless empty death of a Jewish woman. I only wish we hadn't come to the day when rabbis, in the name of Halacha, claim that it is appropriate to kill innocent people.

I continue to hope and pray that all of you will define your Americanism, define your Judaism, take the best out of each, and reject that which you feel uncomfortable with. In the end, the values for which we as a people have struggled for thousands and thousands of years will not be solved overnight by a false prophet. You will solve them, the people of Israel will solve them.

Rabbi Kahane replied:

I think that at the very least on this point, I agree with my friend and my fellow alumnus from BTA.

My family was certainly the influence on my life. And my father, of blessed memory, a great Talmid Chacham [sage] was a Jewish activist . . .

My opponent is a product of America, a smattering of Jewishness. I tell you, I appeal to you—time is running out for you living here in America—go home, go home to Israel. And in Israel live the life of a Jew.

Simpleminded solutions are usually rejected by professors. I have greater faith in the Sephardic Jew in Israel who sees my solution as the answer because he doesn't come out of Cambridge. He lived under Arabs. He knows what Arabs are. He never again wants to live under Arabs. Don't be put off by such clichés as, "It's a simpleminded thing." Sometimes simpleminded answers are quite good and quite correct. Sometimes not. Be good Jews, be observant Jews, accept the yoke of heaven, the religious way.

The debate was concluded. There was no vote on who won.

We debated several more times. I doubt we persuaded each other of very much. But I continued to defend his right to speak. The last time we spoke was three days before he was assassinated in November 1990. He was scheduled to speak at Brandeis University, but his speech was canceled at the last minute, allegedly because of security concerns. He asked me to call the Brandeis authorities and threaten to sue. I did and he made his speech. The next speech he gave was in New York City, where a Muslim terrorist shot him dead. That terrorist had a list of other prominent Zionists who he was planning to assassinate. I was informed that I was on the list. Ten years later, Meir's son, Binyamin Ze'ev Kahane, was murdered by Palestinian terrorists on the West Bank. Meir Kahane's political party is now a shadow of its former self.

Time has not been kind to Kahane's brand of Jewish fundamentalism. It did produce Baruch Goldstein, the racist Jewish zealot, who, in 1994, murdered 29 Palestinian Muslims praying at the Cave of the Patriarchs. But he is the exception that proves the rule. Jews have mainly stayed true to their centrist liberal and conservative principles despite the constant fissures for extremists on both sides to abandon them. In 2019, a great controversy erupted both in Israel and throughout the Jewish world when Prime Minister Netanyahu arranged for an extremist right-wing party called Otzma Yehudit, which was reminiscent of Kahane's Kach Party, to merge with a mainstream religious Zionist party, thereby giving it the kind of legitimacy Kahane never had. I joined in the criticism of this dangerous move.

My confrontations with Redgrave and Kahane personified my developing positions with regard to Israel and its critics. I would defend Israel, though not all of its policies. But I would also defend the right of those who demonized Israel—even those who sought its destruction—to express their hateful views. My mother, who was very smart, couldn't accept this cognitive dissonance: "Either you're for Israel or you're against. Don't give me your fancy Harvard talk about free speech. The people you're defending hate us. They want to kill us. They would never defend your right to speech."

She spoke for a lot of people, but I have always defended the rights of those with whom I disagree: from the Nazis marching through Skokie to pornographers, to Redgrave and Kahane. As I told Kahane, "I cannot defend you without also defending the Redgraves of the world. Otherwise, people will think that I'm defending you only because I agree with you. If I were to defend the free speech right only of people I agree with, I would be home watching TV."

My principles have been tested on several occasions. Two years after the Redgrave and Kahane events, the Harvard Law School Forum invited a representative of the PLO to make the case against

Israel. I was asked to make the case for Israel. It was to be the first debate at Harvard involving a leader of the PLO.

I was looking forward to a lively debate. But the State Department refused to grant him a visa. I joined the ACLU in challenging the visa denial. I supported the the right of Harvard students to hear views I despised. Representatives of the Israeli Foreign Ministry were furious at me because they had worked hard to exclude him, but I placed my commitment to free speech above any loyalty to Israel. I would decide for myself, as a private citizen, who to debate and where. A university was the perfect place for such an encounter.

In 2004 when Yasser Arafat died, Palestinian students wanted to have a memorial service at which they raised the Palestinian Authority flag in Harvard Yard. The university refused permission on the ground that it only allowed the flags of countries to be flown from the mast in Harvard Yard. The Palestinian students came to me to defend their freedom of expression. I agreed to challenge the Harvard Policy, but advised them that if they were to be given permission to raise the flag, I would be there handing out leaflets telling the truth about Arafat's murderous background and how he turned down a generous peace offer that would have given the Palestinians a state. We won. They flew the flag. And I handed out leaflets describing Arafat's death as "[u]ntimely—because if he had just died five years earlier, the Palestinians might have a state." The flag and the leaflets were the perfect symbols of the marketplace of ideas at Harvard.

I have drawn the line, however, at debating Holocaust deniers. I had refused to cross this red line for several reasons. First, no rational person can actually believe that there were no gas chambers, no mobile killing units, and no systematic Nazi plan to kill the Jews of Europe. Holocaust deniers are liars and anti-Semites.

Second, to subject the Holocaust to debate—to make its existence a debatable issue—is to demean the memory of the six million who died and the survivors. But to refuse an invitation to debate the Holocaust is to give ammunition to deniers. So in 1991, when I was invited by Bradley Smith—a notorious denier who placed ads in the university newspapers challenging professors to debate—I accepted on one condition: it had to be part of a series of debates. These debates would include the following subjects: the earth is flat; men didn't land on the moon; Elvis is still alive; and the Holocaust didn't happen. It is in that kooky company that Holocaust denial belongs. He turned me down.

In the years following, I had dozens of debates—live and in print—on Israel, both with people to the right of me, like Norman Podhoretz, Pat Buchanan, Dennis Prager and Shmuley Boteach, and to the left of me, like Cornel West, Peter Beinart, Jeremy Ben-Ami, Leonard Fein and Peter Tatchell. I was supposed to debate Professor Edward Said on the hard-left radio show *Democracy Now!*, but at the last minute its biased host, Amy Goodman, pulled a bait and switch and substituted Norman Finkelstein, a failed and discredited academic, who had been fired from several universities.

I also had dozens of invitations to speak about Israel on university campuses and at charitable events. None was more impactful on my personal life than an invitation in 1982 to speak at a Jewish singles brunch in Newton, Massachusetts, sponsored by the Combined Jewish Philanthropies of Boston. My topic was Israel and human rights. Partway through the speech, I spotted a beautiful woman in the audience. I couldn't keep my eyes off her, and as soon as my talk was over, I pushed my way through the crowd and got her name. When I got home, I looked up Carolyn Cohen in the phone book (remember phone books?). There were five Carolyn Cohens in the Boston area. I called the first and asked her to dinner. She told me she couldn't leave the nursing home. The second asked if she could bring her husband. I reached my Carolyn on the third try, and we went to dinner that night—and nearly every night since. So my debates and speeches about Israel paid off, at least for me.

At the same time that I was debating American intellectuals, on both the right and the left, I was criticizing Israel's policies with regard to the building of civilian settlements on the West Bank.

In 1979, I joined 59 other prominent American Jewish figures—including the Nobel Prize winner Saul Bellow, the conductor Leonard Bernstein, the literary critic Alfred Kazin, and the academics Leonard Fein, Martin Peretz, Michael Walzer and Jerome Wiesner—in expressing our "distress" over the building of new Israeli towns on the West Bank that "require the expropriation of Arab land unrelated to Israeli security needs."[7] We suggested that this policy was "morally unacceptable, and perilous for the democratic character of the Jewish State."

The letter was written publicly to Prime Minister Begin, who responded (also publicly) that Jews had an absolute right to live anywhere in "the land of our forefathers," including the West Bank, and that the "right of our people is inseparably bound with the needs and demands of our vital national security"[8]—a highly questionable assertion.

Our letter raised a storm of protests in both Israel and the United States. The inclusion of my name in a *New York Times* report on the controversy caused the rabbi in my parents' Orthodox synagogue—the one in which I grew up and was bar mitzvahed—to call me and the other signers "traitors" to Israel and the Jewish community. But nearly all the signers were staunch Zionists; there were no Chomskys on the list. We honestly believed, and I still believe, that building civilian settlements on the West Bank and in the Gaza Strip was harmful to Israel's moral standing and did not contribute to its security.

I could not then and cannot now defend this policy, though I do not believe it is *the* major barrier to a peaceful two-state solution. The fact that Israel unilaterally abandoned all of its civilian settlements in the Gaza Strip in 2005 and that the vast majority of its West Bank settlers now live in "settlement blocks" close to the Green Line—land that can be swapped for equivalent land in Israel—makes it clear that the primary barrier is the unwillingness of the Palestinians to make the kinds of negotiated compromises that are necessary to reach an agreement. (More on this later.)

My criticism of civilian settlements was not my only point of conflict with the Begin government. I was skeptical about the war in Lebanon, especially after Sabra and Shatila, though I was reluctant to publicly criticize Israeli security and military decisions. But I could not, and did not, defend every military action Israel took. I also could not, and did not, defend every compromise Israel felt it had to make with civil liberties in the name of fighting terrorism, just as I could not, and did not, defend every military decision or compromise the United States made.

I joined then-professor Ruth Bader Ginsberg and several other liberals in supporting the Israeli equivalent of the ACLU—the Association for Civil Rights in Israel—which challenged in court Israel's compromises with civil liberties, and generally won.

My position on Israel guaranteed me enemies on both the right and the left. Right-wing Zionists despised my support for a two-state solution and my opposition to Israel's policies on civilian settlements. They also opposed my willingness to defend the civil liberties and free-speech rights of Israel haters. Left-wing anti-Zionists despised my support for a nation-state of the Jewish people and for Israel's right to defend itself against terrorism and other forms of aggression. The divisions grew even sharper as many on the center left moved further toward the hard left, and many on the center right moved further to the hard right. The center, where I had located myself (center left in my case), was shrinking, and that movement toward extremes made reasoned, nuanced discourse more difficult.

In an effort to maintain centrist support for Israel among law school students and faculty, I worked with several of my students to establish the Harvard Jewish Law Students Association. There was criticism from some faculty members: "Why do you want an all Jewish club at HLS?" they asked. There were already African American and women's law student's associations, but Jews were thought to be different. We believed, however, that the growing opposition to Israel necessitated a collective response. There were other issues as well, including a growing interest in Jewish law and concerns that Jewish applicants were not being treated fairly by some admissions committees. The *Harvard Law School Record* reported:

> *The group's advisor is Criminal Law Professor Alan M. Dershowitz, whom Berlin called the "inspiration" behind the organization. Dershowitz spoke at the organizational meeting emphasizing the need for a group such as this. Dershowitz said that he encouraged the formation of the group to serve as an inspiration to law students and lawyers here and elsewhere. He said groups around the United States have begun to organize by ethnic association, and that historically Jews have been concerned with the rights of all minorities. He said Jews should continue to follow this concern while not neglecting their own legal rights.*

Concern about Harvard's admission policies led to the famous "bagel exchange" that occurred when Dr. Chase N. Peterson, then dean of admissions at Harvard, addressed a group of Jewish faculty members suspicious that Harvard had decided to reduce the number of Jews it would admit. Peterson averred that there was no particular "docket" or area of the country whose quota of admissions had been reduced. Rather, he said, it was "the doughnuts around the big cities" that were not "as successful with the Harvard Admissions Committee as they used to be . . ." He said that "now we have to be terribly hard on people with good grades from the good suburban high schools, good, solid, clean-nosed kids who really don't have enough else going for them." The doughnuts, said Peterson, included such areas as Westchester County and Long Island, suburban New Jersey and Shaker Heights, Ohio. When he described these areas to the Jewish faculty members, the *Crimson* reports, one stood up and said, "Dr. Peterson, those aren't doughnuts, they're bagels."

Our association was open to anyone interested in Jewish and Israeli issues, but naturally it attracted Jewish students from all backgrounds and ideologies. I was its first faculty advisor. The idea spread quickly, and by 1983 we convened the first National Jewish Law School Student Network conference with representatives from 20 law schools. I was the speaker at the first conference. Today nearly every law school has a branch.

Several years later, I helped to organize the first Chabad at Harvard, under the direction of Rabbi Hirschy Zarchi. Chabad is a branch of Orthodox Judaism, sometimes called Lubavitch, which conducts outreach to Jews of all religious and nonreligious persuasions. Its motto is that at Chabad, "every Jew is family." There are now dozens of Chabads, in every major university. They have become centers of pro-Israel advocacy through the United States. I myself am no longer Orthodox—though I continue to attend services in an Orthodox synagogue—but I have deep admiration for those who keep the tradition, especially when they are not judgmental about those of us who express our Jewishness differently.

At the same time that academic and public attitudes among the chattering classes were moving away from the center, both the Israeli and U.S. governments were moving toward center-left positions with the election of Yitzhak Rabin as prime minister and Bill Clinton as president.

9

Oslo and the Murder of Rabin

1992 WAS A good year for centrist liberalism. Yitzhak Rabin was elected to replace Yitzhak Shamir, and Bill Clinton was elected to replace George H. W. Bush. The negotiations that led to the Oslo Accords were about to begin. The first violent intifada, which had caused more than 2,000 deaths, was coming to an end. The prospects for a peaceful resolution of the conflict were looking brighter than ever. Both President Clinton and Prime Minister Rabin were determined to break the deadlock. Even Yasser Arafat seemed closer to accepting a compromise resolution than ever before.

I had met Bill Clinton during the summer of 1994, when I invited him to attend Rosh Hashanah services on Martha's Vineyard, where he was vacationing with his family. He accepted and invited my wife, my son Elon, and me to join him and Hillary for dinner after services. After that, we had numerous meals and drinks with them and other guests—including at the White House—during his presidency. I had met Yitzchak Rabin when he was still a general and on numerous occasions thereafter, both in Israel and in the United States.

In 1993, the Oslo Accords were signed after months of secret talks between Israel and the PLO. Although the Oslo Accords left many issues, such as the status of Jerusalem, unresolved, they provided for mutual recognition between the Palestinian Authority and Israel and an ongoing process that would produce an agreed-upon two-state solution and the resolution of key issues.[1] The famous handshake at the White House was seen around the world. It showed that Rabin—who correctly regarded Arafat as a cold-blooded murderer of Jewish men, women and children—was willing to make compromises, both moral and political, that could resolve the age-old conflict over the Holy Land.

But these positive developments did not have any discernable positive impact on Israel's acceptance among hard-left academics around the world. To the contrary, as Israel offered compromises in the interests of peace, the efforts by the hard left to demonize, delegitimize and isolate Israel only increased.[2] This perverse dynamic—demonstrating that the hard-left opposition was not to Israel's policies but rather to its very existence—has continued to this day.

The early to mid-1990s were busy times for me professionally. A few years earlier, I had won the Claus von Bülow case, and my son Elon had produced an Academy Award–winning film called *Reversal of Fortune*, starring Jeremy Irons (who won the Oscar for Best Actor), Glenn Close (who played Sonny von Bülow) and Ron Silver (who played me). I had also published the *New York Times* number-one bestseller *Chutzpah*. These developments brought me a considerable amount of media attention. As a result, I was retained to represent Leona Helmsley, Michael Milken, Mike Tyson, O.J. Simpson, Mia Farrow, Jim Bakker and other high-visibility clients. Despite my busy schedule of classes and cases, I continued to devote a considerable portion of my time to defending Israel in the court of public opinion.

As the demonization of the nation-state of the Jewish people increased around the world, particularly among the hard left and academics, my involvement increased. Israel remained, and remains, a priority in my professional and private life, despite—perhaps because of—the increasingly difficult challenges faced by liberal supporters of Israel.

Radical leftists chose to downplay Rabin's effort to make peace and instead focused on Israel's imperfections, while ignoring or excusing the crimes of the Palestinian leadership. Anti-Israel groups conducted "apartheid week" events, demanded divestment from Israeli companies and companies that did business with Israel, and shouted down pro-Israel speakers in an effort to prevent their views from being heard.

On November 4, 1995, Israel—and the world—suffered a cataclysmic loss with the assassination of Prime Minister Yitzhak Rabin at a peace rally in Tel Aviv. His assassin was an Orthodox Jew named Yigal Amir, a hyper-nationalist, and an opponent of Rabin's peace efforts.

The impact of this murder on Israel is incalculable. It is the Israeli analogue to the assassination of Abraham Lincoln 130 years earlier. Both killings changed the course of history, for the worse.

The crime impacted me personally in several distinct ways. Eight days before Rabin was killed, Israel's ambassador to the United States had asked me to meet with the prime minister when he was scheduled to speak in Boston later that month. I asked the ambassador what the subject of the meeting would be, and he told me that the prime minister was deeply concerned about the increasingly virulent level of rhetoric in Israel and the fact that certain fringe religious and political figures were advocating violence against government officials. He wanted to discuss whether there were ways of constraining the level of vitriol without infringing on the right of free speech.

I agreed to meet with Rabin and wrote the appointment in my calendar. I also did some research on Israeli law in preparation for the meeting. But it was not to be. Rabin was murdered a week before his scheduled trip to Boston. I could never erase the scheduled meeting from my appointment book or from my mind.

Then a week after the murder, on a Sunday morning, family members of the accused killer knocked on the door of my home, with no appointment, and asked me to represent Amir. I met with them, and they told me that Amir had in fact pulled the trigger, but that he was legally innocent, because the killing was justified under the Jewish law of rodef—a concept akin to preventive or anticipatory self-defense, or defense of others. This concept, which derives from a biblical passage as interpreted by Jewish sages, including Maimonides, authorizes the killing of a person who is about to do great harm to the community.[3] They told me that their relative believed Rabin was about to make a peace with the Palestinians that involved giving back "sacred" land captured by Israel during the Six-Day War. He also believed that this would endanger the lives of Israelis, and so he set out to stop it by killing the rodef who was, in his view, endangering his land and people.

The trial of Rabin's killer promised to be among the most interesting of my career and among the most important in the history of the Jewish state. Although the crime did not carry the death penalty (Israel has abolished the death penalty except for the Nazi genocide against the Jewish people, under which Adolf Eichmann was hanged), the case fit many of the criteria I generally consider in taking a case. It was challenging and historically significant—but I decided not to take it.

The reason was that it involved the kind of political defense that I abhor. If every citizen had the right to decide who was a rodef deserving of death, there would be anarchy. The "rule of personal politics" would replace the rule of law. The rodef defense was not, in my view, a legitimate legal defense, and I, as a lawyer, was not obligated to present it.

I had a more personal reason as well for turning down this case. I deeply admired Rabin, and I supported his efforts to make peace. We had known each other for a long time, though not well, and he had consulted with me regarding several issues. Indeed, he was seeking my advice on the very issue that may have led to this death.

Standing next to Rabin when the fatal bullets were fired was the man who would succeed him as prime minister, my friend Shimon

Peres. He represented an approach to the peace process that was essentially similar to that of Rabin, but he lacked Rabin's popular appeal. So within a year, he was defeated by the younger, more charismatic and more conservative Benjamin Netanyahu, who was also a close personal friend. My early acquaintance with Bibi had ripened into a warm friendship during his tenure as Israel's representative to the United Nations. We have maintained this friendship until today, despite our differences over Israel's settlement policies and other issues, including his apparent willingness to work with the racist Otzma Party.

It was widely predicted that Peres would win the election. In the run-up to the vote, I was asked to speak at the policy conference of the American Israel Public Affairs Committee (AIPAC). Many in that organization, like many in Israel, were moving to the right, so I went out of my way to ask my audience to commit themselves to supporting whichever candidate and party won the election, believing at the time that Peres would win. There was some grumbling from right-wing members, who also expected Peres to win, but most accepted that AIPAC should not take sides in Israeli domestic politics.

Netanyahu won a narrow victory and was able to form a government that lasted for three years, until he was defeated by Ehud Barak in 1999. Netanyahu's election was influenced by the immigration into Israel of nearly a million Soviet Jews in the previous several years. This amazing influx of many highly talented Jews was the epitome of the Zionist dream: to ingather persecuted Jews into the nation-state of the Jewish people. I had worked hard—politically, diplomatically and legally—to help open the exit door for Soviet Jews, and I was proud of the small role I had played in that historic event—including direct advocacy to Soviet leader Mikhail Gorbachev in the Kremlin—that helped to turn Israel into a "startup nation." But not surprisingly, it also moved the Israeli electorate to the right. When people have been as brutally repressed as Soviet Jews had been by communism, it was only natural for them to be suspicious of left-wing parties and more comfortable with a conservative like Netanyahu.

In a subsequent debate between Peter Beinart, the former editor of the *New Republic* and a vocal critic of Israel, and myself, Beinart began by saying how much he admired me for the work I had done to help Soviet Jews immigrate to Israel. Then, in the same breath, he condemned me for supporting Israel as it moved to the right. I pointed out the obvious contradiction in his two statements. It is the very fact that a million Soviet Jews immigrated to Israel that moved Israeli politics to the right. I asked him whether he would want to deport or disenfranchise the million Soviet Jews so that Israel could move back to its traditional left-wing orientation. He laughed, but he failed to respond to my deeper point: that Israel is a democracy in which the majority view prevails. It is also a Zionist country, which includes as one of its primary goals to serve as a place of refuge for repressed Jews, such as those who had suffered discrimination in the Soviet Union. Zionism, a sanctuary for repressed Jews, and liberalism do not always work in tandem, especially when Zionist ingathering of endangered Jews results in a greater number of illiberal voters. Many of the Jews who fled communist oppression are naturally averse to the left, but their children and grandchildren may well move closer to the center and even to the left. That is what happened to Cuban refugees in Florida, and there are indications that it may be happening to former Soviet Jews in Israel. For those of us who would like to see Israel move leftward, our only options are to educate and persuade the younger generation, not to bemoan the political movement rightward by survivors of Soviet repression.

Netanyahu understood this post-Soviet dynamic and used it to his advantage. There were other reasons as well—both domestic and international—for Netanyahu's victory, but this new demographic reality was among them. So was his personal charisma and sharp political instincts. Netanyahu's surprise victory energized right-wing support for Israel in the United States, while at the same time energizing hard-left opposition to the Israeli government. Clinton was still the U.S. president, and he had mixed feelings toward the new prime minister. I discussed Clinton's fraught relationship with the newly elected prime minister and encouraged Clinton to keep an open mind despite his early reservations. For Clinton, Yitzhak Rabin, and his successor Shimon Peres, represented the true Israel. He identified much more with the heavily accented Rabin and Peres than with his perfectly accented contemporary Netanyahu. I was friendly with both of them, and my friendship was used by both, especially when the relationship became testy.

I was in Israel for the spring semester of 1996 doing research for a book when Netanyahu was elected. He invited me and my wife and daughter to his office on a Friday afternoon. We stood outside of the King David Hotel trying to hail a cab, but all the cabdrivers were heading home for the Shabbat weekend. It looked like we might be late for our appointment with the prime minister. Suddenly, a car pulled up. It was the mayor of Jerusalem, Ehud Olmert, who was driving around his city to make sure all the trash had been collected before Shabbat. He shouted to me, "Alan, you'll never get a cab on a Friday afternoon. Where do you need to go?" I told him, and he agreed to drive us there. As I got into his car, a cabdriver pulled over, shouting, "Hey, mayor, I don't try to run Jerusalem, why are you trying to be a cabdriver? Stop taking business from me." I gave the driver $10, and he drove away, but not before giving the mayor the finger.

When I got to the prime minister's office, we schmoozed and took some pictures. Then Bibi invited me to his secure private office. "There's been something I have been wanting to ask you," he said. I expected him to solicit my advice on some critical security or political issue. He put his arm around me and whispered in my ear, "So, did O.J. do it?" I was taken aback, but I quickly responded, "Well, there's been a question I've been wanting to ask you, Mr. Prime Minister: Does Israel have nuclear weapons?" Bibi looked at me sternly and said, "You know I can't answer your question." I looked back at him and said, "Aha! And you know I can't answer your question." Bibi understood, and we both laughed.

Netanyahu had campaigned against the Oslo Accords and taken a harder line than his predecessors did on the peace process, and especially on the occupation and settlement building. He regarded himself as a center-right pragmatist who wanted peace, but only if Israel's security was not compromised. His coalition partners included some who were considerably to his right, especially with regard to the West Bank settlements. The new prime minister surprised the world, and disappointed his hard-right supporters, when he signed the Hebron Protocol with Yasser Arafat, just months after taking office. The protocol ceded control of over 80 percent of Hebron—the holiest biblical city in the Torah and the burial place of Jewish patriarchs and matriarchs—to the Palestinian Authority. It also called for the rollback of Israeli troops in other areas of the West Bank. Beyond its specific changes, it reflected a more positive approach by Netanyahu to the peace process, despite opposition by a significant number of his own cabinet (7 out of 18). President Clinton strongly supported the Hebron Accord, but he opposed the continued expansion of settlements on the West Bank, on the Gaza Strip and in East Jerusalem.

This tension within the Netanyahu government and between Bibi and Bill Clinton characterized much of his first term as prime minister. (He would be elected to a second term in 2009, after a decade out of office.) I recall a dinner on Martha's Vineyard with the president and Mrs. Clinton and several other couples at the home of a mutual friend shortly after Netanyahu's first election. Our host, who was Jewish, was railing against Netanyahu's apparent unwillingness to move the peace process forward. I began to answer him, when Clinton said, "Let me take this."

The president, who had a somewhat tenuous personal relationship with Netanyahu, especially compared to his close friendship for and admiration of his predecessors Rabin and Peres, explained to our host how difficult it was for Israeli prime ministers to get anything done: "My cabinet has to carry out my wishes. If they disagree and refuse, they're gone. My cabinet is on my side. They support me. They want me to succeed. In Israel, every member of Bibi's cabinet has his or her own political agenda. They are rivals. They want to replace Bibi. They are perfectly willing not only to stab him in the back, but in the front—in full view of the world. It is a cabinet of convenience—a coalition cabinet that holds the sword of Damocles over the current government, because if a few of them quit, the government fails. So Bibi's hands are tied by his far-right coalition members."

Our host then asked the president, "We give Israel so much assistance, can't you just tell Netanyahu to make peace with the Palestinians?"

The President smiled and replied, "It's relatively easy with Jordan and Egypt. I can call the king and president and they can usually get it done. But when I call the Israeli prime minister and ask him to do something, he says, 'I have to get the approval of the security cabinet, the large cabinet, the Knesset and then sometimes the Supreme Court. We have to do polling. I'll try my best.'"

"The problem with Israel," the president said emphatically, "is that it's a democracy, damn it!" We all laughed and even the belligerent host shook his head, as if to say, "OK, now I understand."

Clinton was right. Unlike the Arab states, where the leaders can do the bidding of the United States if they choose to, Israel is a democracy whose leader must follow the will of its citizens. But it's also a democracy with a deeply flawed structure, at least when it comes to getting things done. The coalition system of governance allows a small minority to hold the majority hostage to its extreme demands, especially when these demands are *not* to do things that the majority would like to see done. The minority in a coalition government has veto power over many actions of the prime minister and his party, even if these actions reflect the will of a majority or plurality of the citizens.

Because of my close relationship with both Netanyahu and Clinton, I played an informal role in advising them and in facilitating communications between them. When Bibi made his first official visit to the United States during the Clinton presidency, he made the mistake of meeting with the Reverend Jerry Falwell, the founder of the Moral Majority and a virulent critic of President and Mrs. Clinton. Falwell was pushing a video titled *The Clinton Chronicles* that falsely portrayed the Clintons as drug dealers and murderers. The Clintons were furious that Netanyahu had begun his U.S. visit at a Falwell event. The event had been added at the last minute on the recommendation of Israel's ambassador Eliyahu Ben-Elissar, who was not familiar with American politics or the Falwell–Clinton animosity. All he knew was that Falwell represented Evangelical Christians, who were quickly becoming a dominant factor in the Republican Party's increasingly vocal support for Israel in general and for Netanyahu in particular. This factor did not alleviate the anger felt by the Clintons about the Falwell meeting. Bibi asked me to convey to the Clintons that he intended no disrespect for the president or his wife. I communicated this message and others in the months to come.

During his first term, Netanyahu was prevented by his coalition from taking any giant steps that might have moved the peace process forward, such as placing restrictions on settlement building. But Netanyahu did not place impassable barriers in the way of a two-state solution either. Indeed, I think it is fair to say that Netanyahu's first term—especially his signing of the Hebron Accord—helped pave the way toward the Camp David proposals of 2000–2001, put forward by his successor Ehud Barak. But it was Barak's electoral victory over Netanyahu that set the stage for the most generous peace offer the Palestinians would receive up to that time.

10

Clinton and Barak

Palestinians Reject Peace, and the Birth of BDS

THE ELECTION OF Ehud Barak—a war hero/peacemaker in the mold of Yitzhak Rabin—boded well for a continuation of the process that had begun with the Oslo Accords. Barak had served with distinction in an antiterrorist unit of the IDF, famously dressing as a woman in a 1973 raid into Lebanon that killed several key terrorists. He was later promoted to chief of staff of the IDF. When he retired, he waited the prescribed time period before entering politics as a member of the Labor Party. He was elected prime minister in July 1999, while President Clinton still had a year and a half left in his second term. Clinton's impeachment process had ended months earlier, and the president was determined to use his remaining months to secure a deal between Israel and the Palestinians. His first term had begun with the Oslo Accord that created a process designed to lead to a final status agreement. It would be fitting to end his second term with the Holy Grail that had eluded past presidents: a two-state solution to the century-old conflict that would cement his foreign policy legacy.

I had worked behind the scenes with Clinton's legal team, as well as with the president himself, on the Starr investigation, the impeachment and the Senate vote. I had also written a book—*Sexual McCarthyism*—and had appeared on television defending Clinton. So I had the president's ear, and I used it to make the case both for Israel and for an agreement that assured Israel's security.

I also tried, unsuccessfully, to get the president to commute the life imprisonment sentence of Jonathan Pollard, who had pleaded guilty to spying for Israel. I tell the full story of my involvement in the Pollard case in my book *Chutzpah*. Briefly, Pollard had worked for U.S. Navy Intelligence and provided Israel with intelligence material that he believed was necessary to its defense but that was being withheld by the Defense Department. He agreed to plead guilty and cooperate fully in exchange for a promise that the government would not seek life imprisonment, but the prosecutor and the secretary of defense, Caspar Weinberger, broke that promise. I urged Clinton on several occasions throughout his eight years in office to commute the sentence. Clinton wanted to commute the sentence to time served, but the CIA chief, George Tenet, threatened to resign in protest if he did. So, much to my regret, he didn't.

Bill Clinton loved Israel. His attachment to the nation-state of the Jewish people was deeply emotional, as well as intellectual. He told me how his Baptist minister had instilled in him a love of Israel and the Jewish people from an early age. He had enormous respect and affection for Yitzhak Rabin, whose death had a deep impact on him. When he bid Rabin farewell at his funeral in Jerusalem with the Hebrew words "Shalom chaver"—"Farewell and peace my friend"— his emotions were captured by the cameras for all to see. He had persuaded his friend to take the politically risky course of shaking hands with Yasser Arafat on the White House lawn when the Oslo Accords were signed. These accords, which were controversial both in Israel and among American Jews, laid the foundation for a two-state solution by recognizing the Palestinian Authority and its right to limited self-governance in areas of the occupied territories. Rabin's agreement to these controversial provisions, punctuated by his handshake with the man who was responsible for the murder of so many Jews, became an emotional issue in the next election. There were some who believed that it was the handshake with a mass murderer who had called for Israel's destruction that sealed Rabin's fate. But it was also this handshake that held out the hope that enemies could put the bloody past behind them and build a peaceful future. Time was short, though, because Barak assumed the office of prime minister just six months or so before the 2000 presidential campaign season would consume the attention of America and 15 months before Clinton would become a lame-duck president.

Clinton and Barak worked hard to bring the parties together. Clinton pressed Barak to make concessions, and Barak—using an acquaintance of mine to poll the reactions of Israeli citizens to proposed compromises—agreed to offer Arafat nearly everything he was seeking. Though there is some dispute as to precisely what was offered and when, no one disagrees that the offer included statehood for the Palestinians on more than 90 percent of the West Bank and the entire Gaza Strip.[1] Although some Palestinian supporters have denied this, President Clinton and those who participated in the negotiations have confirmed the basic outline of the various offers.

Unbeknownst to Clinton and Barak, a prominent American was working behind the scenes to undercut their peace efforts. He was warning Arafat that if he accepted the Clinton–Barak offers, he would surely be assassinated. The American who was advising Arafat to reject the American–Israeli offer was none other than former president Jimmy Carter.

Carter wanted the credit for solving the Israeli–Palestinian conflict. Indeed, he made the following boast to the *New York Times*: "Had I been elected to a second term with the prestige and authority and influence and reputation I had in the region, we could have moved to a final solution."[2]

Carter had no love for Israel and Israeli leaders, blaming them and them alone for the ongoing conflict. When Arafat finally rejected the generous Clinton–Barak peace offers, Carter mendaciously claimed that it was Barak, not Arafat, who walked away from the negotiations. Carter, who was not there, was willing to take the word of Arafat—a serial liar—over the word of Dennis Ross, a seasoned diplomat who had worked on Middle East issues for several administrations, was there and later wrote a detailed account of the negotiations that contradicted Carter's placing the blame on Israel.[3] By blaming Israel and Israel alone for the failure, Carter also contradicted Arab leaders, such as Prince Bandar of Saudi Arabia, who had told Arafat, "I hope you remember, Sir, what I told you. If we lose this opportunity, it is not going to be a tragedy, [it] is going to be a crime."[4] When Arafat rejected the offer without even making a counteroffer, Bandar called Arafat's rejection "a crime against the Palestinians—in fact against the entire region."[5]

Carter's interference with efforts by the sitting U.S. president to achieve a peaceful resolution, as well as siding with Arafat over Clinton, reflected his strong bias against Israel. This bias was long-standing and pervasive, manifesting itself in many of his actions, beginning with a meeting he had with Golda Meir when he scolded her for Israel's "secular" culture and warned that "Israel was punished whenever its leaders turned away from devout worship of God."[6] He had nothing good to say about other Israeli leaders, though he praised Arafat, Syrian dictator Hafez al-Assad and other tyrannical and terrorist Arab leaders. When Carter visited the Middle East in 2008, he made a point to lay a wreath at Arafat's grave, but he did not visit Rabin's grave or those of Arafat's many Jewish victims.

I was not aware of these biases when I campaigned for Carter in 1976 or even when he helped bring Begin and Sadat to Camp David. The real extent of his anti-Israel feelings did not become public until his pernicious role in the Clinton–Barak peace process became known.

I had met Carter in early 1976, when he sent me a handwritten note telling me that he was "impressed with [my] ideas on crime and punishment," which I had expressed in a recent *New York Times Magazine* article. He asked for my help with "other ideas" that would be very valuable to [him]" in his campaign. A "cc" on the bottom of the page to "Stu" indicated that he had sent a copy to Stuart Eizenstat, his chief domestic assistant. Stu, my former student, was a committed Jew and a strong supporter of Israel, but his role in the Carter administration was primarily domestic. He did play a positive role in the Camp David Accords, and has since written an excellent book about the Carter presidency in all its complexity.[7]

After Carter wrote his letter to me, Stuart called and told me that Carter was coming to speak at Harvard and wanted to meet me. I agreed.

I liked the gracious Southerner and consented to work on his campaign. In June of that year, *Newsweek* ran a cover story on "Carter's game plan" that included a page on "the Carter brain trust." I was featured in that story, with my photograph (beard, long hair, and aviator glasses) and a report that I was a key part of the brain trust and a member of Carter's "task force on criminal justice." Following Carter's election and inauguration, my name was included on several lists of lawyers the president was considering for Supreme Court appointments if any vacancies were to occur. (None did.)

When Anatoly (later Natan) Sharansky was arrested in the Soviet Union in March 1977 and charged with spying for the United Sates, I went to the White House to urge Carter to formally deny that Sharansky had spied for us. I, along with Professor Irwin Cotler, was representing Sharansky as part of my decade-long defense of many Soviet dissidents and refuseniks. Stuart advised me that it would be difficult, since no president ever admits or denies that anyone is an American spy. But after considerable efforts on Stuart's part and mine, President Carter agreed to issue an unprecedented denial, saying that he was "completely convinced" that Sharansky was innocent—a denial that may have saved Sharansky's life. Eventually Sharansky was released from the Gulag, due to the combined efforts of his wife, Avital, his lawyers, and pressure from the United States and Israel. Sharansky arrived in Israel to a hero's welcome and soon became a political and moral leader, much admired by American presidents and Israeli prime ministers alike.

Several years after meeting Carter, I closely followed the Camp David meetings between Israeli prime minister Menachem Begin and Egyptian leader Anwar Sadat. My friend Aharon Barak was Israel's chief legal advisor at the talks, Stuart was an important advisor to Carter, and another former Harvard Law student, Osama El-Baz, was one of the leaders of the Egyptian negotiating team. Once peace was finally achieved, I was invited to the White House ceremony on March 26, 1979.

Despite Carter's success in helping to bring about peace between Israel and Egypt, I campaigned for Senator Ted Kennedy when he decided to challenge Carter for the 1980 presidential nomination. I had served as a lawyer during the Chappaquiddick investigation after he had driven off a bridge, which resulted in the death of Mary Jo Kopechne, and we had become friends. I traveled on the campaign trail with Ted and his wife at the time and made speeches for him. When he lost to Carter in the primaries, I campaigned for Carter's reelection, which he lost to Ronald Reagan. I did not see Carter for several years after that until he wrote his controversial book titled *Palestine: Peace Not Apartheid*. More about that later (but now back to the Clinton–Barak peace efforts).

For whatever reason, Arafat decided to reject the generous peace offers. He did not offer counterproposals or explain why he was turning down the opportunity for statehood for his people. He simply walked away and immediately initiated a second intifada, in which thousands of Israelis and Palestinians were killed. Arafat employed the pretext that Ariel Sharon had visited the Temple Mount, but proof has since emerged that the intifada was carefully planned well before Sharon provided the phony excuse to start the bloodshed. Arafat did not give back the Nobel Peace Prize he had been awarded for signing the Oslo Accords and rejecting terrorism.

At the same time that the Israeli government was offering the Palestinians a state and Arafat was committing "a crime against the Palestinians" by rejecting Ehud Barak's generous offer, anti-Israel activists were plotting the economic destruction of the nation-state of the Jewish people through the bigoted tactic of boycotts, divestments and sanctions. This plot, called BDS, was hatched at an anti-Semitic hate fest in Durban, South Africa, in 2001. Its grandparents on one side were the Nazis who organized the boycott of Jewish businesses, academics and artists in the 1930s. Its grandparents on the other side were the Muslim leaders who organized the Arab boycott of all Israeli and Jewish commerce in the years following the establishment of Israel. Its parents are the contemporary bigots who only single out Israel for boycott and seek to use BDS to end the existence of the world's only nation-state for the Jewish people.

The illegitimate birth of this tactic reflects the anti-Semitic goal of its founders and leaders: to isolate, delegitimize and ultimately destroy the state of Israel and replace it with another Muslim-Arab state. Anyone who supports BDS is thus complicit—knowingly or out of willful blindness—in the world's oldest bigotry.

The goal of the so-called "Durban strategy" was to turn Israel into a pariah state. Based on the inapt South African paradigm, it provided the blueprint for the ensuing boycott of Israel by falsifying parallels between the former's apartheid regime and Israel's territorial dispute with the Palestinians. As a result, calls for "anti-apartheid boycotts" became the battle cry of the broad Israel boycott strategy. The apartheid analogy is absurd on its face and refuted by the facts on the ground: Israeli Arabs—even Palestinians on the West Bank—have more rights and benefits than Palestinians in any other country.

The countries, entities and NGOs participating in the UN conference accused Israel of racism, apartheid, genocide and creating a holocaust. Led by Yasser Arafat and his nephew, Nasser al-Kidwa, the Palestinian UN delegation—in conjunction with Western NGOs and nations belonging to the Organisation of Islamic Cooperation—oversaw the conference's final declaration of principles. It stated:

> *[We] call upon the international community to impose a policy*
> *of complete and total isolation of Israel as an Apartheid state*
> *as in the case of South Africa which means the imposition of*
> *mandatory and comprehensive sanctions and embargoes, the full*
> *cessation of all links (diplomatic, economic, social, aid, military*
> *cooperation and training) between all states and Israel.*

In the highly anti-Semitic milieu of the Durban Conference, U.S. secretary of state Colin Powell ordered the American delegation to stage a walkout. This was his reason:

> *Today I have instructed our representatives at the World*
> *Conference Against Racism to return home. . . . I know that you*
> *do not combat racism by conferences that produce declarations*
> *containing hateful language, some of which is a throwback to*
> *the days of "Zionism equals racism"; or supports the idea that we*
> *have made too much of the Holocaust; or suggests that apartheid*
> *exists in Israel; or that singles out only one country in the*
> *world—Israel—for censure and abuse.*[8]

Congressman Tom Lantos, the only Holocaust survivor to have served in the U.S. Congress, was a U.S. delegate at the Durban Conference. Writing about the blatant anti-Semitism he witnessed there, Congressman Lantos said,

> *Another ring in the Durban circus was the NGO forum . . . the*
> *forum quickly became stacked with Palestinian and fundamentalist*
> *Arab groups. Each day, these groups organized anti-Israeli and*
> *anti-Semitic rallies around the meetings, attracting thousands.*
> *One flyer, which was widely distributed, showed a photograph*
> *of Hitler and the question "What if I had won?" The answer:*
> *"There would be NO Israel . . ." An accredited NGO, the Arab*

Lawyers Union, distributed a booklet filled with anti-Semitic caricatures frighteningly like those seen in the Nazi hate literature printed in the 1930s. Jewish leaders and I who were in Durban were shocked at this blatant display of anti-Semitism. For me, having experienced the horrors of the Holocaust first hand, this was the most sickening and unabashed display of hate for Jews I had seen since the Nazi period.[9]

In the wake of these "gains" made at the Durban conference, Qatari-born, Israeli-educated Omar Barghouti cofounded the Palestinian Campaign for the Academic and Cultural Boycott of Israel (PACBI) in April 2004, which was tasked with "overseeing the academic and cultural boycott aspects of BDS."[10]

The movement was formally launched in July 2005—just as Israel was ending its military occupation of Gaza and uprooting all of its settlements there—and was endorsed by over 170 Palestinian political parties, organizations, trade unions and movements.[11]

Since 2004, Barghouti—who himself received his advanced degree at Tel Aviv University (a fact that flies in the face of his claim of a state-sponsored system of apartheid in Israel)—has been the key driving force behind the global BDS campaign. It is ironic that the leading advocate of a worldwide boycott of Israel—who has said that "all Israeli academics" are members of the "occupation reserve army"—was himself unwilling to disrupt his own education and boycott the "Zionist" institution from which he received his higher education.[12]

Central to Barghouti's tactic has been the engagement of European governments, NGOs and grassroots organizations, as well as university campuses across the United States, in order to push the BDS campaign and grow its support base. As part of his overarching tactic of equating the global BDS campaign with the anti-apartheid movement in South Africa, Barghouti also formed a strategic "alliance" with South African human rights and anti-apartheid activist Archbishop

Desmond Tutu. Like Barghouti, Archbishop Tutu has a sordid history of demonizing Jews and their nation-state.[13]

As we will see later, I was invited to debate Barghouti at Oxford Union, but the founder of BDS refused to debate me because, according to his criteria, I—as an American Jewish supporter of Israel—am subject to his boycott. He also refused to join me in a discussion sponsored by the Young Presidents' Organization (YPO), insisting that he conclude his presentation first so that it would not be seen as a debate, discussion or encounter with me. His bigoted boycott is also directed against non-Israeli Jews, such as the singer Matisyahu—but not (at least according to some leaders of BDS) against Israeli Arabs.[14] In other words, this is a religious, not a national, boycott. That is anti-Semitism, pure and simple. BDS has increasingly been a hotbed of anti-Semitic activity and regrouped bigots of all stripes who feel comfortable with the language used by its leaders.

It is abundantly clear that Barghouti is against the existence of Israel as the nation-state of the Jewish people in any form. He confirmed this in a 2008 column when he declared,

> *It was born out of ethnic cleansing and the destruction of the indigenous Palestinian society, Israel is the state that built and is fully responsible for maintaining the illegal Jewish colonies. Why should anyone punish the settlements and not Israel? This hardly makes any sense, politically speaking . . . why should European civil society that fought apartheid in South Africa accept apartheid in Israel as normal, tolerable or unquestionable? Holocaust guilt cannot morally justify European complicity in prolonging the suffering, bloodshed and decades-old injustice that Israel has visited upon Palestinians and Arabs in general, using the Nazi genocide as pretext.[15]*

Barghouti neglects to mention the role of the Palestinian leadership during the 1930s and 1940s, who had formed an alliance with the Nazi regime in general and Adolf Hitler in particular. The Grand Mufti of Jerusalem, Haj Amin Al-Husseini, collaborated with the Nazis to prevent Jewish refugees from seeking sanctuary in what became Israel. He was instrumental in having Jews, who were on their way out of Europe, sent to death camps. After the war, he was declared a war criminal for recruiting thousands of Muslim Yugoslavs to murder Jews in Croatia and Hungary. Despite his Nazi collaboration—or perhaps because of it—he became and remained a hero to most Palestinians, many of whom hung his picture in their homes. He helped design an Arab fez adorned with a Swastika that his Palestinian followers wore (I saw that fez in a private collection of Nazi-Arab memorabilia). Following the Holocaust, Al-Husseini received asylum in Egypt, where he organized other German Nazis to help in efforts to destroy Israel.[16] So "Holocaust guilt" among the Palestinian leadership was an entirely appropriate factor to consider—though certainly not the only one—in supporting the establishment of two states for two peoples in mandatory Palestine.

Proponents of the boycott against Israel call their bigoted campaign "the BDS Movement." But in reality, there is no such thing. A "movement" suggests universality, such as the feminist movement, the gay rights movement and the environmental movement. If there were a BDS movement that sought to achieve equality, justice and freedom, it would rank every nation on earth by reference to two overriding criteria:

1. the seriousness and pervasiveness of its violation of basic human rights to equality, justice and freedom;
2. the inaccessibility of the victims to judicial, media and political relief.

A true movement would then prioritize its protest activities—its boycotts, divestments and sanctions—according to the universal mantra of all true human rights movements: namely "the worst first."

It would not pick only one country, point out its imperfections, and focus ALL of its protest activities on that one country to the exclusion of all others. Ranked according to the universal criteria outlined above, the list of countries with horrible human rights records and little or no access to relief would be quite long. It would include North Korea, Iran, Cuba, China, Zimbabwe, Myanmar, Belarus, Russia, Turkey, Saudi Arabia, Pakistan, the Philippines, Venezuela and Kuwait, among many others. Israel would be near the very bottom of any objective list, ranking behind every Arab, Muslim, African and Asian country, as well as several Eastern European countries.

No reasonable person, including many supporters of BDS, would dispute this assessment. Even Peter Tatchell, a supporter of BDS whom I debated at Oxford Union in 2015, acknowledged this when he wrote,

> *While I oppose Israel's occupation, I find it strange that some people condemn Israel while remaining silent about these other equally or more oppressive occupations. Many of Israel's critics are also silent about neighboring Arab dictatorships. And where are the protests and calls for boycotts against the tyrannies of Saudi Arabia, Iran, Burma, Zimbabwe, North Korea, Uzbekistan, Bahrain, Syria and elsewhere? Why the double standards?*

Indeed, the only nation subjected to the so-called BDS "movement" is the nation-state of the Jewish people. When only Muslim states were subject to the Trump administration's travel ban, the left was outraged. Why is there no similar outrage at subjecting only the nation-state of the Jewish people to BDS? Many of those who most loudly support boycotting Israel demand that we end boycotts of Cuba, Iran, North Korea and other tyrannical regimes. How can they justify this double standard? There is something very wrong with that picture.[17]

From its very beginning, I have taken a lead in opposing BDS. I have written dozens of columns, delivered hundreds of speeches, debated numerous supporters of BDS, consulted with lawyers who have litigated against BDS, advised legislators who have proposed statutory bans against BDS, spoken to university administrators who oppose student and faculty BDS initiatives, supported political candidates who have campaigned against BDS, encouraged alumni donors who want to pressure their universities against accepting BDS, purchased products that have been targets of BDS, invested in financial companies that have resisted demands to divest from Israeli companies, and counseled students who are confused about the issue. I have also urged artists and entertainers to go out of their way to perform in Israel. One great musician, the pianist Evgeny Kissin, has gone even further. Although he does not live in Israel, Kissin—who I count as a friend—became an Israeli citizen in protest against the boycotting of Israeli artists. Now, anyone who subscribes to that bigoted boycott will not have the pleasure of hearing Kissin play.

In 2014, I wrote an article, which has been widely republished and circulated, for *Haaretz*, outlining the "ten reasons why BDS is immoral and hinders peace."[18]

1. ***BDS immorally imposes the entire blame for the continuing Israeli occupation and settlement policy on the Israelis.*** *It refuses to acknowledge the historical reality that on at least three occasions, Israel offered to end the occupation and on all three occasions, the Palestinian leadership, supported by its people, refused to accept these offers. There were no BDS threats against those who rejected Israel's peace offers. Under these circumstances, it is immoral to impose blame only on Israel and to direct a BDS movement only against the nation-state of the Jewish people that has thrice offered to end the occupation in exchange for peace.*

2. *The current BDS tactic, especially in Europe and on some American university campuses, emboldens the Palestinians to reject compromise solutions to the conflict.* Some within the Palestinian leadership have told me that the longer they hold out against making peace, the more powerful will be the BDS movement against Israel. Why not wait until BDS strengthens their bargaining position so that they won't have to compromise by giving up the right of return, by agreeing to a demilitarized state, and by making other concessions that are necessary to peace but difficult for some Palestinians to accept? BDS is making a peaceful resolution harder.

3. *BDS is immoral because its leaders will never be satisfied with the kind of two-state solution that is acceptable to Israel.* Many of its leaders do not believe in the concept of Israel as the nation-state of the Jewish people.

4. *BDS is immoral because it violates the core principle of human rights: namely, "the worst first."* Israel is among the freest and most democratic nations in the world. It is certainly the freest and most democratic nation in the Middle East. Its Arab citizens enjoy more rights than Arabs anywhere else in the world. Yet Israel is the only country in the world today being threatened with BDS. When a sanction is directed against only a state with one of the best records of human rights, and that nation happens to be the state of the Jewish people, the suspicion of bigotry must be considered.

5. *BDS is immoral because it would hurt the wrong people.* It would hurt Palestinian workers who will lose their jobs if economic sanctions are directed against firms

that employ them. It would hurt artists and academics, many of whom are the strongest voices for peace and an end to the occupation. It would hurt those suffering from illnesses all around the world who would be helped by Israeli medicine and the collaboration between Israeli scientists and other scientists. It would hurt the high tech industry around the world because Israel contributes disproportionally to the development of such life-enhancing technology.

6. ***BDS is immoral because it would encourage Iran**—the world's leading facilitator of international terrorism—to unleash its surrogates, such as Hezbollah and Hamas, against Israel, in the expectation that if Israel were to respond to rocket attacks, the pressure for BDS against Israel would increase, as it did when Israel responded to thousands of rockets from Gaza in 2008–2009.*

7. ***BDS is immoral because it focuses the world's attention away from far greater injustices, including genocide.** By focusing disproportionately on Israel, the human rights community pays disproportionately less attention to the other occupations, such as those by China, Russia, and Turkey, and to other humanitarian disasters such as that occurring in Syria.*

8. ***BDS is immoral because it promotes false views regarding the nation-state of the Jewish people, exaggerates its flaws and thereby promotes a new variation on the world's oldest prejudice, namely anti-Semitism.** It is not surprising therefore that BDS is featured on neo-Nazi, Holocaust denial, and other overtly anti-Semitic websites and is promoted by some of the world's most notorious haters such as David Duke.*

9. **BDS is immoral because it reflects and encourages a double standard of judgment and response regarding human rights violations.** *By demanding more of Israel, the nation-state of the Jewish people, it expects less of other states, people, cultures, and religions, thereby reifying a form of colonial racism and reverse bigotry that hurts the victims of human rights violations inflicted by others.*

10. **BDS will never achieve its goals.** *Neither the Israeli government nor the Israeli people will ever capitulate to the extortionate means implicit in BDS. They will not and should not make important decisions regarding national security and the safety of their citizens on the basis of immoral threats. Moreover, were Israel to compromise its security in the face of such threats, the result would be more wars, more death, and more suffering.*

In 2018, I published a book titled *The Case Against BDS: Why Singling Out Israel for Boycott Is Anti-Semitic and Anti-Peace.* In it, I urge students and others to use their moral voices to demand that both the Israeli government and the Palestinian Authority accept a compromise peace that assures the security of Israel and the viability of a peaceful and democratic Palestinian state. I urge that the way forward should not be by immoral extortionate threats that do more harm than good but by negotiations, compromise and goodwill.

We are winning the war against BDS on campuses, insofar as no mainstream university has boycotted or divested from Israel. But the goals of BDS go beyond these specific outcomes. They include poisoning the minds of students with false accounts of Israel's "apartheid," "genocide" and other sins. (More on this to come.) It is for that reason that I decided to write *The Case for Israel.*

At about the time the Clinton–Barak peace offer was being rejected and the second intifada and BDS weapons were being aimed at Israel, a Harvard student came to see me during the 10 days of Repentance between Rosh Hashanah and Yom Kippur, when Jews are supposed to seek forgiveness for sins of commission and omission. The student asked me to forgive him for his sin of omission in failing to stand up for Israel when his professors or fellow students unjustly condemned the Jewish state. He told me that he was quite knowledgeable about the Israeli–Palestinian conflict, having spent a gap year in Israel and having also attended a Zionist high school. I asked him why he didn't stand up for Israel, and he replied sheepishly, "If I'm perceived as a supporter of Israel, I won't get dates. It's not cool to be a Zionist."

My immediate response was humorous. "Why don't we start a campaign: Support Israel—Date a Zionist Tonight?" He didn't laugh. It was becoming a serious issue on campus. Students were reluctant to stand up for Israel, some out of fear of losing popularity, others out of lack of the knowledge necessary to rebut the growing anti-Israel rhetoric. It was already becoming clear to me that college campuses would become one of the front lines in the war for public opinion on the question of Israel. Moreover, a number of pernicious myths had grown up around the Arab–Israeli conflict, some of them due to ignorance and others promulgated knowingly by anti-Israel activists and propagandists.

The Case for Israel therefore grew out of my desire to write an accessible primer on the core issues in this debate. My target audience was university students, and I arranged with my publisher to make copies available at a reduced cost for them. I was pleasantly surprised when the book not only became a campus bestseller but also landed on the *New York Times* bestseller list for general audiences.

The format of the book was simple and accessible. Each of its 32 short chapters begins with an accusation against Israel commonly made on campuses and in hard-left media. The accusation is followed by a paragraph describing and quoting the accusers. Then comes a paragraph summarizing "the reality." Finally, several pages document "the proof" of the reality.

For example, chapter 5 begins with the following accusation: "While the Arabs were willing to share Palestine with the Jews, the Jews wanted the entire country for themselves." The accuser was Edward Said, a prominent anti-Israel Columbia University professor who, at the time, had considerable influence over faculty and students. I then disproved the accusation with documentary and other historical evidence. It was important to disprove the myths and lies promulgated by Said and other respectable academics, who were using their respectability and popularity on campus to make the case against Israel, based largely on false information. I believed then, and I believe now, that the proper response to false information is competition in the marketplace of ideas rather than attempts to censor the falsehoods. For the most part, truth tends to prevail in the marketplace, if there is hard evidence to support it.

Other accusers included Noam Chomsky, Norman Finkelstein and other hard leftists who accused Israel of apartheid, Nazism and other sins.

Because of its simple format, *The Case for Israel* became a bestseller and an accessible "bible" for defenders of Israel, who would carry it around and turn to the relevant chapters whenever a false accusation was leveled against the Jewish state. I am proud to say that it had a significant impact on campuses, empowering pro-Israel students to respond to the increasingly shrill and mendacious accusations being directed at Israel.

I spoke about the book on numerous campuses. The response from students was very heartening, despite the protests that accompanied my appearances. Perhaps the most gratifying response came from a young man named Kasim Hafeez. Here is his story in his own words:

Growing up in the Muslim community in the UK I was exposed to materials and opinions at best condemning Israel, painting Jews as usurpers and murderers, and at worse calling for the wholesale destruction of the "Zionist Entity" and all Jews.

My father [was even] more brazen in his hatred, boasting of how Adolf Hitler was a hero, his only failing being that he didn't kill enough Jews.

[One day] I found myself in the Israel and Palestine section of a local bookstore and picked up a copy of Alan Dershowitz's The Case for Israel. *Given my worldview, the Jews and Americans controlled the media, so after a brief look at the back, I scoffed thinking "vile Zionist propaganda."*

As I read Dershowitzs' arguments and deconstruction of many lies I saw as unquestionable truths, I searched despairingly for counterarguments, but found more hollow rhetoric that I'd believed for many years. I felt a real crisis of conscience, and thus began a period of unbiased research. Up until that point I had not been exposed to anything remotely positive about Israel.

Now I didn't know what to believe. I'd blindly followed others for so long, yet here I was questioning whether I had been wrong. I reached a point where I felt that I had no other choice but to see Israel for myself, only that way I'd really know the truth. At the risk of sounding cliché, it was a life-changing visit.

I did not encounter an apartheid racist state, but rather, quite the opposite. I was confronted by synagogues, mosques and churches, by Jews and Arabs living together, by minorities playing huge parts in all areas of Israeli life, from the military to the judiciary. It was shocking and eye opening. This wasn't the evil Zionist Israel that I had been told about.

After much soul searching, I knew what I had once believed was wrong. I had been confronted with the truth and had to accept it.

I had to stand with Israel, with this tiny nation, free,

democratic, making huge strides in medicine, research and
development, yet the victim of the same lies and hatred that
nearly consumed me. . . .
    This isn't about religion and politics; it's about the truth.

I'm proud of having played a small part in Hafeez's search for the truth. Several other erstwhile anti-Israel activists told me that my book had changed their minds as well.

The Case for Israel made me a popular speaker on campuses throughout the United States and around the world. I felt a deep responsibility to make the centrist-liberal case for Israel in as many forums as possible. This endeavor took considerable time and effort, but despite my full-time teaching schedule and part-time legal practice, I prioritized my advocacy for Israel because of my strong feelings about the unfairness of the attacks on Israel. There was another reason why pro-Israel campus groups invited me to speak: on many campuses, there were no professors who were willing to make the case for Israel—even the centrist two-state solution case. I was the default choice. It was shocking to me that on campuses with a significant number of Jewish faculty, not a single professor was willing to stand up for Israel. Some of these silent scholars supported Israel in private, but they refused to become publicly identified with Zionism. I should not have been surprised, since even tenured professors are rarely willing to challenge hard-left "political correctness" lest they alienate colleagues and students.

This lack of public support for Israel among university faculty reflects a broader phenomenon. The anti-Israel faculty on most campuses are better organized and more willing to speak out than the pro-Israel faculty. They also present a more united front and a singular program: the end of Israel as the nation-state of the Jewish people and the illegitimacy of Zionism as a national liberation movement. The pro-Israel faculty are deeply divided, from the J Street left to the pro-settlement right. Moreover, many fear reprisals from their better-organized anti-Israel colleagues and students. And their fear is understandable, if not commendable. Being perceived as a Zionist carries with it, on many campuses, risks of unpopularity, lower student evaluations and other consequences, as I will document below. But tenured professors who privately support Israel—without supporting all of its policies—should show more courage in expressing their pro-Israel views, not in the classroom, where the expression of political preferences has no proper place, but in the public square.

The risks to professors were substantial even during the period when Prime Minister Ehud Barak was offering the Palestinians a state. They became even greater when Barak, the candidate of the left-leaning Labor Party, was defeated for reelection by the right-wing coalition headed by Ariel Sharon.

11

Sharon and Bush

Partners in the War on Terror

YASSER ARAFAT'S REJECTION of Ehud Barak's peace offer, followed by the bloody second intifada, considerably weakened the Israeli peace camp. Most Israelis no longer believed that Arafat was a potential peace partner. Many now believed that signing the Oslo Accords had been a mistake and that Israel needed to protect itself from terrorism and other threats by showing strength. They wanted a government headed by a prime minister who projected toughness and self-determination. No one fit this bill better than General Ariel Sharon, Israel's most famous military hero, whose only flaw was that he was too tough: he had been removed from his post as minister of defense for his indirect responsibility in not preventing the Phalangist massacres at Sabra and Shatila back in 1982.

Sharon's fame and infamy as a military genius was known throughout Israel. His exploits were the stuff of novels and films: how he disobeyed orders during the Yom Kippur War and surrounded and trapped the Egyptian army; how he disobeyed orders in Lebanon and had his troops move more deeply into that country; how, as a young soldier, he had conducted retaliatory raids in response to terrorist attacks on Israeli civilians; how he had done nothing to stop the Phalangist massacres in Sabra and Shatila. After leaving military service, he became an equally controversial political leader, and he soon helped form the Kadima Party, which was more to the center than his former party, Likud, which he had left.[1]

"To every thing there is a season," wrote the author of Ecclesiastes. And this was the season for Sharon, the warrior. No one expected him to suddenly become a man of peace or to compromise. But as with Begin and Egypt, Sharon surprised the world by calling for a Palestinian entity on the West Bank and by endorsing the roadmap for peace proposed by the United States, Russia and the European Union. His biggest surprise took the form of Israel's unilateral withdrawal from the Gaza Strip in 2005.

Sharon dismantled all the Jewish settlements in the Gaza Strip, over the strong objection of their nearly 9,000 residents. He also ended the military occupation there, removing every soldier and military base. Although the Israeli Defense Forces maintained security control over the air, sea and land borders to prevent terrorism, the residents of the Gaza Strip were free to create a "Singapore on the Mediterranean." They could have used hothouses and agricultural equipment left behind by Israel, as well as the financial support they received from Europe, Arab states and the United Nations to create a thriving economy.[2] Instead, they voted for Hamas, then murdered or expelled Palestinian Authority functionaries before turning the Gaza Strip into a launching pad for thousands of rockets, dozens of terror tunnels, hundreds of incendiary kites and other cross-border attacks on the civilian residents of cities and towns in close proximity.[3]

Sharon's decision to leave the Gaza Strip unilaterally, without any peace deal with the Palestinians, was intended to be a first step in a more general unilateral approach to separating Israel from the Palestinians. Four Jewish settlements in the northern West Bank were also dismantled. The building of a long security barrier separating Israel from the West Bank, which began before Sharon took office, accelerated under his watch. Although its major purpose was to prevent the infiltration of terrorists, the wall's route was seen by many as a new unilaterally imposed "boundary" between Israel and the Palestinian entity from which Israel would disengage. It was also seen as part of the overall process of separation that could lead to a de facto two-state solution.

The entire enterprise of unilateral disengagement was extremely controversial both within Israel and among the Palestinian leadership. Pro-settlement Israelis were furious at Sharon's decision to dismantle existing settlements. Some security-minded Israelis were understandably concerned that ending the military occupation of the Gaza Strip would make the border areas more vulnerable to rocket attacks. Many Israelis were upset that Israel was getting nothing in return for these concessions.

Nor did Israel receive the praise it rightfully deserved. Despite taking these risks for peace, efforts to isolate and demonize Israel—through BDS, UN resolutions and demonstrations—only increased. There was no correlation between Israel's positive actions on the one hand and the condemnation it received on the other, especially from the hard left. The security barrier on the West Bank—which was mostly a sophisticated electronic fence, with solid walls placed in areas from which rifle shots were aimed at Israeli civilians—was called an apartheid wall, despite the reality that it dramatically reduced terrorist attacks and saved lives on both sides.

The absence of a positive response to Sharon's unilateral steps only made them—and him—more controversial, especially among the Israeli right, which accused him of becoming a traitor to their cause. But his support among centrist Israelis increased as he responded vigorously to continuing terrorist attacks while at the same time seeking to disengage from the Palestinians. Sharon maintained a positive relationship with President George W. Bush despite his opposition to the U.S. invasion of Iraq.

The controversy hit home in 2005 when I received an honorary doctorate from Bar-Ilan University.[4] My uncle Zecharia, my father's youngest and only living brother, believes that Israel has the right to build settlements in all of the historical areas that are part of the Jewish patrimony, and he was furious at Sharon for withdrawing from some areas. He had attended all the prior ceremonies at which I had been honored, but he refused to attend this one because of the prime minister's decision to attend. He only came to the reception, after Sharon had flown off in his helicopter.

I met privately with Sharon just before the stroke that disabled him in 2006 and ended his prime ministership. We discussed his unilateral approach, and he asked me my opinion. I told him that I completely supported the dismantling of the settlements, since I had opposed their establishment in the first place. He told me that he had favored the settlements from the beginning—especially those in areas he regarded as essential to Israel's security—but he felt the time had come to separate from the Palestinians and that dismantling some of the non-security-related settlements was necessary to secure this separation. He showed me a map and pointed to several areas in the West Bank in which he intended to dismantle more settlements. The map made it clear, at least to me, that he viewed the security barrier as serving two purposes: prevention of terrorism and a rough boundary for unilateral disengagement.

Before I met Sharon, I didn't expect to like him. He struck me, from a distance, as arrogant and difficult. He had a reputation for ignoring or circumventing the orders of higher-ups, which he had done during the Yom Kippur War and the First Lebanon War. In some important respects, his character conformed to some Israeli stereotypes: much like the sabra, Israel's national fruit, Sharon was prickly on the outside, but sweet on the inside. Until we met in person, I had only seen the outside.

Sharon had a reputation for being brusque and arrogant. In person, at least to me, he was warm and personable. At first, he talked down to me, as if reading from a scripted briefing he had given many times to prominent Jewish visitors from abroad. But I politely interjected, reminding him that I had written several books and numerous articles on what he was telling me. "Can we get to tachlis?" I asked, using a Yiddish term that roughly suggests, "Cut the B.S. and let's get to the point." He laughed and replied, "Good, I like tachlis." We proceeded to have a good substantive discussion of the merits and demerits of unilateral steps designed to create de facto separation on Israel's terms, without the need for negotiation with or agreement from the Palestinians. "I would love to make a mutual deal, like we did with Egypt and Jordan," he said, "but the Palestinian leadership is weak, and they cannot say yes. It may be easier for them to passively accept my unilateral acts than for them to affirmatively agree to them, even if they get less."

It was an interesting perspective, one I had not heard previously. I wasn't sure whether time would prove it right or wrong, but I was not in a position to argue with a man who knew the Palestinian leadership much better than I did.

We had one more conversation before his stroke. One Friday afternoon, I was visiting a group of friends in Tel Aviv who gathered every week for tea, vodka and political conversation—a so-called "parliament." I had been scheduled to meet again with Sharon that day, but his lawyer had canceled the meeting because I was representing an Israeli businessman who was a potential witness in the ongoing investigation of the prime minister and his sons for financial corruption. The lawyer thought it would be a bad idea for us to meet while the investigation was in progress, even though we would be discussing other issues. I agreed.

Just before the Sabbath began, the phone of one of the men attending the parliament rang. He spoke in Hebrew and then handed the phone to me: "Someone wants to speak to you." "Who?" I asked. "A friend," he replied. I took the phone and heard the familiar raspy voice of the prime minister: "Shalom. This is the man you're not supposed to talk to, just calling to wish you Shabbat Shalom." With that, he hung up. It was the last time we spoke.

When he suffered his stroke, Christian Evangelist Pat Robertson—a fellow Yale Law School graduate, who had interviewed me for his show on several occasions—declared that it was God punishing Sharon for abandoning the Gaza Strip and parts of the West Bank. Most of the rest of the world saw Sharon's stroke as a tragedy that might have prevented further withdrawals and further steps toward some sort of rapprochement.

Like Israel itself, Sharon's legacy is somewhat mixed. His military tactics helped Israel during the Yom Kippur War but hurt Israel in Lebanon. Before he became prime minister, his politics—especially his aggressive support for settlements—made the quest for peace more difficult. But when he ascended to the prime ministership, his decision to end the Gaza occupation and withdraw from settlements there gave the Palestinians an opportunity to secure the benefits of self-rule—an opportunity they frittered away by abandoning peace and turning instead to Hamas and terrorism. Sharon was (along with Shimon Peres) the last of the founding generation of Israelis. He will have a positive place in Israel's complicated and ever-changing history.

12

Olmert Attacks Syrian Nuclear Reactor, Offers Peace

Deputy Prime Minister Ehud Olmert became acting prime minister after Sharon's debilitating stroke. Olmert, who I first met when he was the popular mayor of Jerusalem, helped found the Kadima Party with Sharon and served as the prime minister's second in command. After serving as acting prime minister, he led his Kadima Party to an electoral victory before assuming the role of prime minister for nearly three years, a role he held until he stepped down as a result of the investigation that ultimately led to his conviction and imprisonment on charges of corruption. But his three-year term was among the most consequential in Israel's history.

Perhaps the most significant act undertaken by Olmert was the successful attack on a nuclear reactor being built by North Korea in Syria. Olmert, who had a close relationship with President George Bush, had suggested that the United States bomb the reactor, but Bush refused and told Olmert not to do it, suggesting tough diplomacy instead. But Olmert decided that the facility had to be destroyed—and it was, in a precision bombing raid named "Orchard" on September 6, 2007.

There were no public outcries from Syria or North Korea, because neither wanted to acknowledge the reactor's existence. Israel, too, remained silent about what it had done.

Intelligence sources have reported that the air strike was assisted by Special Forces on the ground that pinpointed the target, and by Israel's electronic warfare system that had infiltrated Syria's air defenses and fed them false information while Israeli fighter jets were in the air.

Just imagine how different and even more deadly the subsequent Syrian civil war would have been if Hafez al-Assad had possessed sophisticated nuclear weapons instead of the chemical barrel bombs he used on his own people. Despite President Bush having urged Olmert not to bomb the Syrian facility, the United States came to appreciate that he had done the right thing and had potentially saved many lives. This was especially true when, several years later, ISIS captured the area where Syria had been preparing to create a nuclear arsenal.[1]

In March 2018, Israeli censors finally allowed the government to acknowledge publicly what everyone knew: that the Israeli air force had destroyed the Syrian reactor. A few days later, I conducted the first English-language interview with Olmert about his decision and its implementation.

The interview was part of an Israeli TV show I moderated each week via Skype, titled *One on One with Alan Dershowitz*, in which I ask and answer questions with Israeli guests. The producer is Danny Grossman, a former top gun in both the U.S. and Israeli air force. Danny is also my go-to guy in Israel, arranging all my interviews and visits when I make my frequent trips there. He has been an indispensable associate and friend.

In this interview, Olmert—also an old friend—was candid in assessing the risks Israel faced and proud of the role he had played in protecting Israel from a Syrian nuclear threat. He credited his close personal relationship with President Bush for the positive U.S. response when the attack was a fait accompli. I too knew President

Bush despite my legal role against him in the Florida recount case, representing voters in Palm Beach County who were arguing that the so-called butterfly ballot had caused them inadvertently to cast their vote for a candidate for whom they did not intend to vote. We first met through our mutual friendship with Anatoly Sharansky. Bush wrote me a lengthy handwritten letter about our mutual friend, which included the following:

> *Like you, I care deeply about human dignity and justice. Thanks as well for representing Natan. When I was in Europe, I saw a copy of his book* [The Case for Democracy] *on the desk of the P.M. of Slovakia, was questioned about it at the E.U., and know it was referenced in European press on my trip. Truth is powerful.*
>
> *Best Regards,*
> *George Bush*

I spent some time with President Bush in Israel when we were both there celebrating Israel's sixtieth birthday in 2008. During that visit, Sharansky, Vaclav Havel and I were on a panel discussing human rights. Afterward, we all got into an elevator with Mikhail Gorbachev. I had previously met Gorbachev in the Soviet Union when I was there defending dissidents. He pointed at me and said, "You're the big-shot lawyer who tried to get these people out of prison. You did a good job, but I did a better job. I'm the one who got them out." Havel then turned to Gorbachev and asked, "Why didn't you get us out sooner?," to which Gorbachev replied, "I'm not that good."

Not all of Olmert's military decisions were as successful and uncontroversial as Operation Orchard. The 34-day Lebanon War, which began on July 12, 2006, and ended with a UN-brokered ceasefire on August 14, 2006, was started by a Hezbollah incursion into

Israel during which three Israeli soldiers were killed and two kidnapped. Several more were killed in a failed attempt to rescue the kidnapped soldiers.[2]

Israel then launched air attacks and a ground invasion, and Hezbollah fired thousands more rockets at Israeli civilian targets, killing and injuring many. Israel, which regarded Hezbollah as the real power in Lebanon, attacked parts of the Lebanese infrastructure, including its international airport, which—like other Lebanese structures—had mixed military-civilian use and were thus legitimate military targets. In the end, thousands of Lebanese and Israeli civilians were temporarily displaced. As usual, the number and proportion of Lebanese civilians and fighters were hotly disputed—because Hezbollah fighters were civilians by night and terrorists by day—but a total of approximately 1,000 Lebanese were killed. For Israel, 121 soldiers and 46 civilians were killed, with more than 4,000 civilians injured.

The indecisive military outcome was unpopular in Israel and led to protests and the establishment of a commission—headed by retired justice Eliyahu Winograd—that deemed the war as a "missed opportunity" without "a defined military victory." In my interview with Olmert, I raised this issue, and he told me that he believed the war had accomplished what he had set out to do: deter further incursions into Israel from Lebanon.

The international reaction—especially in the media and on campuses—was critical, focusing on the Lebanese civilian casualties and damage to the infrastructure.

While I could not defend everything that Israel had done—or the wisdom of Israel's full-scale response to a cross-border raid by Hezbollah—I did try to explain why there were so many more Lebanese than Israeli civilian casualties. Israel goes to great effort and expense to protect its civilian population, constructing shelters and underground medical facilities, whereas Hezbollah deliberately uses Lebanese civilians as human shields to protect its fighters. Moreover, Hezbollah uses civilian structures—homes, hospitals, schools, shops—as launching places for its rockets. Israeli video footage, obtained for me by Danny, vividly showed how Hezbollah would place mobile launchers in civilian garages and other spaces, exit those spaces to fire the missiles and then retreat to them. Israel tried to avoid unnecessarily destroying civilian structures, but under the law of war, mixed-use structures were legitimate targets as long as reasonable efforts were made to minimize civilian casualties. But for most of the media[3] and on campuses, the body count was all that mattered, even if Hezbollah deliberately conducted its asymmetrical warfare so as to maximize the disparity between Lebanese civilian casualties and those of Israel.

I have pointed out in my writings that the media, and sometimes even academics, misunderstand the legal concept of *proportionality*. No nation is required by international law to limit its military actions to proportionate responses to enemy aggression. It may respond with disproportionate force as long as that force is directed at *military* targets. The legal requirement of proportionality relates to the use of military force that may result in *civilian* casualties. International law requires that when civilian deaths or injuries are contemplated in an attack against legitimate military targets, such anticipated civilian casualties should be proportional to the value of the military objectives sought. For example, if the leaders of a dangerous terrorist cell were hiding in a civilian building, it would be permissible to target those leaders, even if it was anticipated that a small number of civilians might be killed or wounded. But if one terrorist was hiding in a hospital or school, it would not be permissible to risk the lives of patients or students to target that one terrorist.

When Israel invaded the Gaza Strip in 2008, following an increase in Hamas rocket attacks on Israeli civilian targets, there were claims of disproportionality. "Operation Cast Lead," as it was called, began on December 27, 2008, and ended three weeks later. It led to the notorious *Goldstone Report* in September 2009. The report was commissioned by the United Nations Commission on Human Rights.[4] The commission was widely discredited because its members and chairpersons included some of the worst human rights offenders in the world, such as Iran, Syria, Belarus, China, Russia, Venezuela, Cuba, Saudi Arabia and Iraq. In order to lend credibility to the report it commissioned on Gaza, it appointed Richard Goldstone to be its chairman. It was a cynical, if brilliant, choice. Goldstone was a prominent Jew from South Africa, much of whose family lived in Israel. He had served as a judge during the apartheid period in South Africa, but had redeemed himself by his commitment to human rights following Nelson Mandela's assumption to the presidency of South Africa. But Goldstone was also ambitious to achieve status within the UN structure.

I wrote a 50-page[5] rebuttal to that error-filled report, which contributed to Richard Goldstone's decision to retract its most damning conclusions.

According to the report, Israel used the more than 8,000 rocket attacks on its civilians merely as a *pretext*, an *excuse*, a *cover* for the real purpose of Operation Cast Lead, which was to target innocent Palestinian civilians—children, women, the elderly—for death. The report said that this criminal objective was explicitly decided upon by the highest levels of the Israeli government and military and constituted a deliberate and willful war crime. The report found these serious charges "to be firmly-based in fact" and had "no doubt" of their truth, but it cited no credible evidence that actually supported its questionable conclusions.

The same *Goldstone Report*, in contrast, concluded that Hamas was not guilty of deliberately and willfully using the civilian population as human shields. It found "no evidence" that Hamas fighters "engaged in combat in civilian dress," "no evidence" that Palestinian combatants "mingled with the civilian population with the intention of shielding themselves from attack," and no support for the claim that mosques were used to store weapons.

The report was demonstrably wrong about both of these critical conclusions. The hard evidence conclusively proved that the exact opposite was true, namely that (1) Israel did not have a policy of targeting innocent civilians for death—indeed, the IDF went to unprecedented lengths to minimize civilian casualties, including phoning, leafleting and firing nonlethal warning "bombs" to advise civilians to leave buildings that were being targeted—and (2) that Hamas did have a deliberate policy of having its combatants dress in civilian clothing, fire their rockets from densely populated areas, use civilians a human shields and store weapons in mosques.[6]

What is even more telling than its erroneous conclusions, however, was its deliberately skewed methodology, particularly the manner in which it used and evaluated similar evidence very differently, depending on whether it favored the Hamas or Israeli side.

I wrote a detailed analysis of the Goldstone methodology, which is available online.[7] It was sent to the secretary general for inclusion in critiques of the *Goldstone Report* received by the United Nations. This analysis documents the distortions, misuses of evidence and bias of the report and those who wrote it. It demonstrates that the evidence relied on by the report, as well as the publicly available evidence it deliberately chose to ignore, disproves its own conclusions.

The central issue that distinguished the conclusions the *Goldstone Report* reached regarding Israel, on the one hand, and Hamas, on the other, is intentionality. The report credits the most serious accusations against Israel, namely that the killing of civilians was intentional and deliberately planned at the highest levels. The report also discredits the most serious accusations made against Hamas, namely that their combatants wore civilian clothing to shield themselves from attack, mingled among the civilian populations and used civilians as human shields intentionally. These issues are, of course, closely related.

If it were to turn out that there was no evidence that Hamas ever operated from civilian areas, and that the IDF knew this, then the allegations that the IDF, by firing into civilian areas, deliberately intended to kill Palestinian civilians would be strengthened. But if it were to turn out that the IDF reasonably believed that Hamas fighters were deliberately using civilians as shields, then this fact would weaken the claim that the IDF had no military purpose in firing into civilian areas. Moreover, if Hamas did use human shields, then the deaths of Palestinian civilians would be more justly attributable to Hamas than to Israel.

Since intentionality, or lack thereof, was so important to the report's conclusions, it would seem essential that the report would apply the same evidentiary standards, rules and criteria in determining the intent of Israel and in determining the intent of Hamas.

Yet a careful review of the report made it crystal clear that its writers applied totally different standards, rules and criteria in evaluating the intent of the parties to the conflict. The report resolved all doubts against Israel in concluding that its leaders intended to kill civilians, while resolving all doubts in favor of Hamas in concluding that it did not intend to use Palestinian civilians as human shields.

Moreover, when it had precisely the same sort of evidence in relation to both sides—for example, statements by leaders prior to the commencement of the operation—it attributed significant weight to the Israel statements while entirely discounting comparable Hamas statements. This sort of evidentiary bias, though subtle, permeates the entire report.

In addition to the statements of leaders, which are treated so differently, the report takes a completely different view regarding the inferring of intent from action. When it comes to Israel, the report repeatedly looks to results, and from those results, it infers that they must have been intended. But when it comes to Hamas, it refuses to draw inferences regarding intent from results. For example, it acknowledges that some combatants wore civilian clothes, and it offers no reasonable explanation for why this would be so other than to mingle indistinguishably among civilians. Yet it refuses to infer intent from these actions. Highly relevant to the report's conclusion that militants did not intend for their actions to shield themselves from counterattack is that the Goldstone investigators—who included Goldstone himself and several professional Israel bashers—were "unable to make any determination on the general allegations that Palestinian armed groups used mosques for military purposes," "did not find any evidence to support the allegations that hospital facilities were used by the Gaza authorities or by Palestinian armed groups to shield military activities," did not find evidence "that ambulances were used to transport combatants or for other military purposes," and did not find "that Palestinian armed groups engaged in combat activities from United Nations facilities that were used as shelters during the military operations." There is, however, hard evidence—including videos and photographs—that Hamas did operate in mosques and near hospitals and schools.

When the report was dealing with Israeli intentions, it relied on highly questionable circumstantial inferences: since Israel's rockets are relatively accurate, the fact that some hit civilians led to the inference that they were intentionally targeted rather than accidently hit, despite the universally accepted reality that in the fog of war, the most sophisticated weapons sometimes hit unintended targets. But when the report considered Hamas, it ignored the circumstantial evidence, even though it was much stronger in suggesting intent. It is beyond obvious that militants fire rockets from the vicinity of mosques or hospitals not because it is easier to launch rockets near community institutions, but only because of the special protections afforded to hospitals and religious centers in war.

The report—commissioned by an organization with a long history of anti-Israel bigotry and written by biased "experts" with limited experience—was one-sided and wrong in its fundamental conclusions. This should not be surprising since conclusions can be no better than the methodology employed, and the methodology employed in this report was fundamentally flawed. It was as if two different people, with different evidentiary standards, were tasked with writing the report: one the Israel portion and the other the Hamas portion. But it was Richard Goldstone, its chairman, who was fully responsible.

In op-eds and media appearances, I challenged Goldstone to explain the evidentiary bias that is so obviously reflected in the report. I said that the burden was on him to justify the very different methodologies used to arrive at the report's conclusions regarding the intentions of Israel and the intentions of Hamas. I argued that failure to assume that burden would constitute an implicit admission that the conclusions reached in the *Goldstone Report* were not worthy of consideration by people of goodwill.

A debate was arranged by students at Fordham Law School, where Goldstone was a visiting professor. He was invited to defend his report, but he was a no-show, claiming some excuse. So I placed his report on the chair that had been reserved for him and "debated" *it*! I invited students and faculty in the audience to take his side during the question period, but none did.

I had been on friendly terms with Richard Goldstone—I was not a close friend but an admiring colleague—until he signed the report. My criticism of the report, and of him for signing it, were so deep that our friendship could not survive the dispute. I questioned not only his "findings" but his motivations as well. I saw him as an opportunist who placed his ambitions above his commitment to truth. To advance in the world of international diplomacy and law, especially within the structure of the United Nations, a Jew had to lean over backward—in this case doing triple somersaults—to prove the absence of any pro-Israel leanings. In performing these contortions, Goldstone scored points with the UN bureaucracy, but he lost the respect of many of his colleagues, even some who were critical of Israeli actions in Gaza. No reasonable, objective observer could accept the two major conclusions of the *Goldstone Report*: that there was evidence that the Israeli military deliberately targeted civilians in an effort to kill as many innocent noncombatants as possible, and that there was no evidence that Hamas terrorists used

Gaza civilians as human shields. Not only was there *no* evidence that the former proposition was true, but there was substantial evidence that it was false. Consider the very different conclusion drawn by Colonel Richard Kemp, the former commander of British Forces in Afghanistan: "I don't think there has ever been a time in the history of warfare when an army has made more efforts to reduce civilian casualties and deaths of innocent people than the IDF is doing today in Gaza."[8]

The evidence that Hamas used civilians as human shields was overwhelming and indisputable, including admissions—indeed proud proclamations—by Hamas officials describing human shields as martyrs. According to a translation by the Middle East Media Research Institute, on February 29, 2008, Fathi Hamad, a Hamas member of the Palestinian Legislative Council, stated,

> *For the Palestinian people, death has become an industry, at which women excel, and so do all the people living on this land. The elderly excel at this, and so do the mujahideen and the children. This is why they have formed human shields of the women, the children, the elderly, and the mujahideen, in order to challenge the Zionist bombing machine. It is as if they were saying to the Zionist enemy: "We desire death like you desire life."*

There were also videos of Hamas rockets being fired from civilian homes, schools and hospitals, as well as photographic evidence of civilian buildings used as storage facilities for rockets and other weapons.

When the war was over, I wrote a book defending Israel's actions, entitled *The Case for Moral Clarity: Israel, Hamas and Gaza*. Its cover was a cartoon depicting an armed Israeli soldier standing *in front* of a baby carriage to protect the baby and a Hamas fighter standing *behind* a baby carriage, using the baby to protect himself as he fired rockets at Israeli civilians. It made my point more powerfully than any words. And it undercut the conclusions of the *Goldstone Report* more powerfully than any argument.

Eventually, Richard Goldstone disassociated himself from the report's conclusion, but not before it falsely persuaded so many people that Israel bore primary responsibility for the deaths in Gaza.

The wars in Lebanon and Gaza were not Prime Minister Olmert's only problems. His term ended ingloriously with his resignation, forced by the criminal charges he faced.[9] He was accused of corruption for alleged actions he took before he became prime minister. His resignation was not only a personal tragedy but also a tragedy for Israel, the Palestinians and the prospects for peace. Shortly before he resigned, he had offered the Palestinians a deal even better than the one criminally rejected by Yasser Arafat seven years earlier.[10] Although President Mahmoud Abbas had sufficient time to accept the offer, he did not. Nor did he formally reject it. When Olmert was replaced by Netanyahu, the deal was no longer on the table.

I visited Ehud Olmert in prison. I was allowed the visit because I had informally advised his lawyer, who was appealing the conviction. It was devastating to see this great man who I knew and admired for more than two decades in a prison cell. (In Israel, when you ask for a politician's cell number, it isn't always for his phone!)

I was taken to Olmert by a young guard, who I was told was an Israeli Druze. I was quite shocked to see the former prime minister of the nation-state of the Jewish people being ordered around by a young Druze man. Although the Druze, in general, are loyal to Israel and serve in its military, they are closer in ethnicity to Israel's Arabs than to its Jewish population. I guess I should not have been surprised, since the panel that convicted Moshe Katsav, Israel's former president, of sexual crimes included an Israeli Arab. So much for any claim of apartheid.

I spent several hours discussing the political situation with Olmert. He is not a fan of Prime Minister Benjamin Netanyahu, but he wished him well in his efforts to govern a country with millions of prime ministers, generals and opinionated know-it-alls, from taxi drivers to prison guards.

An anti-Semitic pro-Palestinian propaganda poster featuring a caricature of Dershowitz.

‣ Dershowitz family photo, summer 1950. Alan is wearing the Palmach shirt.

‣ Family portrait at Yom Kippur with Justice Goldberg and Mrs. Goldberg.

President Clinton and the First Lady attend Rosh Hashanah services on Martha's Vineyard with the Dershowitz family, 1994.

‣ Dershowitz (and son Elon) showing Prime Minister Netanyahu one of Dershowitz's books at the Prime Minister's Residence, 2010.

‣ Dershowitz, Elie Wiesel and his wife, and Sara Netanyahu in the front row for Prime Minister Netanyahu's speech to Congress, March 3, 2015.

Dershowitz interviewing Golda Meir for *The Advocates*, 1970.

Dershowitz discussing Iran with President Obama and his Middle East team, 2012.

‣ Dershowitz with his wife Carolyn on a camel at the Pyramids.

‣ Dershowitz outside the gates at Terezín.

▲ Dershowitz being led away after declaring he planned to challenge Iranian President Mahmoud Ahmadinejad about his views on the Holocaust and Israel minutes before the meeting between Swiss President Hans-Rudolf Merz and the Iranian president in Geneva, Switzerland, on April 19, 2009. *(Reuters)*

▾ Dershowitz meets with Israeli Prime Minister Shimon Peres.

13

Obama and Netanyahu Disagree on Iran and Jerusalem

In 2008, Barack Obama, who I had known as a law student, was elected president of the United States. When he was a student, his mentor was Professor Charles Ogletree, an African American colleague and brilliant criminal lawyer. Obama would visit Ogletree's office, which was in the same suite as mine. Charles was often late for appointments because he ran a clinical program that sometimes ran over. So Obama, garbed in his signature leather jacket, would wait for him, and we chatted while he waited. I liked him and saw his obvious leadership qualities and intelligence.

I was therefore deeply gratified by his later emergence in national politics as a dynamic young figure in the Democratic Party. I naturally couldn't vote for him when he ran for the Senate in Illinois, but I campaigned for him. When he ran for president in 2008, I supported Hillary Clinton, who I knew much better, in the primaries. But after he won the nomination, I campaigned enthusiastically for him in the general election.

My support for this young, relatively unknown candidate—whose record on Israel was sparse—instigated a firestorm of criticism from right-wing Zionists, and even from some concerned centrists. I felt it necessary to explain and justify my support for Obama over Senator John McCain from an American liberal and Zionist perspective.

First, I much favored Obama's policies on issues unrelated to Israel, such as the Supreme Court, the rights of women and gay people, separation of church and state, as well as the economy and environment. But I also preferred Obama to McCain on the issue of Israel. The reason is that I thought it would be better for Israel to have a liberal supporter in the White House than to have a conservative supporter. I believed that Obama's views on Israel would have a greater impact on young people, on Europe, on the media and on others who tend to identify with the liberal perspective. Although centrist liberals in general tend to support Israel, I acknowledged that support from the left seemed to be weakening as support from the right strengthened. I hoped that the election of Barack Obama—a liberal supporter of Israel—would enhance Israel's position among wavering liberals.[1]

During his first term, Obama supported Israel in a variety of important ways. He helped Israel militarily by funding the "iron dome," a sophisticated anti-rocket technology; supporting Israel's defensive incursion into Lebanon; opposing the *Goldstone Report*; increasing financial aid to the IDF and preventing the United Nations from passing one-sided resolutions against Israel. But he strongly—more strongly than his predecessors—opposed Israel's settlement expansion. This put him in conflict with many, though not all, Jewish supporters.

It also put him in conflict with Benjamin Netanyahu, whose second term as prime minister coincided with Obama's presidency.

I continued to support Obama because I, too, was critical of settlement expansion by the Netanyahu government, but other Jewish leaders began to waiver in their support. To deal with Jewish criticism, Obama counted on J Street—a new left-leaning organization that labeled itself "pro-Israel and pro-peace."

J Street was founded near the end of Prime Minister Olmert's term by Jeremy Ben-Ami—a left-leaning Democrat. But it increased its profile considerably when Netanyahu became prime minister. J Street initially saw its role as siding with Obama and giving him Jewish "cover" in his confrontations with Netanyahu regarding settlements and the peace process. Over time, and in an effort to build a base on the hard left of the Jewish community, J Street took anti-Israel positions that even Obama could not support. The *Goldstone Report* was one such issue: J Street brought Richard Goldstone to the Capitol to present his outrageously false conclusions to members of Congress.

But generally J Street toed the Obama line on divisive issues, such as the Iran deal and the Security Council resolution declaring Jerusalem's historically Jewish areas—such as the Western Wall, the Jewish Quarter and the access roads to Hebrew University and Hadassah Hospital—to be "illegally occupied" by Israel.

With regard to Iran, I came face to face with Ahmadinejad. In 2009, I traveled to Geneva to protest a meeting of the UN Human Rights Council, which had invited Mahmoud Ahmadinejad, the Holocaust-denying president of Iran, to deliver the key address. My wife and I were having a drink in the lobby of our hotel when Ahmadinejad and his entourage paraded through. I approached one of his handlers, introduced myself, and told him that I challenged the president to a debate about the Holocaust. His handler asked, "Where, at Harvard?" I replied, "No, the debate should be at Auschwitz; that's where the evidence is." He said he would communicate my offer to the president, who, he told me, was on the way to a press conference. I went and tried to ask Ahmadinejad directly whether he would debate me. I was immediately hauled off by the Swiss police, removed from the hotel and told I would not be allowed to return "for security reasons." I insisted that "security reasons" did not justify protecting the president from a hostile question. I called someone I knew in the Obama administration, who phoned the U.S. consulate in Geneva, and I was allowed back into the hotel with an apology. The photograph of me being removed from the hotel was flashed around the world with the following caption:

> *Harvard Law professor Alan Dershowitz is led away after declaring he planned to challenge Iranian President Mahmoud Ahmadinejad about his views on the Holocaust and Israel minutes before a meeting between President Hans-Rudolf Merz and the Iranian president in Geneva, Switzerland, on April 19, 2009.*[2]

We were not allowed into the chamber where Ahmadinejad was speaking so I led a march into the chamber. Several delegations were absent, and we took their seats. As soon as Ahmadinejad denied the Holocaust, which he did near the beginning of his speech, I stood up and shouted "Shame!" and walked out, passing directly in front of his lectern. Many others walked out as well, including several European delegations. Ahmadinejad's talk was a fiasco, and was reported as such by the media. He had made a fool of himself—with our help.

In 2010, the "human rights" conference was in New York at the UN headquarters. I delivered the following words:

> *One important reason why there is no peace in the Middle East can be summarized tragically in two letters, UN. The building dedicated in theory to peace has facilitated terrorism, stood idly by genocide, given a platform to Holocaust deniers, and disincentivized the Palestinians from negotiating a two-state solution . . . How dare states such as Saudi Arabia, Cuba, Venezuela, Zimbabwe, Iran, Bahrain, Syria, Belarus, and other tyrannies too numerous to mention lecture Israel about human rights? How dare states such as Turkey, that have attacked their own Kurdish minorities and Armenian minorities, and Russia, which has attacked its own Chechnyan minority . . . lecture Israel about peace?*

Is there no sense of shame . . . ? Has the word hypocrisy lost
all meaning . . . ? Does no one recognize the need for a single,
neutral standard of human rights? Have human rights now
become the permanent weapon of choice for those who practice
human wrongs? For shame. For shame.

Shortly after Benjamin Netanyahu was elected to his second term as prime minister, he made me an offer that gave me an existential identity crisis. He urged me to become Israel's ambassador to the United Nations. He said that I was the only person about whom there was a consensus within his security cabinet. I was honored beyond belief to be asked to serve in this important role. Nothing would have given me more personal or professional pleasure than to stand in the well of the United Nations and defend the nation-state of the Jewish people against the defamation and blood libels that are spewed out daily in that chamber of hatred against Israel. My father always taught me to stand up for the underdog, and there is no bigger underdog than Israel at the United Nations, where every year more resolutions are directed against this tiny democracy than all the other countries of the world together. I had written several books and articles on the subject, and I welcomed the enormous responsibility of becoming the spokesperson against anti-Israel bigotry at the United Nations. But as soon as the offer was made, I knew deep in my heart that I would reluctantly have to decline it.

For me, an American Jew, to become the official UN representative of another country would raise the specter of "dual loyalty," a charge frequently made by Israel haters against American Jews who support Israel. At the time, it did not appear that there would ever be any conflicts over the positions of the United States and Israel at the United Nations, because the United States almost always voted with Israel. It would later turn out that during Obama's second term, such conflicts did arise, especially with regard to Iran and the Security Council resolution. But even if there were no actual conflicts, the perception that an American Jew had switched sides and was representing the nation-state of the Jewish people would have given solace to those who have long claimed that American Jews have more loyalty to Israel than to the United States. I explained all this to Netanyahu, but he persisted and asked me to come to Israel and give him the opportunity to change my mind.

I flew to Israel and had a long dinner with the prime minister. He offered compelling arguments as to why my presence in the United Nations would be good for Israel, for the United States, for world Jewry, for American Jews and for peace. He also argued that I should not turn down the job because of what anti-Israel bigots would think and say. "They will think and say it even if you don't take the job." Netanyahu is an extremely persuasive man. But in the end, I persuaded him that I could better serve our mutual interests by retaining my role as an independent and liberal defender of Israel. He reluctantly accepted my decision, but he asked me if I were willing to take on another job. I asked him what it was. He said, "I need you to be Israel's unofficial ambassador to the Jews of America, especially the young ones. America's political support for Israel is every bit as important as its military support, and the two are, of course, related. Please help keep American Jews supportive of our small country." I promised I would, and he gave me a big hug—the first time he had ever shown such physical affection during the many decades that we had known each other.

Even as I walked back to my hotel, I was uncertain whether I had done the right thing. Intellectually, I was satisfied with my decision, but emotionally it left a big question mark. I knew I would be missing a great deal by turning down this unique opportunity. Fortunately, the man Netanyahu picked instead of me—Ron Prosor—performed brilliantly at the United Nations and served his country with great distinction. Israel certainly did not suffer from my decision. But declining the offer did not diminish my advocacy. I traveled around the world making the liberal case for Israel, especially when the IDF was criticized for defending their civilians against terrorist attacks.

On June 13, 2014, the commander of the southern region for the Israel Security Agency (ISA), together with the commander of the Gaza Division of the Israel Defense Forces (IDF), took me into a Hamas tunnel that had recently been discovered by a Bedouin tracker who served in the IDF. The tunnel was a concrete bunker that extended several miles from its entrance in the Gaza Strip to its exit near an Israeli kibbutz kindergarten.

The tunnel had one purpose: to allow Hamas death squads to kill and kidnap Israelis. The commander told me that Israeli intelligence had identified more than two dozen additional tunnel entrances in the Gaza Strip. They had been identified by the large amounts of earth being removed to dig them. Although Israeli intelligence knew where these entrances were, they could not order an attack from the air, because the openings were built into civilian structures such as mosques, schools, hospitals and private homes. Nor could Israel identify their underground routes from Gaza into Israel, or their intended exit points. Israeli scientists and military experts had spent millions of dollars in an effort to develop technologies that could find these tunnels that were as deep as a hundred feet beneath the earth, but they had not succeeded in finding a complete solution to this problem.[3] The planned exits from these tunnels—each had several—were also a Hamas secret, hidden deep in the ground and incapable of being discovered by Israel until the Hamas fighters emerged. At that point it would be too late to prevent the death squads from doing their damage.

I was taken into the tunnel and saw the technological innovations: tracks on which small trains could transport kidnapped Israelis back to Gaza; telephone and electrical lines; crevices beneath schools and other civilian targets that could hold explosives; and smaller offshoot tunnels leading from the main tube to numerous exit points from which fighters could simultaneously emerge from different places. Building these tunnels cost Hamas a small fortune, which came from funds that could have been used to educate, employ and heal the residents of Gaza. It also cost a considerable number of lives and limbs, resulting from frequent accidents that occurred during the dangerous task of excavation and construction. But Hamas's priority was death rather than life.

As soon as I went down into the tunnel, I realized that Israel would have no choice but to take military action to destroy them. Israel had a technological response—though imperfect—to Hamas rockets. Its Iron Dome missile defense system was capable of destroying approximately 85 percent of Hamas rockets fired at its population centers.[4] Moreover, it could attack rocket launchers from the air with sophisticated GPS-guided bombs. But it had no complete technological answer—at least not yet—to these terror tunnels.

At the time, the media reported that Hamas was possibly planning a Rosh Hashanah massacre during which hundreds of terrorists would simultaneously emerge from dozens of tunnels and slaughter hundreds, if not thousands, of Israeli civilians and soldiers.[5] If this report had been true, as many in Israel believed it was, the Rosh Hashanah massacre would have been the equivalent of a hundred 9/11s in the United States. Even if it was an exaggeration, the tunnels certainly provided Hamas with the capability of wreaking havoc on Israeli citizens. There were other reports as well of planned attacks through the tunnels. As one resident of Sderot put it, "We used to look up to the sky in fear, but now we are looking down at the ground."[6]

To me, the only questions were when Israel would act, how it would act, whether it would be successful, and what the consequences would be. Could any nation tolerate this kind of threat to its citizens? Has any nation in history ever allowed tunnels to be dug under its border that would permit death squads to operate against its people?

I discussed these issues with Prime Minister Netanyahu at his home several days later, and it became clear that the Israeli government had been concerned about the security threats posed by these terror tunnels ever since one had been used to kidnap the young soldier Gilad Shalit and kill two of his compatriots.

Ironically, it was while we were in the tunnel that we learned that three Israeli high school students had been kidnapped. Their kidnapping and subsequent murder was the beginning of what turned into Operation Protective Edge, which ended with the destruction of most of the tunnels by special IDF explosive units.

Israel was widely condemned for its military operations in Gaza, with little concern expressed for those Israeli civilians whose lives had been placed in danger by those deadly tunnels.

In a book called *Terror Tunnels: The Case for Israel's Just War Against Hamas*, I made the case that Israel was justified—legally, morally, diplomatically and politically—in responding to the dangers posed by the tunnels and the rocket attacks that preceded and followed their discovery. I also explained why so many of the media, academia, the international community and the general public seemed to blind themselves to the dangers posed by Hamas and blamed Israel for actions they would demand their own governments take were they faced with comparable threats.

The "blame Israel" reaction has serious consequences, not only for Israel but also for the people of Gaza, and for the democratic world in general. Blaming Israel only encourages Hamas to repeat its "dead baby strategy" and other terrorist groups to emulate it. The strategy operates as follows: Hamas attacks Israel either by rockets or through tunnels, thereby forcing Israel to respond to protect its citizens. Because Hamas fires its rockets and digs its tunnels from densely populated civilian areas rather than from the many open areas of the Gaza Strip, the inevitable result is that a significant number of Palestinian civilians are killed. Hamas encourages this result, because it knows the media will focus more on the photographs of dead babies than on the cause of their death: namely, the decision by Hamas to use these babies and other civilians as human shields. Hamas quickly produces the dead babies to be shown around the world while at the same time preventing the media from showing its rocket launchers and tunnels in densely populated areas. The world is outraged at the dead civilians and blames Israel for killing them. This only emboldens Hamas to repeat its strategy following short cease-fires, during which they re-arm and regroup.

In 2018 and 2019, Hamas sent thousands of civilians, including young children and mothers carrying babies, to the fence adjoining Israeli population centers. Their goal was to break down the fence and attack Israeli civilians. Inevitably, some Palestinian children were killed and injured. The media responded precisely as Hamas intended.

I tried to warn the world—in my book and media appearances—that unless Hamas's dead baby strategy is denounced and stopped by the international community, the media, the academy and good people of all religions, ethnicities and nationalities, it will be "coming soon to a theater near you." Hamas repeatedly employs this despicable and unlawful strategy because it works. It works because despite the material losses Hamas suffers in its repeated military encounters with Israel, it always wins the public relations war, the legal war, the academic war and the war for the naïve hearts if not always wise minds of young people. And if it is indeed winning these wars—if its dead baby strategy is working—why not repeat it every few years? That's why cease-fires between Israel and Hamas always entail Israel "ceasing" and Hamas "firing"—perhaps not immediately, but inevitably. And if it works for Hamas, why shouldn't other terrorist groups, like ISIS and Boko Haram, adapt this strategy to their own nefarious goals? The United States is also blamed—to a lesser extent than is Israel—when its military, despite efforts to minimize civilian casualties, produces them anyway because their enemies employ human shields as well.

The only way to end this cycle of death is to expose the dead baby strategy for what it is—a double war crime whose ultimate victims are civilian children, women and men.

I had, and have, only one weapon in this ongoing war: my words. During the course of Operation Protective Edge, I tried to make the case for Israel's just war against Hamas's double war crime strategy. I wrote more than two dozen op-eds, participated in several debates and television interviews, and spoke to numerous audiences. My goal was to show that Israel's military actions in defense of its citizens have been just and that they have been conducted in a just manner. They are no less just than the military actions being conducted by the United States and its allies against ISIS, al-Qaeda, and other terrorist groups. And they have been carried out at least as justly, with a lower percentage of civilian-to-combatant casualties.

Yet Israel has been unjustly condemned from too many corners, thus encouraging Hamas to continue its despicable and unlawful strategy. I argued that for the sake of justice and peace, the world must stop applying a double standard to the nation-state of the Jewish people.

Books and op-eds are comparatively weak instruments for affecting the course of international affairs. Nevertheless, I believe that my advocacy—and that of others such as Bret Stephens, Irwin Cotler and the late Elie Wiesel—for Israel's military response to the Hamas terror tunnels helped to sway general public opinion in favor of Israel. So did the Obama administration's lack of criticism of Israel's military actions before, during and after Operation Protective Edge.

It was for that reason, among others, that I was inclined to support Obama's quest for reelection in 2012, though I had some doubts about his policy with regard to Iran.

In the spring of 2012, I was in Israel. The U.S. election was beginning, and Iran was rattling its weapons. My wife and I were having dinner at a Georgian restaurant and bar in Tel Aviv when my cell phone rang. The restaurant, which was filled with young émigrés from the former Soviet Union, was noisy and raucous, with vodka-inebriated patrons dancing and singing. I could hardly make out what the caller was saying, but I did hear the words "White House" and "president." I walked outside, where the overflow crowd was still loud but I could hear the caller repeating that the president wanted to talk to me. I told her that I couldn't hear clearly from where I was, but that I would be back in my hotel in half an hour. Could the president call me then? Her tone of voice suggested that she was not used to being asked to have the president try again, but she told me he would.

We raced back to our hotel and the president called. He inquired as to whether I had met with the prime minister and I told him I had. He asked me what the most important issues on Netanyahu's mind were, and I replied,

"Number one is Iran."

He followed up, "What's number two?"

I replied "Iran," and continued: "If you want to know what number three is, it's Iran. So is number four, five, six."

"I get the point," he said with a slight laugh. "Can you come see me in the Oval Office, when you get back, to discuss Iran? I want to tell you what we're doing."

We then schmoozed for a few minutes about how much he had enjoyed his visit to Israel and whether my wife was having a good time.

A few weeks later, I was sitting alone with the president in the Oval Office, engaged in a serious discussion about Iran, sanctions, containment, prevention and preemption. Prime Minister Netanyahu was expressing concern to anyone who would listen about Iran's nuclear weapons ambitions. There was talk of a possible deal, but it was light on specifics. I expressed my concerns to the president. He replied: "Alan, you've known me for a long time, and you know I don't bluff. You can count on what I'm telling you. I will never allow Iran to develop a nuclear arsenal, no matter what it takes. My policy is not 'containment' of a nuclear Iran, it's prevention."

I told him that I wasn't worried about Iran developing or acquiring a nuclear bomb during his watch. What worried me was that they could spin enough centrifuges to be ready to transition from civilian to military use in the near future, when his term was over. Obama assured me that both the United States and Israel had sufficient intelligence on the ground and cyber capabilities to make sure that didn't happen. He also said that the sanctions then in place would disincentivize the mullahs from challenging his policies, and that the international community had enough leverage to make a good deal with the Iranian regime, if the Iranians were prepared to negotiate in good faith.

I expressed my own skepticism and relayed the even greater skepticism I had heard from Netanyahu. He said he understood. "There is no perfect solution," he acknowledged, referring to the experience of prior administrations with North Korea. "But we won't allow Iran to become North Korea. I will not take the military options off the table as a last resort, but I will try not to have to use it."

I reminded him of the wise statement that George Washington—whose portrait was in full view—had made about how the best way of avoiding war is to be prepared to wage it. He assured me, "We are prepared, but we are also prepared to negotiate, to sanction and to take other actions."

He then looked me straight in the eye and said, "I want you to know, and I want your friend Bibi to know, I have Israel's back and I will always have Israel's back. You can count on that."

I wasn't sure what to make of his commitment. Many American Jewish and Israeli leaders were growing suspicious of Obama in relation to Israel. They worried that in a second term he would care more about his legacy, of which a deal with Iran would be a prime component, than about Israel's security down the road. I knew that he wanted me to assure these leaders that they could trust him in his final four years.

I had several more White House (and Martha's Vineyard) discussions with President Obama and his staff—especially Ben Rhodes, as well as soon-to-be secretary of state John Kerry, an old friend—in the run-up to the 2012 election and thereafter.

I was comforted by the knowledge that the man in charge of

keeping the pressure on Iran through sanctions was David Cohen, who was then undersecretary of the treasury for terrorism and financial intelligence and who would soon become deputy director of the CIA. David was a childhood and law school friend of my younger son Jamin. I had mentored David while he was in law school and in his first jobs. I knew that he had positive views regarding Israel and was a tough negotiator who was committed to preventing Iran from acquiring a nuclear arsenal. We might disagree about the means necessary to achieve that result, but not on the result itself.

The deal that was eventually struck not only disappointed me, it outraged Prime Minister Netanyahu, virtually all Israelis, many Americans and a significant number of senators and House members. David Cohen believed it was a good, if not perfect, deal that would keep Iran from developing a nuclear arsenal for a considerable number of years. Because the president could not get enough votes to make it a binding treaty, or even an act of Congress, he had to settle for an executive order that could be rescinded by any future president (which is in fact what happened). In exchange for lifting sanctions and billions of dollars in cash, Iran promised to stop spinning centrifuges for a limited number of years. At the end of that period, the agreement did not prevent Iran from spinning enough centrifuges to develop a nuclear arsenal.

When President Obama assured me that he had Israel's back and that he would never allow Iran to develop a nuclear arsenal, he may have believed what he was saying. In light of what actually happened, there are three possibilities: The first is that he actually believed it then, believed it when he signed the deal and still believes it now. If that is the case, then he apparently assumed—in a way that could only be called arrogant—that he knew more about Israel's security than the Israeli officials whose job it is to protect Israel. The second possibility is that he believed it then, but was persuaded by Secretary of State John Kerry and other strong advocates of the deal to change his mind. The third is that despite his assurances to me that he never bluffs, he was, in fact, telling me what he knew I wanted to hear in order to ensure my support among American Jews for his reelection. I don't know which of these possibilities is true, but I do know that none of them makes me feel comfortable about having endorsed and campaigned for him in 2012.

I went to Florida to persuade Jewish voters that they could trust Obama. Obama's invitation to meet with me may have grown out of the skepticism I expressed in op eds and his desire to persuade me he could be trusted on Iran. It worked—at least it did then.

I wrote additional op-eds defending the Obama administration's Iran policy:

> It has taken containment off the table and kept the military option on the table. Everyone hopes that the military option will not have to be employed since it would entail considerable loss of life, especially among Israeli civilians who would be targeted by Hezbollah rockets fired in retaliation against any attack on Iran.
>
> But the best way to avoid the need for military action is for the Iranian mullahs to believe that the United States will never allow them to develop nuclear weapons. If they believe that reality then the pain of the sanctions will pressure them to give up their nuclear ambitions. President Obama has clearly stated that he is not bluffing when he says that his administration will never allow Iran to develop nuclear weapons.

Just months earlier I had expressed skepticism about Obama's policy toward Iran in the *Wall Street Journal*, warning that he would be remembered as the Neville Chamberlain of the twenty-first century if he did not stop Iran from developing a nuclear arsenal.[7] I reminded my readers that Chamberlain had done great things for British citizens during the Depression, but history remembers him only for his failure to confront Hitler. "That is his enduring legacy." I warned Obama that "history will not treat kindly" any leader who allows Iran to develop nuclear weapons.[8]

Despite my strong concerns about Obama's Iran policy, I felt comfortable endorsing him for reelection, based in part on his record up to then with regard to Israel's military actions and his firm assurances to me.

The first event that caused me to reconsider my endorsement was the way Obama and several Democratic senators and members of Congress treated the invitation by the Speaker of the House to Prime Minister Netanyahu to address a joint session of Congress about the Iran deal. Generally such invitations are approved in advance by the president, but Obama did not want the highly articulate and knowledgeable Netanyahu to persuade members of Congress to oppose a deal with Iran. He was furious with Netanyahu for appealing directly to Congress. I was told that Obama urged Democratic senators and congressmen and -women to boycott the talk, which several said they would do.

In the *Wall Street Journal*, I made the constitutional case for the power of the legislative branch to invite foreign leaders disagreeing with the presidential decision. I then argued that one should walk out on tyrants, bigots and radical extremists like the United States did when Iran's Mahmoud Ahmadinejad denied the Holocaust and called for Israel's destruction at the United Nations. To use such an extreme tactic against our closest ally, and the Middle East's only democracy, is not only insulting to Israel's prime minister, but it puts Israel in a category in which it does not belong.

I called several of my friends who had indicated they would boycott Netanyahu's speech and urged them to change their minds. "Would you boycott a speech by Putin or Castro?" I asked. They said no, but they insisted that this was different, because the invitation from the Speaker was partisan. I agreed that this was different because Netanyahu was the democratically elected prime minister of an American ally. I changed several minds, the most important of which was that of Congressman Charles Rangel, the head of the Congressional Black Caucus. *Every* member of the Black Caucus had announced that they would boycott Netanyahu's speech because they thought Netanyahu disrespected the first African American president by accepting Boehner's invitation against Obama's wishes. The action risked becoming a "Black-Jewish" split, with ongoing consequences. Rangel agreed and announced that he would attend the talk.

The Center for Public Integrity reported it as follows: "Thank super lawyer Alan Dershowitz—at least in part—for Rep. Charlie Rangel, D-N.Y. suddenly reversing his decision to skip Prime Minister Benjamin Netanyahu's contentious March 3 address to Congress."

Netanyahu made a powerful speech pointing to the dangers of a nuclear Iran. He received, quite deservedly, standing ovations from both sides of the aisle, which reportedly angered Obama even more.

After the talk, Congressman Rangel thanked me for changing his mind: "I learned a lot from Bibi's talk," he told me. Kenneth Bialkin, a major Jewish leader, also thanked me "for performing a service to the entire Jewish community and African American community, because if Rangel had not changed his mind . . . there would have been a very big backlash . . ."

But I could not persuade Senators Elizabeth Warren and Al Franken, who saw the invitation to Netanyahu as partisan. I told them both that this was a red line for me, and that I would no longer contribute to their campaigns or to the campaigns of any other Democrat who showed such disrespect toward the prime minister of Israel. This was the first, but unfortunately not the last, time mainstream Democrats, who were my friends, would break with the long tradition of bipartisan support for Israel.

I was invited by Bibi to sit next to his wife and Elie Wiesel in the front row of the House gallery for his talk. It was an extraordinary speech that electrified Congress and helped persuade a majority of both Houses to oppose the deal.[9] But Obama decided to circumvent Congress, and although the deal had all the hallmarks of a treaty, he signed it as an executive agreement. This meant that it was subject to abrogation by any future president, without any input from Congress.

As I had done several times before, I decided to write a polemical book about the agreement, titled *The Case Against the Iran Deal: How Can We Stop Iran from Getting Nukes?* I knew that Obama would sign the deal, but I wanted to lay out the arguments against it in the event that a future president—who at the time I believed would be Hillary Clinton—might decide to strengthen its provisions. I ended with a constructive proposal that could prevent Iran from becoming a nuclear power without the United States abrogating the deal (which I knew Hillary Clinton would never do as president):

> *Congress now has the power to improve this bad deal in a way that reduces the changes that Iran will obtain a nuclear arsenal. The key lies in the words of the deal itself. . . . In both the preface and the preamble and general provisions, the following commitment is made: "Iran reaffirms that* under no circumstances *will Iran ever seek, develop or acquire any nuclear weapons" [emphasis added]. This noteworthy provision is rarely mentioned by supporters of the agreement.*
>
> *Congress should now enact legislation declaring that this reaffirmation is an integral part of the agreement and represents the policy of the United States. It is too late to change the words of the deal, but it is not too late for Congress to insist that Iran comply fully with its provisions.*
>
> *In order to ensure that the entirety of the agreement is carried out, including that reaffirmation, Congress should adopt the proposal made by Thomas L. Friedman on 22 July 2015 and by myself on 5 September 2013. To quote Friedman: "Congress should pass a resolution authorizing this and future presidents*

*to use force to prevent Iran from ever becoming a nuclear weapons
state. . . . Iran must know now that the U.S. president is
authorized to destroy without warning or negotiation—any
attempt by Tehran to build a bomb."*[10]

Neither Netanyahu nor Obama were happy with my position
on the deal. Netanyahu thought I wasn't being tough enough, while
Obama thought I was being too tough.

My opposition caused Obama and his national security team to
become angry with me. Prior to this, he had invited me to several
White House events, including his annual Chanukah celebration. On
the day of one such celebration, I was in the Oval Office with Obama
when my cell phone rang. The president gave me a look as if to say,
you should leave your phone outside when you're in the Oval. I told
him I was expecting a call from my grandson telling me whether he
had gotten into Harvard. The president told me to take it. Lyle did
get in, and the president and vice president sent their congratulations
to him, with Biden adding, "But he should go to the University of
Delaware. It's a better school."

President Obama also invited my wife and me to the small state
dinner at which he bestowed the Medal of Freedom on our old friend
Shimon Peres. Other guests included Vice President Biden, Secretary of State Clinton and her husband, Senator John Kerry, Elie and
Marion Wiesel. Itzhak Perlman entertained us with beautiful violin
music.

Shimon, who always called me "professor Chutzpah," was then
close to 90 years old. He spoke of his wish to see peace with the Palestinians during his lifetime. Obama, in a jovial mood, pointed to
Shimon's son-in-law, who was also his doctor, and said, "Shimon you
are free to go back to Israel when this dinner is over, but your doctor
stays here in the White House to take care of me. I want to have your
energy and determination when I turn 90."

The only speeches were by the two presidents. The rest of the evening consisted of table-hopping among old friends, exchanging stories, proposals for peace and gossip. The Iran situation figured in virtually every discussion. No one seemed thrilled with it, but most supported it, perhaps out of loyalty to the president. There was considerable goodwill between Shimon Peres's Israel and Barack Obama's America. But Peres's Israel was not Bibi Netanyahu's, and this was the last time during the Obama administration that such goodwill toward Israel would be seen.

President Obama also sent me a very friendly handwritten note on my 75th birthday, wishing me "many more years of adocacy, mischief and great fun!" and ending with his "warm regards."

But following my "advocacy" against his deal—which he perhaps regarded as a bit too much "mischief"—he showed his anger in petty ways, such as disinviting me from the annual Chanukah party. (In contrast, President George W. Bush invited me, despite my strong opposition to his candidacy and to the Iraq war, not to mention my role as one of Vice President Gore's lawyers in *Bush v. Gore*.) Obama also disinvited other Jewish leaders who had opposed the deal.

I didn't care about the childish revenge Obama took against me and other Americans, but I cared deeply about the game-changing revenge he took against Prime Minister Netanyahu and the nation-state of the Jewish people.

In the weeks before the end of his presidency, Barack Obama engineered a Security Council resolution that perniciously changed the status of Jewish Jerusalem. The resolution declared, in effect, that the Western Wall (Judaism's holiest site), the Jewish quarter (in which Jews had lived for thousands of years) and the access roads to Hebrew University (built before Israel became a state and open to all residents of Israel and the West Bank) were illegally occupied by Israel and a "flagrant violation under international law."

This historic and legally flawed conclusion was never before supported by the United States. It was opposed by Congress, the American people and even many within the Obama administration. But

Obama was determined to wreak revenge as he was leaving office on Prime Minister Netanyahu for daring to challenge him on the Iran Deal. Not only did Obama order his representative to the United Nations—Samantha Power, also my former student—not to veto the resolution (which Power was apparently prepared to do), he actually worked behind the scenes to encourage its passage, even when several Security Council members tried to postpone or withdraw it. Although the United States didn't vote for the resolution—it cast a meaningless absention—it pressured several countries that had doubt to vote for it.

I wrote a scathing attack on Obama for changing long-standing American policy in order to exact revenge on Netanyahu and tie the hands of his successors. I urged the next president to immediately and officially recognize Jerusalem as Israel's capital and move its embassy there, arguing that such a move would "dramatically demonstrate that the United States does not accept the Judenrein effects of this bigoted resolution on historic Jewish areas of Jerusalem which are now forbidden to Jews."[11]

My public denunciation of Obama's role in enacting the Security Council resolution was the last straw for both of us. It cooled my long-standing friendship with him. He had broken his promise to me and to the American public. Yes, he did have "Israel's back"—but he painted a target on it and fired a weapon at it as he was leaving office.

It's impossible to know for sure whether Obama's parting shot was directed only against Netanyahu personally or whether it reflected a deeper antagonism against Israel that Obama had kept under the surface until his final weeks in office. I don't know which is worse.

It would be up to the next president to try to undo the damage Obama had peevishly inflicted on Israel and its prime minister.

14

Trump and Netanyahu Agree on Iran and Jerusalem

IN THE 2016 election, I strongly supported Hillary Clinton, who I had known for many years, over Donald Trump, who I had met briefly several times. As a liberal Democrat, I favored Clinton's domestic policies on choice, gay marriage, gun control, environmental policies, taxation and other issues. Because of my family history with regard to immigration—especially my grandfather's role in saving relatives from the Holocaust—I was strongly opposed to Trump's campaign promise to build a wall on the Mexican border. I trusted Clinton on foreign policy, despite the fact that she had served as secretary of state to a president with whom I largely disagreed on foreign policy decisions. I had discussed Iran and Syria with her and was satisfied that her approach would be somewhat different from Obama's.

I was not surprised by Trump's election, having written several months before—when Clinton was ahead in the polls by double digits—that Trump might win, for reasons similar to why Brexit had won and why so many hyper-nationalists and populists were doing well in European elections. I thought that Trump understood this trend, and how it applied to the United States, more clearly than Clinton did.

Not long after his victory, President Trump approached me while I was having dinner with some mutual friends at his Palm Beach hotel. He said that he knew I was a friend of Bibi Netanyahu's and that he wanted to discuss the Israeli–Palestinian issue with me. We had a serious talk that was followed by an invitation to the White House to continue the conversation with Jared Kushner, his son-in-law and senior advisor, and Jason Greenblatt, who was a key player in devising a strategy and plan for reducing the Israeli–Palestinian conflict.

Among the issues we discussed were Trump's campaign promise to recognize Jerusalem as Israel's capital and to move the U.S. embassy there as soon as he was sworn in. I favored the move, but I originally thought it would be better to finalize it as part of a peace deal in coordination with America's other Middle East allies. But after Obama's insidious resolution, I publicly urged the incoming president to restore the status quo by recognizing Jerusalem as Israel's capital immediately. I wrote articles to this effect and spoke to President Trump about it personally.

The Security Council resolution, which declared that "any changes to the 4 June 1967 lines, including with regard to Jerusalem," have "no legal validity," meant, among other things, that Israel's decision to build a plaza for prayer at the Western Wall constituted, in the words of the text, a "flagrant violation of international law." This resolution was, therefore, not limited to settlements in the West Bank, as the Obama administration later claimed. It applied equally to the very heart of Israel.

Before June 4, 1967, Jews were forbidden from praying at the Western Wall, Judaism's holiest site. They were forbidden to attend classes at the Hebrew University at Mt. Scopus, which had been opened in 1925; they could not seek medical care at the Hadassah Hospital on Mt. Scopus, which had treated Jews and Arabs alike for many years; and they could not live in the Jewish Quarter of Jerusalem, where their forbearers had built homes and synagogues for thousands of years.

These judenrein (no Jews allowed) prohibitions were enacted by Jordan, which had captured these Jewish areas during Israel's War of Independence in 1948 and had illegally occupied the entire West Bank, an area that the United Nations had set aside for an Arab state.

When the Jordanian government occupied these historic Jewish sites, they destroyed all the remnants of Judaism, including synagogues, schools and cemeteries, whose headstones they used for urinals. Between 1948 and 1967, the United Nations did not offer a single resolution condemning this Jordanian occupation and cultural devastation of historically Jewish Jerusalem.

When Israel retook these areas in a defensive war against Jordan—which Jordan had started by shelling civilian homes in West Jerusalem—and opened them up as places where Jews could pray, study, receive medical treatment and live, the United States took the official position that it would not recognize Israel's legitimate claims to any part of Jerusalem, even Jewish West Jerusalem, which had been part of Israel since it came into existence as a state and which housed its parliament, Supreme Court, prime minister's residence and president's house. It stated that the status of Jerusalem, including the newly liberated Jewish areas, would be left open to final negotiations and that the status quo would remain in place. That is the official rationale for why the United States refused to recognize any part of Jerusalem, including West Jerusalem, as part of Israel. That is why the United States refused to allow an American citizen born in any part of Jerusalem to put the words "Jerusalem, Israel" on his or her passport as their place of birth.

But even that ahistoric status quo was changed with President Obama's unjustified decision not to veto the Security Council resolution. At the time, it was not known that Obama was discreetly pushing for the passage of the resolution, so it was expected that it would be vetoed, as the U.S. has vetoed all prior Security Council resolutions that were one-sidedly anti-Israel. The United Nations all of a sudden determined that, subject to any further negotiations and agreements, the Jewish areas of Jerusalem recaptured from Jordan in 1967 are not part of Israel. Instead, they were territories being illegally occupied by Israel, and any building in these areas—including places for prayer at the Western Wall, access roads to Mt. Scopus, and synagogues in the historic Jewish Quarter—constitute "a flagrant violation under international law." If that indeed was the new status quo, then what incentives would the Palestinians have to enter negotiations? And if they were to do so, they could use these Jewish areas to extort unreasonable concessions from Israel, for which these now "illegally occupied" areas were sacred and non-negotiable.

President Obama's refusal to veto this one-sided resolution was a deliberate ploy to tie the hands of his successors, the consequence of which was to make it far more difficult for his successors to encourage the Palestinians to accept Israel's offer to negotiate with no preconditions. No future president can undo this pernicious agreement, since a veto not cast can never be retroactively cast. And a resolution once enacted cannot be rescinded unless there is a majority vote against it, with no veto by any of its permanent members, which include Russia and China, who would be sure to veto any attempt to undo this resolution.

The prior refusal of the United States to recognize Jerusalem as Israel's capital was based on the notion that nothing should be done to change the status quo of that city, holy to three religions. But the Security Council resolution did exactly that by declaring Israel's de facto presence on these Jewish holy sites to be a "flagrant violation under international law" that "the U.N. will not recognize."

Since virtually everyone in the international community acknowledges that any reasonable peace would recognize Israel's legitimate claims to these and other areas in Jerusalem, there was no reason to make criminals out of every Jew or Israeli who sets foot on these historically Jewish areas. (Ironically, President Obama prayed at the "illegally occupied" Western Wall.) I urged President Trump to recognize Jerusalem as Israel's capitol because such a decision would help to restore the appropriate balance. It would demonstrate that the United States does not accept the judenrein effects of this bigoted resolution. I told him it would be right to untie his own hands and undo the damage wrought by his predecessor.

Some have argued that the United States should not recognize Jerusalem because it will stimulate violence by Arab terrorists. No

American decision should ever be influenced by the threat of violence. Terrorists should not have a veto over American policy. If the United States were to give in to the threat of violence, it would only incentivize others to threaten violence in response to any peace plan.

It is true that on the day the United States moved its embassy to Jerusalem, Hamas engineered massive protests at the Gaza fence, including efforts by terrorists to cross into Israel to kill and kidnap Israeli civilians. I had been near the fence just days earlier, and I was in Jerusalem itself on the day of the move. It was clear that these preplanned actions by Hamas were not in response to the U.S. decision to move the embassy to Jerusalem, since Hamas did not recognize Tel Aviv as part of Israel. The embassy move provided a convenient excuse for Hamas to do what it was already planning to do.

Trump did the right thing by undoing the wrong that Obama had done at the end of his presidency. Yet many left-wing Democrats—even some who had opposed President Obama's decision to push the anti-Israel resolution through the Security Council and who had urged Obama to move the embassy to Jerusalem—thoughtlessly condemned the move without providing coherent arguments. For them, it was enough that it was President Trump who ordered the relocation of the embassy. If the same action had been taken by a President Hillary Clinton, or even by a President Mitt Romney, it would have been greeted with joy and approval. But because it was taken by President Trump, it was viewed by most Democrats, including many Jewish supporters of Israel, as the reckless act of an impulsive man who was blind to the nuances of Middle East diplomacy.

Toward the end of 2017, I was invited by the emir of Qatar to meet with him in Doha, to discuss among other things improving relations with Israel. Having read that Qatar funds terrorist organizations such as Hamas and the Muslim Brotherhood, I was skeptical, but I decided to research the issues surrounding the relationship between Qatar and these extremist groups. As I read more widely on the subject and spoke to experts in the United States and Israel, as well as to government officials in both countries, more nuances and complexities began to emerge.

There was a growing conflict between Qatar on the one hand and Saudi Arabia and the United Arab Emirates (UAE) on the other. This conflict eventuated in an embargo against Qatar by those two countries. The embargo included a blockade of Qatar's flights and shipping, as well as a denial of food shipments and trade between the countries, thus preventing family members who lived in Qatar from attending weddings, funerals and other family events.

My research revealed conflicting factual claims by each side, particularly relating to the funding of terrorism and commercial dealings with Iran. There were also conflicting claims with regard to government-funded television, such as Al Jazeera, Al Arabiya and other media. I had no way of resolving these conflicting claims without hearing all sides of the issues and seeing for myself. I decided, therefore, to accept the emir's invitation. I would ask hard questions and subject all answers to independent confirmation.

I had another reason for making the trip to Doha. Whenever people wanted to boycott Israel, I would urge them to go to Israel, see what is going on, and decide for themselves. I resolved to apply the same criteria to myself: go to Qatar and then make up my mind.

The issue of Al Jazeera and other government-funded media presented a particularly complex issue for me, as a lifelong defender of freedom of the press. Al Jazeera is a government-controlled medium (as are all media in the Middle East other than in Israel) based in Qatar that publishes both in Arabic and English. The English version tends to be somewhat balanced, but the Arabic version tends to be rabidly anti-Israel. The Saudis and Emirates were demanding that Qatar "shut down" Al Jazeera, especially following its support for the Arab Spring in 2010. I could not support such a demand, though I strongly disagreed with much of what was broadcast on Al Jazeera, as well as on Saudi-funded Al Arabiya.

My meeting with the emir was cordial. I asked him to press Hamas to return the bodies of Israeli soldiers who had been killed in Gaza. He said he would try. We discussed many other issues regarding Israel, with inconclusive results.

In May 2018, I agreed to deliver a lecture on the issue of government-sponsored media at the Northwestern University campus in Doha. Several American universities have well-funded campuses in Qatar, taught largely by American professors and attended largely by Arab students. I knew I would confront a hostile audience mainly composed of Qatari undergraduates raised on anti-Israel propaganda. Although my talk was not about Israel—it was about relations between the media, law and government in both democracies and theocracies—students shouted "Zionist go home," "No Zionists in Qatar," as they unfurled a Palestinian flag, marched in front of me and conducted a walkout. The professor who had introduced me whispered, "Tell them you're not a Zionist and that you support a Palestinian State." I stood up and said. "I'm a proud Zionist, and I support two states for two people." I invited the protestors to stay and ask me hard questions about the Israeli–Palestinian issue, but they left and I gave my talk—discussing the complexity of governmental relationships with critical, often hostile, media—to the remaining students and faculty. The questions were respectful and thoughtful.

I believe strongly in dialogue and engagement even with one's enemies, and certainly with leaders who seem willing to listen to constructive ideas and perhaps to change their ways. I wondered why the opposition to my visits by some American Jews had become so strident, emotional and personal. I learned that some of my critics had financial and other ties to the Saudis and Emirates, and that one of them had begged to be invited to travel to Qatar to meet the emir but had been turned down. Whatever the reasons, there was no cause to question my motives, or those of the supporters of Israel who were seeking dialogue with Qatar. As I write these words, the U.S. government is seeking the support of its peace plan from all the Gulf countries. It is a work in progress.

In April 2018, I was invited to spend two days in the White House consulting and advising on the proposed peace plan. My prearranged visit took place—by complete coincidence—on the day that Special Counsel Robert Mueller and federal prosecutors from New York conducted a search and seizure on the offices of President Trump's personal lawyer Michael Cohen. This led to speculation by the media and others that the Israel issue was a "cover" for a secret meeting for me to give Trump legal advice. As Professor Richard Painter, a Minnesota Democrat who was running for nomination as senator on an impeach-Trump platform, put it in a tweet, "Complete B.S. Alan Dersh does not know anything about the Middle-East. This [meeting] was probably about DOJ's criminal investigation and perhaps firing Robert Mueller." I tweeted in reply that I had written numerous books about the Israel–Palestine conflict and that Trump was the fourth president I had advised on the Middle East. But paranoid and uninformed tweeters and commentators like Painter persisted in their ignorant conspiracy theories.

During my two days at the White House, I proposed ideas regarding the refugee issue, the settlements, Jerusalem and how to get the Sunni Arabs to agree to a plan. I also provided insights into the political realities in Israel, based on my knowledge of the players. I told them about a dinner I recently attended in Washington at the home of a prominent Jewish leader with Palestinian president Mahmoud Abbas and his chief negotiator, Saeb Erekat. I had met them both on several previous occasions and had persuaded Abbas to sign in agreement an op-ed I had written proposing a basis for renewing negotiations. I brought the signed op-ed to Netanyahu in the hope that both sides could agree to sit down and talk. I also gave both Abbas and Netanyahu copies of my old friend Larry David's "Palestinian Chicken" episode from *Curb Your Enthusiasm*, suggesting they watch it together. They both laughed, but no negotiations began.

During the Washington dinner, Abbas asked me to "call [my] friend Bibi and tell him to declare once and for all that he unequivocally accepts the two-state solution." I told him that I had already heard Bibi make such a declaration at Bar-Ilan University. He replied, "But he seems to be backing away." I told him I would make the call if he, Abbas, would declare that he recognizes Israel as "the nation-state of the Jewish people." He said he could never recognize Israel as "a Jewish state," because that would deny the right of return to the Palestinian diaspora and deny equal rights to Israeli Arabs. I told him that by not recognizing the nation-state of the Jewish people while demanding a Palestinian state, he was rejecting the UN partition plan that called for two states for two people. He smiled and said, "It is what it is." I asked him if he could accept Israel as "the nation-state of the Jewish people," rather than as a "Jewish state." He said that might be easier to swallow, but he was not ready to do that either. "Would you ever be willing to do that as part of a negotiated peace?" I asked. "Anything is possible," he said, receiving a dirty look from Erekat, who is believed to be less willing to compromise than his boss is.

My two days in the White House were informative and constructive. I spent hours with Jared Kushner, Jason Greenblatt and several staff people tossing ideas back and forth. They knew that my relationships with Israeli leaders, especially Prime Minister Netanyahu, went back many decades, and they appreciated my insights into their personalities, ideologies and political realities. We all understood that coming up with a plan that was acceptable to both sides—and to the other Sunni Arab countries—is a daunting, some say impossible, task. I will never give up or stop trying to help as an advisor and in other ways, regardless of who is president.

After my first day of work on the plan, the president invited me to have dinner with him and three other people in the White House residence. Trump then invited me to accompany him to the Lincoln Bedroom, where he showed me the original version of the Gettysburg Address. He sat down on Lincoln's bed and asked me to join him. We discussed Lincoln, the Middle East and some mutual friends.

The dinner with the president was private and was supposed to remain confidential to avoid speculation about whether he was asking me to become his lawyer. But it was leaked to Maggie Haberman of the *New York Times*. I don't know who leaked it—some speculated that it was President Trump himself—but my phone log was quickly filled with media calls inquiring whether I had been asked to be his lawyer. Without answering that question—which would be inappropriate—I issued a statement saying that I wanted to maintain my independence and ability to comment, objectively and in a nonpartisan way, on the civil liberties issues being raised by the Mueller investigation.

It was, and is, important to me that people understand that I am not a Trump "supporter." I supported, contributed money to, campaigned for and voted for Hillary Clinton. As a liberal Democrat, I oppose many of Trump's policies, including his approach to immigration, gay and transgender rights, choice regarding abortion, taxation, medical care, gun control, separation of church and state and judicial appointments. I have spoken out against these policies loudly and clearly. I have been particularly critical of his immigration policies, especially his zero-tolerance policy that separated children from parents.[1] But I will not allow my disagreements with President Trump to silence my criticisms of the Mueller investigation and of efforts to criminalize the president's exercise of his constitutional authority. I have already written three books on this issue, and I appear regularly on TV and write op-eds discussing similar legal issues, as I would if Hillary Clinton had been elected and Republican partisans were trying to impeach her and "lock her up" for noncriminal acts. The publisher of my book *The Case Against Impeaching Trump* produced two alternate covers: one with "The Case Against Impeaching Clinton" written on it, which I would have written if Hillary had been elected, and a plain brown wrapper cover for *The Case Against Impeaching Trump* that people on Martha's Vineyard could read without being shunned for their purported Trump support.

My predictions regarding the Mueller Report have proved to be largely accurate: I predicted that the contents of the report would be "devastating" politically, but exculpatory legally, and that President Trump would not be impeached and removed because the evidence would not establish any impeachable "high crimes and misdemeanors," as required by the Constitution. The predictions of many pundits who I debated on CNN, MSNBC, ABC and Fox have proved, on the other hand, to be inaccurate. This is not because I am any smarter than they are; it is because I do not substitute wishful thinking for objective legal analysis.

As I did with President Bill Clinton, I serve as an informal conduit between Trump and the prime minister of Israel, and I have conveyed several messages back and forth on a confidential basis.

Will President Trump be good or bad for Israel? Only time will tell. His decision to move the U.S. embassy to Jerusalem was popular among most Israelis and was only minimally criticized by most Sunni countries. The Palestinians were furious. His subsequent decision to recognize Israel's sovereignty over the Golan Heights, which Israel formally annexed in 1981, was also quite popular with Israelis and produced little reaction from neighboring Arab states. Trump's general support for the nation-state of the Jewish people, and the individuals he has put in positions of responsibility relating to the Middle East, bode far better for Israel and for peace than those of his predecessor.

Will the Israeli government be able to accept a peace plan proposed by President Trump? That, too, is uncertain. Netanyahu faces a criminal proceeding that has made his political survival more dependent on coalition members to his far right, who might well oppose a two-state solution that requires giving up land and ending the building of new settlements. I am confident that Bibi himself, if he remained prime minister, would support a two-state solution that did not compromise Israel's security and that allowed the major settlement blocks to become part of Israel in exchange for an equivalent amount of Israeli land being ceded to a Palestinian state.

I speak to Bibi regularly, and I have written critically of the investigation and the proposed prosecution against him, which focus on gifts he received from friends and questionable deals with the media he allegedly discussed.[2] My fear is that if President Trump comes up with a peace plan that Bibi likes but his coalition partners do not, it may be impossible for him to accept it without risking his political position. If he were to lose an election, his replacement might well be to his right, thus making peace more difficult. Were Israel to reject a Trump peace plan, Trump would not take that lightly. Trump does not readily accept rejection of his ideas, especially because he believes Israel "owes" him as a result of the embassy and Golan decisions. That is why I have privately urged Netanyahu's most important right-wing coalition partners to put statesmanship before politics and accept a peace plan that may require "painful compromises," as Bibi has put it, so long as they do not weaken Israel's security.

In May of 2019, I met alone with Prime Minister Netanyahu in his home for more than two hours. We discussed, as we always do, a range of issues relating to U.S.–Israeli relations, including the peace plan. I came away from the meeting encouraged. But shortly thereafter, he failed to form a government and a new election was scheduled. Then, at the end of June, Jared Kushner unveiled the economic portion of the peace plan, which the Palestinians immediately rejected, despite the enormous benefits it would provide to the Palestinian people. They have refused even to negotiate or offer suggestions to improve the plan.

The Trump plan undoubtedly contains elements that bolster Israel's security, while at the same time increasing Palestinian autonomy and economic viability. It is a good plan that should be accepted by Israel, the Palestinian Authority, the Sunni Arab states and the international community. No one ever lost money betting against peace between the Israelis and their neighbors, largely because the Palestinian leadership has never "missed an opportunity to miss an opportunity." But if they forego this one, as they did in 1948, 2001 and 2008, they will have no one except themselves to blame for the lack of progress toward a resolution of the conflict.

15

The New Anti-Semitism

Taking the Fight to Campus and Congress

THERE IS NOTHING really new about the "new" anti-Semitism. It is the old wine of Jew-hatred bottled under a new label of anti-Zionism and "intersectionality."

There have been several distinct but sometimes overlapping types of anti-Semitism over time.

The first is traditional right-wing fascist Jew hatred that has traditionally included theological, racial, economic, social, personal and cultural aspects. This type has decreased since the end of World War II, but it rears its ugly and violent head from time to time, as it recently did in Pittsburgh, Charlottesville and near San Diego. We are seeing a resurgence of this today in Greece, Hungary, Austria, Poland and other European countries with rising right-wing parties, some of which are anti-Muslim in addition to anti-Jewish.

The second is Muslim anti-Semitism. Just as not all European nationalists are anti-Semitic, not all Muslims suffer from this malady either. But far too many do. It is wrong to assume that only Muslims who manifest Jew hatred through violence harbor anti-Semitic views. Recent polls show an extraordinarily high incidence of anti-Semitism—hatred of Jews as individuals, as a group and as a religion—throughout North Africa, the Middle East and Muslim areas in Europe.[1] This hatred manifests itself not only in words but often in deeds, such as taunting Jews who wear kippot, vandalizing

Jewish institutions and directing occasional violence at individual Jews. Among a small number of extremists, it also results in the kind of deadly violence we have seen in Paris, Brussels and other parts of Europe. Several decades ago, it manifested itself in attacks on synagogues by Palestinian terrorists, some of whom were operating on behalf of the Palestine Liberation Organization.

Third, there is hard-left anti-Semitism. Although this goes back in time to Voltaire, Marx, Stalin and others, the new anti-Semitism is different in that it often disguises itself as anti-Zionism. This bigotry is seen in the double standard imposed on everything Jewish, especially the nation-state of the Jewish people. It is also reflected in blaming "Jewish power" and the "pushiness" of Jews in demanding support for Israel.

The ultimate form of this pathology is the absurd comparison made by some extreme leftists between the extermination policies of the Nazis and Israel's efforts to defend itself against terrorist rockets, tunnels, suicide bombers and other threats to its civilians. Comparing Israel's actions to those of the Nazis is a not-so-subtle version of Holocaust denial. Because if what the Nazis really did was what Israel is now doing, there could not have been a Holocaust or an attempt at genocide against the Jewish people. A variation on this perverse theme is apartheid denial: by accusing Israel—which accords equal rights to all its citizens—of apartheid, these haters deny the horrors of actual apartheid, which was so much more terrible than anything Israel has ever done.

Fourth, and most dangerous, is eliminationist anti-Zionism and anti-Semitism of the kind advocated by the leaders of Iran, Hezbollah, Hamas and the Islamic State. Listen to Hezbollah leader Hassan Nasrallah: "If [the Jews] all gather in Israel, it will save us the trouble of going after them worldwide," or, "If we search the entire world for a person more cowardly, despicable, weak and feeble in psyche, mind, ideology and religion, we would not find anyone like the Jew. Notice I didn't say the Israeli."

These variations on the theme of anti-Semitism have several elements in common. First, those who subscribe to them tend to engage in some form of Holocaust denial, minimization, glorification or comparative victimization. Second, they exaggerate Jewish power, money and influence. Third, they seek the delegitimization and demonization of Israel as the nation-state of the Jewish people. Fourth, they impose a double standard on all things Jewish. Finally, they nearly all deny that they are anti-Semites who hate all Jews. They claim that their hatred is directed against Israel and Jews who support the nation-state of the Jewish people.

This common core of the "new" anti-Semitism—we love the Jews, it's only their nation-state that we hate—is pervasive among many European political, media, cultural and academic leaders. Polls among Germans showed that a significant number of the children, grandchildren and great-grandchildren of Nazi supporters didn't want to hear about Nazi atrocities, but they believed what Israel was doing to the Palestinians was comparable to what the Nazis had done to the Jews.

This then is the European problem of anti-Semitism that many European leaders are unwilling to confront, because they have a built-in excuse! It's Israel's fault—if only Israel would do the right thing with regard to the Palestinians, the problem would be solved.

Tragically, it won't be solved, because the reality is that hatred of Israel is not the cause of anti-Semitism. Rather, it is the reverse: anti-Semitism is a primary cause of hatred for the nation-state of the Jewish people.

The university campus has become an important battlefield for the new anti-Semitism, as well as a platform for efforts to end bipartisan support for Israel. Current students are future leaders. This is already becoming evident by the election to Congress of several young leftists who want to end the long-standing bipartisan support for Israel.

Just as classic anti-Semitism has gone through different historical phases, so too have the continuing efforts to destroy the nation-state of the Jewish people. The initial phase—from 1948 to

1973—manifested itself through military attacks from Arab armies, especially Egypt, Syria and Jordan. Although this effort came close to succeeding in the Yom Kippur War, it ultimately failed, and its failure was reflected in peace treaties with Egypt and Jordan as well as an informal cold peace with Syria. The second phase—which began even before Israel's Declaration of Independence and continues to some degree even today—is the attempt to destroy or at least weaken Israel through persistent terrorism. The height of this campaign began with the first intifada, started in 1987, in which approximately 150 Israelis, mostly civilians, and 1,000 Palestinians, including many civilians, were killed.[2] It ended with the termination of the second intifada between 2000 and 2005, in which more than 1,000 Israelis, mostly civilians, and more than 3,000 Palestinians, including many civilians, were killed.

The deaths and injuries alone do not tell the whole story of these terrorist campaigns. They changed life both in Israel and in the Palestinian areas. The second intifada ended shortly after Arafat's death. No coincidence. Although terrorism persists, it has been reduced considerably by the security barriers—mostly high-tech electronic fences—that Israel has erected along its borders. Current terrorism emanates primarily from Gaza in the form of rockets, incendiary kites, terror tunnels and other cross-border attacks, which Israel has managed to control through technological superiority, with its Iron Dome defense, anti-tunnel technology and drones.

The third phase in Palestinian efforts to destroy, or at least delegitimize, Israel is much more subtle and difficult to counter by traditional defense tactics. It is directed at the future leaders of the United States and Western Europe, who are now university students. It has taken the form of campaigns to boycott, divest and sanction (BDS) Israel and *only* Israel, to have the international community treat Israel as an apartheid pariah state in the way South Africa was treated, to turn students and faculty against the nation-state of the Jewish people and, most disturbingly, to end the American tradition of bipartisan support for Israel and to turn the Democratic Party into the kind of anti-Israel party that the Labour Party has become in Great Britain.

When I taught first-year criminal law students on their first day at Harvard Law School, they would look at each other and see 150 frightened young women and men anxious about being subjected to the rigorous questioning of the Socratic Method. I would see something different: a future president of the United States; a future editor of the *New York Times*; a future chief justice; a future managing partner of Goldman Sachs; a future king of Saudi Arabia; a future secretary general of the United Nations.

Those are the kinds of future leaders that Harvard and other elite universities teach. And many of those future leaders are being "taught"—propagandized—by hard-left professors who express their extreme anti-Israel views as "truths," both in the classroom and outside of it.

Anti-Israel advocacy among hard-left professors has been common since the mid-1970s, following the break in relations between the Soviet Union and Israel as well as Berrigan's anti-Zionist and anti-Semitic screed. Until recently, this one-sidedly anti-Israel position was limited to a relatively small number of radical students and a larger number of vocal radical professors, who were still a minority in most faculties. But during the last several years, this phenomenon has spread to mainstream students and faculty—not all, but many— through what is called "intersectionality."

Intersectionality is a radical academic construct that argues that all forms of oppression are inexorably linked—capitalism, colonialism, imperialism, racism, anti-Islamism, heterosexualism and, of course, Zionism—and that the oppressors of all victimized groups are essentially the same. This pseudo-academic "theory," which has no empirical or scientific basis, resonates on campuses where "identity politics" have often replaced individual merit. Indeed, the very concept of "meritocracy" has become a "politically incorrect" equivalent of all the above "isms." The villains of identity politics are the "privileged classes," which include white, heterosexual, male students and faculty. The most targeted privileged group on many campuses are Jewish students, especially those who support Israel and who are "accused" of Zionism.

In 2017, at the University of Illinois, flyers were plastered around campus calling for the "end of Jewish privilege." The flyer stated in bold letters that "ending white privilege starts with ending Jewish privilege." The posters had outlines of silhouettes with Stars of David printed on their chests and an arrow pointing to them with the accompanying caption: "the 1%." Although some of the posters identified Black Lives Matter as sponsors, it isn't clear whether they were distributed by extreme right-wing groups using hard-left anti-Semitic tropes or by hard-left anti-Semites. In some respects, it doesn't really matter because many on the hard right and hard left share a disdain for Jews, their nation-state and so called "Jewish privilege." Klansman David Duke, Nation of Islam leader Louis Farrakhan, the former Republican presidential candidate Pat Buchanan, the co-chairwoman of the Women's March, Linda Sarsour, and the darling of the progressive wing of the Democratic Party, Congresswoman Ilhan Omar, have much in common when it comes to Zionism, anti-Zionism and anti-Semitism. That is why Duke has praised Omar, a Muslim woman, despite his long history of anti-Muslim bigotry.

At Hunter College, it was clear who was condemning "the Zionist Administration" for raising tuition and other evils. It was also clear that "Zionist" was a euphemism—a politically correct cover—for "Jew," since the president of Hunter was Jewish. I don't know whether she was a Zionist, and it doesn't really matter, since raising tuition at Hunter was not part of any Zionist plot. That anti-Semitic statement was signed by students for Justice in Palestine in 10 New York City colleges—all with substantial Jewish enrollment. The bigoted statement was intended to link the "victims" of a tuition rise in New York with the "victim" of "oppressions" in Gaza.[3] Quite a stretch, unless you believe that "Zionists" are behind all the evils in the world, as Professor Hamid Dabashi of Columbia tweeted: "Every dirty treacherous ugly and pernicious act happening in the world just wait for a few days and the ugly name of 'Israel' will pup [pop up] . . ."

The same bigoted professor recently compared Israel with ISIS, tweeting that the "murderous thugs" of the jihadist group "conquered parts of Syria and declared a 'caliphate.'" He continued, "Their ISRAELI counterparts meanwhile conquered parts of Syria and declared it part of their Zionist settler colony . . . The only difference: ISIS does not have a platoon of clean shaven and well coiffured [sic] columnists at the *New York Times* propagating the cause of the terrorist outfit as the Zionists columnists do on a regular basis."[4]

The linking of unrelated "victimizations," despite their tenuous connections, is reflective of a broader trend in hard-left politics, whereby increasingly radical activists demand that the demonization of "Zionism"—often used as a euphemism for Jews—be included, indeed featured, in the package of causes that must be embraced by anyone claiming the label of "progressive." Lumping seemingly disparate groups under the "umbrella of oppression" leads to the forming of alliances between causes that, at best, have nothing to do with each other and, at worst, are averse to one another's stated mission. Their only common feature is that in order to join them, one must demonize the nation-state of the Jewish people and its national liberation movement.

The following are among many examples of radical leftists conflating unrelated grievances: the linking of our government's handling of the Flint water crisis to the "severe" water crisis in Gaza; the shooting of black men by policemen in America to the shooting of terrorists in Gaza; the denial of healthcare to patients with preexisting conditions in America to the terrible conditions in Gaza hospitals caused by Hamas diverting resources from healthcare to rockets and tunnels; the discrimination against LGBTQ people in America to the discrimination against Palestinians on the West Bank.

During a recent interview on PBS, Jonathan Haidt—social psychologist and professor of ethical leadership at New York University's Stern School of Business—said this about the conflation of various left-wing causes under the banner of intersectionality:

> *There is a good kind of identity politics, which is, you know, if black people are being denied rights, let's fight for their rights. But there is a bad kind, which is to train students, train young people to say let's divide everybody up by their race, gender, other categories. We'll assign them moral merit based on their level of privilege. Okay, now let's look at everything through this lens. Palestinians are the victims. So therefore, they are the good and the Jews or the Israelis are the bad. All social problems get reduced to this simple framework.*

The essence of anti-Semitism is the bigoted claim that if there is a problem, then Jews must be its cause. And not just some Jews, but "the Jews" as a collectivity. This presumption of collective action, and collective guilt, always marks the sometimes subtle shift from legitimate criticism of individual actions by Jews to anti-Semitic conspiracy theory. In the Middle Ages, "the Jews" were blamed for the bubonic plague. The Nazis later blamed "the Jews" for Germany's economic collapse after World War I. Today, many hard-left activists explicitly or implicitly blame "the Jews" and "the Zionists" for many of the evils of the world, including climate change.[5] British Labour parliamentarians—and former cabinet member Clare Short—blamed Israel for "undermin[ing] the international community's reaction to global warming" and for causing the "bitter division and violence in the world." She has said that Israel may one day be the cause of the world ending. We Jews have so much power! I'm reminded of the old joke of two Jews in the early 1930s sitting in a Viennese café reading newspapers—one is reading a Yiddish paper, the other a Nazi paper. The first turns to the second and asks, "Why are you reading that Nazi rag?" The second replies, "When I used to read the

Yiddish paper, all I would see was pogroms, Jews starving and other bad news. Now I read in the Nazi paper how Jews are all powerful and control the world. I prefer the good news!"

Jewish students on many campuses are excluded from joining "progressive" groups unless they pass the intersectionality purity test: they must renounce Zionism and support for Israel. Rabbi Susan Talve, a longtime activist on race issues in the St. Louis area, was told that her advocacy for Israel was incompatible with the objectives of Black Lives Matter: "Solidarity from Ferguson to Palestine has become a central tenet of the movement," she was informed, because "Israel and U.S. state oppression are deeply interconnected." Similarly, a student who attended a Black Lives Matter rally at Northwestern University was told, "You support Israel, so you cannot also support us."

Supporters of the LGBTQ community in Israel learned this lesson when BDS activists, together with a local Black Lives Matter chapter, broke up a gay pride event because it featured a presentation by an Israeli group. The protestors claimed that the event organizers had engaged in "pinkwashing" the Israeli occupation by showing solidarity with the Israeli LGBTQ community. Pinkwashing is the claim that Israel, which has one of the best records with regard to LGBTQ issues, only supports the rights of LGBTQ individuals as a cover—a whitewash with a pink hue—for its terrible treatment of Palestinians. Under this absurd theory, whenever Israel does anything good, it must have an evil hidden motive.

Members of the National Women's Studies Association (NWSA) who also support Israel have been similarly excluded. When that organization voted to endorse BDS, one anti-Israel activist explained, "What is significant about this particular resolution is the rationale: one cannot call themselves a feminist . . . without taking a stand on what is happening in Palestine." Apparently, one can call oneself a feminist without taking a stand on Syria, Russia, China, Saudi Arabia, Turkey, Venezuela, Belarus and other nations that grossly violate human rights, including women's rights. According to Linda Sarsour, one can even be a feminist while expressing sexist views—such as calling for Ayaan Hirsi Ali and other female critics of her views to have "their vaginas [taken] away'"—but not while supporting the only country in the Middle East where women have equal rights with men.

Jewish participants at the Chicago "Dyke March"—a parade geared toward that city's lesbian community—were told to leave the parade because their flag, which had a Star of David printed on top of the LGBTQ rainbow flag, "made people feel unsafe." ("Unsafe" is the current weaponized mantra of the hard left.) They were also told that the march was supposed to be "anti-Zionist" and "pro-Palestinian," so Zionists were not welcome.

The International Women's Strike recently published its platform, which singles out Israel from among all the countries in the world for special condemnation. The platform demands the "decolonization" of Palestine and the dismantling of all "walls, from prison walls to border walls, from Mexico to Palestine." No mention was made of the walls that imprison gays in Iran, dissidents in China, feminists in Gaza or Kurds in Turkey. Only the walls erected by the United States and Israel.

Criticizing Israel's settlement and occupation policies is fair game. But singling out Israel for "decolonization" when it has repeatedly offered to end the occupation and to create a Palestinian state on the West Bank and Gaza, and when other countries continue to colonize, can be explained in no other way than its detractors applying a double standard to Jews and their state.

Palestinian-American activist Linda Sarsour, who helped organize the Women's March on Washington in January, responded in *The Nation* to criticism of the anti-Israel plank appearing in a feminist platform:

> When you talk about feminism you're talking about the rights of all women and their families to live in dignity, peace, and security. It's about giving women access to health care and other basic

rights. And Israel is a country that continues to occupy territories in Palestine, has people under siege at checkpoints—we have women who have babies on checkpoints because they're not able to get to hospitals [in time]. It just doesn't make any sense for someone to say, "Is there room for people who support the state of Israel and do not criticize it in the movement?" There can't be in feminism. You either stand up for the rights of all women, including Palestinians, or none. There's just no way around it.

Sarsour was responding directly to an op-ed published by Emily Shire in the *New York Times*, in which she asked why women must choose between their Zionism and feminism. The op-ed included the following:

My prime concern is not that people hold this view of Israel. Rather, I find it troubling that embracing such a view is considered an essential part of an event that is supposed to unite feminists. I am happy to debate Middle East politics or listen to critiques of Israeli politics. But why should criticism of Israel be key to feminism?

There is nothing wrong with feminists demanding healthcare for Palestinian women, as long as they also demand healthcare for the women of other countries that deny such care to women. But to single out only women allegedly denied healthcare by the nation-state of the Jewish people—which provides better healthcare to Arabs than any Arab country—is not feminism. It is anti-Semitism.

This type of repressive ideological packaging has left progressive Jews and liberal supporters of Israel in an increasingly uncomfortable position. On the one hand, they care deeply about causes such as women's rights, criminal justice reform, income inequality, environmental protection and LGBTQ rights. On the other, they find themselves excluded from the groups that advance those very causes, because, as Jewish progressives, while they are often critical of specific Israeli policies regarding settlements and the occupation, they refuse to renounce Zionism as a national liberation movement of the Jewish people.

For hard-left activists, this sort of nuanced position is impossible to accept. Their hostility toward Israel does not stem from any particular Israeli actions or policies. Even if Israel were to withdraw from the West Bank, destroy the security barrier and recognize Hamas as a legitimate political organization, it would still not be enough. For those radicals, it is not what Israel *does*; it is about what Israel *is*: the nation-state of the Jewish people, or, to use hard-left terminology, an imperialistic apartheid and genocidal colonialist enterprise. The Black Lives Matter policy platform offers a perfect example of such extreme rhetoric: it states that U.S. military and economic support for Israel makes American citizens complicit in "the genocide taking place against the Palestinian people." I have supported the *concept* of black lives mattering as much as white lives, but I cannot and will not support an *organization* that maliciously has accused Israel of genocide for defending its citizens from terrorism and military attacks. Regardless of how much good BLM may do to reduce police misconduct against African Americans, there must be zero tolerance for the kind of anti-Semitism reflected in their platform. Black lives do matter, but so do Jewish lives.

Intersectionality—which was prominently featured in posters at the 2016 Democratic Convention—has been particularly pronounced on college campuses, where a host of academic groups have passed resolutions in favor of BDS. Many of these organizations have also endorsed the Palestinian Campaign for the Academic and Cultural Boycott of Israel (PACBI), which encourages participants to engage in McCarthyist blacklisting of Israeli academic institutions and to oppose all "normalization" activities, which seek to bring Israelis and Palestinians together in seeking peace.

Intersectionality groups—representing women, African Americans, LGBTQ and other disenfranchised people—are gaining influence on campuses throughout the world. Students want to be aligned with "progressive" causes, and they are being told—falsely—that they cannot be true progressives unless they renounce Israel and Zionism. That is why, in recent years, I have felt a special obligation as a *liberal* supporter of the nation-state of the Jewish people and of its national liberation movement to speak in defense of Israel and Zionism on university campuses around both the country and the world.

Accordingly, I have accepted invitations to speak at Yale, Princeton, Columbia, Penn, Johns Hopkins, Colgate, Barnard, Ohio State, the University of Michigan, Michigan State, the University of Florida, the University of Miami, Fordham, the University of Massachusetts, MIT, Boston University, Northeastern, Emory, the College of Charleston, New York University, Cardozo Law School, Brooklyn College, Hunter College, Oxford University, Syracuse University, Hofstra, Liberty, Elon, Pepperdine, Yeshiva, Georgetown, George Washington, Brandeis, Franklin and Marshall, Nova, Hampshire, Duquesne, Gratz, Lafayette, Boston College, Baruch, the University of London, Lyden University, the Technion, Tel Aviv University, Northwestern University, Stanford, Berkeley, UCLA, the University of California at Irvine, McGill University, the University of Toronto, the University of Cape Town, Charles University in Prague, Beijing University and, of course, Harvard. I have also spoken at several high schools and prep schools, including in South Africa and Australia.

Whenever I receive an invitation to speak at a university, I ask the sponsors why they don't invite one of their own professors to make the case for Israel. Often they tell me that there is not a single professor on their campus willing to risk the wrath of anti-Israel colleagues and students. They worry that their evaluations will suffer or that other negative consequences will ensue. Some are prepared to support Israel privately, but not publicly. Courage is not an attribute of most professors, at least when it comes to taking on the powerful anti-Israel forces at many universities. There are some exceptions, but they are all too rare.

Despite the fact that I make the liberal case for a two-state solution and the end of Israeli settlement, I am almost always the object of protests, walkouts and efforts to silence me. On occasion, armed guards are needed to protect me from physical threats.

There have only been two successful efforts by universities to ban or silence me. The first was by the University of Cape Town in South Africa in 2011. Years earlier, I was banned by apartheid South Africa from delivering an anti-apartheid talk at the University of Witwatersrand (WITS) in Johannesburg. The South African consul general would not grant me a visa unless I showed them my speech in advance. I refused. They refused. And I never gave the speech.

In 2011, the University of Cape Town invited me to give a talk. When I arrived, I was greeted by the following headline in the *Cape Times*: "Dershowitz is not welcome here: Harvard Professor Campaigned against Desmond Tutu." The article was in the form of an open letter signed by left-wing anti-Israel academics, lawyers, judges and others, several of whom were Jewish. Its subheadline was accurate: I had written critically of Bishop Tutu for his virulent anti-Zionism, which had morphed into anti-Semitism.

During the struggle against apartheid in South Africa, Tutu emerged as an international paragon, a religious and moral leader often compared with MLK, but since the end of apartheid his bigoted views on Jews, and Israel in particular, have come to the fore.

I argued in op-eds and speeches that Bishop Tutu was no mere anti-Zionist (though Martin Luther King long ago recognized that anti-Zionism often serves as a cover for deeper anti-Jewish bigotry). He minimized the suffering of those murdered in the Holocaust by asserting that "the gas chambers" made for "a neater death" than did apartheid. In other words, Palestinians, who in his view are the victims of "Israeli apartheid," have suffered *more* than the victims of the Nazi Holocaust. He complained of "the Jewish Monopoly of the Holocaust" and demanded that its victims must "forgive the Nazis," while he himself refuses to forgive the "Jewish people" for "persecute[ing] others."[6] This kind of argument is always a telltale sign insofar as it holds the Jewish people collectively responsible for the actions of Israel. Even the German populace that generally supported Nazism was not held responsible for the crimes of the Nazi regime.

Tutu asserted that Zionism has "very many parallels with racism," thus echoing the notorious and discredited "Zionism equals racism" resolution passed by the General Assembly of the United Nations and subsequently rescinded. Without being specific, Tutu accused the Jews of Israel of doing "things that even apartheid South Africa had not done." He said that "the Jews thought they had a monopoly of God—Jesus was angry that they could shut out other human beings"—and that Jews were "opposed to" his God and have been "fighting against" him. He claimed that his God sides with Palestinians, who he compares to the Israelites under bondage in Egypt, and he has sought to explain, if not justify, how Israeli actions lead directly to suicide bombings and other forms of terrorism. He implied that Israel might someday consider as an option "to perpetrate genocide and exterminate all Palestinians."

He complained that Americans "are scared . . . to say it's wrong because the Jewish lobby is powerful—very powerful." He accused Jews—not Israel—of exhibiting "an arrogance—the arrogance of power because Jews are a powerful lobby in this land, and all kinds of people woo their support."

He compared Israel to Hitler's Germany, Stalin's Soviet Union and apartheid South Africa, saying that they too were once "very powerful" but eventually "bit the dust," as will "unjust" Israel.

He denied that Israel is a "civilized democracy" and singled out Israel—one of the world's most open democracies—as a nation guilty of "censorship of their media." He has urged the Cape Town Opera to refuse to perform *Porgy and Bess* in Tel Aviv and has called for a total cultural boycott of Jewish Israel, while encouraging performers to visit the most repressive regimes in the world.

He has been far more vocal about Israel's imperfections than about the genocides in Rwanda, Darfur and Cambodia. He has repeatedly condemned Israel's occupation of the West Bank without mentioning the many other occupations in the world today. When confronted with his double standard against Jews, he justified it on theological grounds: "Whether Jews like it or not, they are a peculiar people. They can't ever hope to be judged by the same standards which are used for other people." There is a name for non-Jews who hold Jews to a double standard: it is anti-Semite.

Tutu has acknowledged that he has frequently been accused of anti-Semitism, to which he has offered two responses: "Tough luck," and, "My dentist's name is Dr. Cohen." Most disturbingly, Tutu seems to be gleeful about singling out Jews for special condemnation. He seems to enjoy making cruel comments about Jews, Israel, the Holocaust and Zionism.

I stand by criticism of Bishop Tutu, and I'm proud of having the courage to go after a Nobel Prize–winning icon, including in South Africa, where he is generally revered. I wish others would tell the truth about Tutu's sordid history with Jews while at the same time applauding his anti-apartheid activities. There must be zero tolerance for anti-Semitism and other bigotry, regardless of its source. But when the source is someone as influential as Bishop Tutu is, both in South Africa and throughout the world, it is especially important to tell the truth about his anti-Jewish bigotry.

As a result of my writings against this South African icon, the University of Cape Town canceled the talk I was invited to give. Their phony excuse: there was too little interest. My talk was then moved to another venue not far from the campus: more than 1,000 people attended.

The second successful effort to silence me took place in 2009 at the University of Massachusetts–Boston campus. I was invited by student groups to give a talk advocating a two-state solution to the Israeli–Palestinian conflict.

Halfway through my talk, a group of students led by an anti-Israel

Jewish professor began to shout me down and drown me out with boos and chants. I welcome sporadic booing, directed at particular points with which the booers disagree. This was not that. It was a concerted effort to drown me out and prevent the other students from hearing my points.

This is a common tactic on the student left these days, known as deplatforming. In this case, the strategy worked. Instead of shutting down those who sought to censor me, the moderator—a high-ranking official of the university—called an end to the event, not allowing me to finish my presentation. It was a victory for censorship and a defeat for the First Amendment and the very idea of the university itself as a forum for the exchange of ideas and open debate.

I could have sued the university, because it is a public school governed by the First Amendment, but I decided not to for two reasons. First, I had already completed a substantial portion of my presentation when I was shut down; and second, the moderator claimed he stopped the event for my "safety," since the booers were rowdy and threatening. Although the safety issue was almost certainly a pretext, it would have made it more difficult to prevail. I could have been asked, on cross-examination, if I had ever been threatened with violence for my views on the Middle East, and I would have had to say that I had been. I would also have had to say that in several of my university talks, armed guards were either on the stage or nearby in order to protect me from threatened or feared violence.

There were two attempts at campuses of the University of California—also a public school—to ban or silence me. Both failed. The first was much like the one that succeeded at the University of Massachusetts. It took place on the Irvine campus, where again student groups invited me to make the case for Israel.

The large auditorium was filled with students who appeared to fall into three categories. To the left of the lectern were 100 or so students carrying pro-Israel signs, some wearing kippot. To the right were approximately the same number of students carrying pro-Palestinian and anti-Israel signs, some wearing the green colors of Palestine. In the middle, there were several hundred students who did not take sides. They were there to listen and learn. This self-selected seating arrangement, with pro- and anti-Israel groups sitting on different sides of the room, was becoming more common on campuses.

I began by asking the pro-Israel students how many of them would accept the two-state solution, with a nonviolent Palestinian state on the West Bank. Nearly every hand went up.

I then asked the pro-Palestinian students how many of them would accept Israel, if it ended the occupation and settlements and accepted the two-state solution. There was rumbling and discussion, but in the end, not a single hand went up.

I looked to the center of the auditorium, where students who did not align themselves with either side were listening with interest, and said,

> *This is not a dispute between pro-Israel and pro-Palestinian advocates. It's a dispute between pro-Israel and anti-Israel students. The pro-Israel students are also pro-Palestine. They support a Palestinian state, as I do. The pro-Palestinian students seem not to want an Israeli state, even if there is also a Palestinian state.*

I was applauded by many of the center students. My little exercise had neatly illustrated the difference between the two sides and also undermined the claims of pro-Palestinian activitists that they are not opposed to the existence of Israel.

When I began my substantive talk, several of the pro-Palestinian students tried to shout me down, by persistent booing, chanting and screaming. But this time the moderator, who was prepared to deal with the disruption, asked the police to remove the disrupters. I was able to complete my talk, and I received a standing ovation from most of the students.

Shortly after my talk, Michael Oren—an Israeli historian who was then serving as his country's ambassador to the United States—was invited to speak about Israel in the same auditorium. A group of students from the Muslim Student Union set out to prevent him from speaking. They did not try to hide their intention. Here is how the dean of the Law School described it:

> *The Muslim student Union orchestrated a concerted effort to disrupt the speech. One student after another stood and shouted so that the ambassador could not be heard. Each student was taken away by the police only to be replaced by another doing the same thing.*

The students were disciplined by the university for their actions, though the nature and degree of the discipline has been kept confidential. Campus sources have characterized it as a "slap on the wrist." After learning of the careful planning that went into the concerted effort to prevent Oren from speaking and the subsequent cover-up, District Attorney Tony Rackauckas courageously filed misdemeanor charges against those who were arrested.

The decision resulted in an outcry by radicals, many of whom favor censorship of pro-Israel speakers. In a letter to the DA signed by many well-known anti-Israel zealots, the incident was described as merely a protest rather than a determined effort to silence the speaker.

The fact that radical anti-Israel zealots would view censorship of a pro-Israel speaker as a form of legitimate "protest" comes as no surprise. But the fact that the letter of support was signed by two leaders of the American Civil Liberties Union shocked many people. I have been a supporter of the ACLU for half a century, and I was a national board member. I supported the right of Nazis to march through Skokie, and I defended the right of the most virulent anti-Israel speakers to participate in the marketplace of ideas. The ACLU policy has always been to oppose concerted efforts to prevent speakers from delivering their remarks. While sporadic heckling and jeering that merely demonstrates opposition to the content of the remarks is constitutionally protected, the ACLU has always condemned systematic efforts to prevent speakers from delivering their talk—except apparently, when the speaker is pro-Israel.

After being criticized for supporting censorship, one of the ACLU leaders sought to justify his signing of the letter with the following logic: "The district attorney's action will undoubtedly intimidate students . . . and discourage them from engaging in any controversial speech or protest for fear of criminal charges."

In fact, the opposite is true. Letting these students off would only encourage other students around the nation—and the world—to continue with efforts to prevent pro-Israel speakers from delivering their speeches and opinions. The ACLU should support a clear line between occasional heckling and outright censorship. It should not support concerted efforts to silence speakers. In the end, the offending students were successfully prosecuted and given suspended sentences.

The next effort to ban me took the form of a legal barrier when I was invited by Jewish student groups to give a talk at Berkeley in 2018. The Berkeley campus had been roiled by controversies about speakers invited by conservative groups and efforts by extreme leftist groups, such as Antifa, to stop them from speaking. In response, Berkeley enacted a new rule requiring eight weeks prior notice before anyone could speak at a campus event, *unless* an official invitation came from a university department.

On its face, this rule seemed content-neutral, since it applied equally to liberals and conservatives, pro-Israel or anti-Israel speakers. But in practice, it was anything but neutral. University departments at Berkeley routinely invited left-wing and anti-Israel speakers but not conservative or pro-Israel speakers. (This was common around the country, which I learned firsthand when the political science department at my alma mater Brooklyn College officially sponsored anti-Israel speakers but refused to sponsor me.) So the effect of the rule—whether intended or unintended, and many believed it was intended—was to allow left-wing and anti-Israel speakers *immediate* access to students (as well as the official imprimatur of university departments) while requiring conservative or pro-Israel speakers to go through hoops and *wait* eight weeks, which often meant that, before any talk could be arranged, the semester would be over (as it would have been if I had had to wait eight weeks).

When I was invited, the Jewish groups asked several departments to sponsor my talk. None would, though several had recently sponsored anti-Israel speakers.

Because Berkeley is such a large and influential campus, I decided to sue the university for violating my First Amendment rights, as well as those of the students who wanted to hear me. As soon as I announced my intention to sue, the dean of the Law School extended me an invitation, thus negating the suit.

My talk on the two-state solution was protested and leafleted by radical students. I invited the protestors to come and listen, promising to take their critical questions first and to take no friendly questions until I had answered all the critical ones. They refused and walked out. The speech was well received by the audience, but not by the school newspaper's editorial cartoonist, who did not attend but drew an anti-Semitic caricature of me. Here is how it was described by a student who wrote a letter to the newspaper:

> In the cartoon, Dershowitz is depicted with a hooked nose and a body of a large amorphous black sphere. His exaggerated head and contorted legs and hands evoke images of a spider. The rhetoric of Jews as "invasive" insects in society, trying to take over resources and power, had long been used to justify violence, persecution and murder. The two elements of the cartoon, with Dershowitz's face in the front and the black body in the back, plays into the anti-Semitic trope of Jews as shape-shifting, sub-human entities using deception and trickery in order to

*advance their own agendas. This rhetoric is nowhere more
common than in Nazi propaganda, and can be traced far beyond
WWII in European and American media.*

In another letter to the editor, the university's chancellor, Carol
Christ, wrote the following:

> *Your recent editorial cartoon targeting Alan Dershowitz
> was offensive, appalling and deeply disappointing. I condemn
> its publication. Are you aware that its anti-Semitic imagery
> connects directly to the centuries-old "blood libel" that falsely
> accused Jews of engaging in ritual murder? I cannot recall
> anything similar in the* Daily Cal, *and I call on the paper's editors
> to reflect on whether they would sanction a similar assault on
> other ethnic or religious groups. We cannot build a campus
> community where everyone feels safe, respected and welcome if
> hatred and the perpetuation of harmful stereotypes become an
> acceptable part of our discourse.*

It was shocking to me that this vile caricature—which would fit
comfortably in a Nazi or white nationalist publication—was published
in "the official paper of record of the City of Berkeley" (according to
the editor). The cartoon resembles the grotesque anti-Semitic blood
libel propaganda splashed across *Der Stürmer* in the 1930s, which depicted Jews drinking the blood of Gentile children. Canards about
Jews as predators—prominently promulgated by the tsarist forgery,
the *Protocols of the Elders of Zion*—were anti-Semitic back then and
are still anti-Semitic today, whether espoused by the extreme left or
the extreme right.

Moreover, the anti-Semitic cartoon was printed in reaction to a
speech in which I advocated a Palestinian state, an end to the occupation, and principles in opposition to Israeli settlement policies. It's
hard to imagine a position more favorable to Palestinian claims and

aspirations. Apparently, even this is not enough to warrant a hearing from radical activists.

Nonetheless, just as I have long defended the rights of Nazis to march in Skokie and elsewhere, I defend the right of hard-left bigots to produce this sort of anti-Semitic material, despite it being hate speech. Those who condemn hate speech when it comes from the right should also speak up when hate speech comes from the left. The silence from those on the left is steeped in hypocrisy. It reflects the old adage: free speech for me but not for thee.

The best response to bigotry is the opposite of censorship: it is exposure and shaming in the court of public opinion. I opposed removing the offensive cartoon, as some suggested. I wanted it to be widely circulated for all to see and criticize. It was not removed.

Writing in the *Daily Cal*, students from a pro-Israel organization at Berkeley did just that: they debunked the claim that the cartoonist and the student paper editors at the *Daily Cal* could not have known that this cartoon was steeped in traditional anti-Semitic stereotyping, considering its deep roots in European, and even American, publications.

The students also wrote about the "pain" the anti-Semitic cartoon had caused them:

> *To a Jewish student on this campus, seeing this cartoon in the* Daily Cal *is a reminder that we are not always welcome in the spaces we call home.*
>
> . . .
>
> *Telling Jews that we can or cannot define what is offensive to us, because of our status as privileged minority in the United States, is anti-Semitic.*

Some students also pointed to the swastika that had defaced my picture on a poster outside Berkeley Law School as evidence of a pervasive anti-Semitism disguised as anti-Zionism on that campus. A poster for my talk at Johns Hopkins was similarly defaced: someone drew a Hitler-type moustache on my lip.

Sadly, though not surprisingly, the *Jewish Forward*—a century-old Jewish publication that had become a megaphone for anti-Israel bigotry under the editor at the time—denied that the imagery was anti-Semitic and justified its publication:

> *The mere appearance of blood near a Jew is not a blood libel. The State of Israel has an army, and that army sometimes kills Palestinians, including women and children. When you prick those people, I am told, they bleed. It is perverse to demand of artists that they represent actual, real Israeli violence without blood, just because European Christians invented a fake accusation.*

The *Forward* also argued that the cartoon was a legitimate criticism of my talk. But the cartoonist admitted that he didn't hear my talk. Nor did the *Daily Cal* report on it.

I doubt the *Forward* would publish an op-ed that justified comparable images of women, blacks or gays. But for them, Jews and Zionists are fair game for bigotry.

When the Columbia University chapter of Amnesty International invited me to deliver a talk on human rights in the Middle East, I immediately accepted. As a supporter of the two-state solution and an opponent of many of Israel's settlement decisions, I regard myself as a moderate on these issues.

That was apparently too much for the national office of Amnesty International. They demanded that their Columbia chapter disinvite me. They did not want their members to hear my perspective on these issues.

Their excuse was two old and out-of-context quotes suggesting that I favored torture and collective punishment. The truth is that I am adamantly opposed to both. I have written nuanced academic articles on the subject of torture warrants as a way of minimizing the evils of torture,[7] and I have written vehemently against the use of collective punishment of innocent people—whether by means of the boycott movement against all Israelis or the use of collective punishment against Palestinians. I do favor holding those who facilitate terrorism responsible for their own actions.[8]

As an outspoken Zionist who supports Israel's right to exist as the nation-state of the Jewish people, I have been sharply critical of Amnesty's one-sided approach to the Israeli–Palestinian conflict. For example, I wrote an article criticizing Amnesty's report on honor killings in the West Bank. An honor killing occurs when a woman has been raped and her family then kills her because of the shame her victimization has brought on them. Despite massive evidence to the contrary, Amnesty mendaciously claimed that honor killings had increased in the West Bank since the Israeli occupation and that the fault for this increase in Arab men killing Arab women somehow lay with Israel. The reality is that there are far fewer honor killings in the West Bank than there are in adjoining Jordan, which is not under Israeli occupation, and that the number of such killings in the West Bank has been reduced dramatically during the Israeli occupation. But facts apparently mean little when Israel is involved.[9]

The national office of Amnesty International did not want their members to hear my views on Israel or my criticisms of their organization. This is despite the fact that I was a strong supporter in its early days, before it became so one-sided and began supporting BDS against only Israel. They were afraid to have their Jewish members at Columbia hear the truth. They feared an open marketplace of ideas, so they tried to shut me down by denying the right of their Columbia chapter to sponsor my talk.

Fortunately, another Columbia student group immediately invited me to speak, and some members of Columbia Amnesty, to their credit, came to listen. They asked me hard questions, which I tried to answer with facts and logic. Some agreed with me, while others disagreed. That is the nature of open dialogue, which Amnesty International claims to champion—except when it comes to their own organization.[10]

When I was invited to debate in favor of the motion "Is BDS Wrong?" at the Oxford Union in 2015, I fully expected to lose the vote of the hundreds of students and faculty members of the oldest debating society in the world. "Israel always loses at Oxford," I was warned by colleagues who had debated other Israel-related issues. Nonetheless, I decided to participate. BDS was quickly gaining support throughout Europe and in the United States, and I saw this debate, which would be widely covered and available on the internet, as an opportunity to change some minds.

I proposed as my opponent Omar Barghouti, the Qatar-born, Israeli-educated, cofounder and spokesperson of the BDS campaign, whom I had many times attacked in print, but he refused to debate me. The Union then selected Noura Erakat, a Palestinian American human rights attorney who has been a vocal supporter of BDS.

When she backed out at the last minute, I began to get suspicious. Was the BDS organization boycotting me? After all, BDS advocates have called for "common sense" academic boycotts against individuals who they feel are too vocal in their support for Israel, in addition to a blanket boycott of all Israeli academic institutions.

After speaking with the organizers of the debate at Oxford, I concluded that I was in fact being boycotted.

The Union then selected Peter Tatchell, a distinguished and popular British human rights activist, who has participated in 30 Union debates, most of which he has won. Tatchell accepted. The debate was held in the beautiful, wood-paneled, old auditorium that had featured debates over the years by many world leaders. The overflow crowd reflected the widespread interest in the issue.

I knew I was in for a difficult time, especially when most of the questions from the students seemed hostile toward Israel, though polite. Mr. Tatchell's main argument was that BDS was a nonviolent form of protest against Israel's occupation and settlement policies that mirrored the boycott campaign against apartheid South Africa and followed the principles of Mahatma Gandhi and Martin Luther King. He was articulate in arguing that boycott tactics generally were a nonviolent alternative to war and terrorism.

I argued that BDS was not an alternative to war but rather an alternative to peaceful negotiations by the Palestinian leadership. This is because the BDS campaign is firmly opposed to the two-state solution. Barghouti confirmed as much when he wrote and said, "Definitely, most definitely, we oppose a Jewish state in any part of Palestine." Thus, I argued that the BDS campaign makes it more difficult for the Palestinian leadership to accept the kind of painful compromise that both sides must agree to if there is to be a negotiated resolution.

Many liberal activists such as Mr. Tatchell—whose advocacy on behalf of LGBTQ rights I greatly admire—have made common cause with BDS, hoping to pressure Israel to end the occupation and afford greater self-determination to Palestinians in the West Bank. They seem to believe that a campaign advocating nonviolent tactics is the best way to achieve a lasting peace. But BDS itself is radically opposed to any negotiated settlement.

Mr. Tatchell and many pro-BDS academics also feel that Israel has committed human rights violations both in the occupation of the West Bank and in its prosecution of the armed conflict in Gaza. So, I issued the following challenge to the audience and to any opponent: name a single country in the history of the world that faces threats comparable to those faced by Israel but has a better record of human rights, of compliance with the rule of law and of seeking to minimize civilian casualties.

I invited the audience members to shout out the name of a country.

Complete silence. Finally, someone shouted "Iceland," and everyone laughed.

In the end, our case against BDS won by a significant majority.

Our side won not because of the comparative skill of the debaters—
Tatchell was superb—but because I was able to expose the moral
weakness of the BDS campaign itself.

Whenever I am protested at universities, I am accused of hav-
ing denied Norman Finkelstein his academic freedom. Finkelstein
was a popular anti-Israel speaker who traveled the country accusing
Israel of being worse than Nazi Germany. Protestors hand out leaflets
claiming that I was instrumental in getting Finkelstein fired from
DePaul University, which had denied him tenure. The claim was that
I opposed him because he had attacked my book *The Case for Israel*.
Here is what happened.

As soon as *The Case for Israel* hit the bestseller lists in 2003, Noam
Chomsky tasked his acolyte Finkelstein with attacking it, as Chomsky had tasked him with attacking other pro-Israel books. Finkelstein
then claimed in his writing and public appearances, quite absurdly,
that I hadn't even written or read the book. The implication was that
some Israeli intelligence agency wrote it and had me sign it. The problem for him is that I don't type or use a computer, so every word of the
text was handwritten by me—and I still have the original, handwritten manuscript. He then falsely claimed that I had plagiarized it.[11]

My first reaction was to ignore the attack, as I generally ignore the
numerous made-up stories about me that are common on neo-Nazi
and Holocaust-denial websites. For example, a story on a conspiracy
website Rense had accused me of murdering my first wife. It had
"photographs" of her and my children, but those depicted were not
my family members. Those in the image had stereotypical Jewish
faces with long noses and other "Jewish" characteristics. After receiving complaints, the site changed it, but it kept the accusations
that I had beaten my first wife, causing her to be hospitalized. Of
course, there was no truth to anything in the article, which can still
be found on the internet. Back to the false accusations of plagiarism,
I realized its underlying purpose was not so much directed at me as
it was at young, untenured academics who might consider writing or

speaking in support of Israel. Its goal was to send a powerful message to such academics that if you write in support of Israel, you, too, may be accused of plagiarism and fraud. Finkelstein and Chomsky knew they couldn't destroy me because I have the means to fight back, but they could deter others who lack such means. For an untenured assistant professor to be accused of such dishonesty could be an academic death sentence, even if the accusation was baseless. As Churchill once quipped, "A lie makes its way halfway around the world before the truth can get its pants on." And Churchill said this before the advent of the internet. Today a lie makes its way completely around the world, and the truth—which is often less interesting than the lie—makes it to the bottom of a Google search.

My response took two forms: one defensive and the other offensive. I asked Harvard to investigate the phony plagiarism charge, which they did and concluded it had absolutely no basis. Then I went after Finkelstein.

I decided that the best weapon to use against Finkelstein was his own words. Accordingly, I compiled and circulated a list of some of Finkelstein's most absurd statements about Israel and the alleged "international Jewish conspiracy" that supports Israel. I made my list available for distribution to pro-Israel activists on campuses at which Finkelstein was speaking.

Finkelstein has claimed that Israel's human rights record is worse than that of the Nazis. "[I] can't imagine why Israel's apologists would be offended by a comparison with the Gestapo." He said that Israel's human rights record is "interchangeable with Iraq's" when it was ruled by Saddam Hussein. He supports Hezbollah, an anti-Semitic terrorist group whose goal is to destroy Israel and commit genocide against the world's Jews, and which has repeatedly launched rocket attacks against Israel from its bases in Lebanon. "The honorable thing now is to show solidarity with Hezbollah as the U.S. and Israel target it for liquidation. Indeed, looking back, my chief regret is that I wasn't even more forceful in publicly defending Hezbollah against terrorist intimidation and attack." He also supported Gaddafi's Libya: "Libya had nothing to do with it [the blowing up of Pan Am 103, for which Libya has acknowledged responsibility] but they are playing along." He seemed to justify bin Laden's terrorism against the United States by saying, "We deserve the problem on our hands because some things bin Laden says are true."

Finkelstein has further argued that the international Jewish conspiracy is responsible for a raft of books and films that advance awareness of the Holocaust, including Steven Spielberg's movie *Schindler's List*, Leon Uris's book *Exodus*, Andrew Lloyd Webber's musical *Cats*, and the NBC series *Holocaust*. In Finkelstein's own words,

> *Who profits [from the movie]? Basically, there are two beneficiaries from the dogma: American Jews and the American administration.*
>
> *The name of the character [in Uris's novel* Exodus*] is Ari Ben Canaan because Ari is the diminutive for Aryan. It is the whole admiration for this blond haired, blue eyed type.*
>
> *In 1978, NBC produced the series* Holocaust. *Do you believe it was a coincidence, 1978? Just at this time, when peace negotiations between Israel and Egypt took place in Camp David?*

Nor are seemingly innocent productions above suspicion, such as Andrew Lloyd Webber's blockbuster musical *Cats*, based loosely on the book by T.S. Eliot (himself a notorious anti-Semite): "Some people think that *Cats* is a code word for K-A-T-Z, Katz."[12]

Finkelstein has also demeaned Holocaust survivors:

> *I'm not exaggerating when I say that one out of three Jews you stop in the street in New York will claim to be a survivor.*
>
> *"If everyone who claims to be a survivor actually is one," my mother used to exclaim, "Who did Hitler kill then?"*

According to the *Guardian*, "Finkelstein says . . . that most 'survivors' are bogus."

Along with these incriminating statements, I circulated a list of what other serious scholars had said about Finkelstein's writing, beginning with Peter Novick, the prominent University of Chicago historian who Finkelstein said had inspired him:

> *As concerns particular assertions made by Finkelstein . . . ,*
> *the appropriate response is not (exhilarating) "debate" but*
> *(tedious) examination of his footnotes. Such an examination*
> *reveals that many of those assertions are pure invention. . . .*
> *No facts alleged by Finkelstein should be assumed to be really*
> *facts, no quotation in his book [about the Holocaust] should*
> *be assumed to be accurate, without taking the time to carefully*
> *compare his claims with the sources he cites. Finkelstein's book*
> *is trash.*

The *New York Times* review of Finkelstein's book by the distinguished Brown University professor Omer Bartov characterized it as

> *a novel variation on the anti-Semitic forgery, "The Protocols of*
> *the Elders of Zion." There is also something indecent about it,*
> *something juvenile, self-righteous, arrogant and stupid.*
>
> *This book is, in a word, an ideological fanatic's view . . . by*
> *a writer so reckless and ruthless in his attacks. . . . [His theory*
> *is] both irrational and insidious. . . . An international Jewish*
> *conspiracy verges on paranoia and would serve anti-Semites.*

Finally, I showed how Finkelstein's work is relied on by neo-Nazis, citing the distinguished writer Gabriel Schoenfeld: "Crackpot ideas, some of them mirrored almost verbatim in the propaganda put out by neo-Nazis around the world."

As a result of my decision to fight back against Finkelstein's attack, I received a letter from Patrick Callahan, one of Finkelstein's colleagues in the DePaul political science department and its former chairman. Finkelstein was being considered for tenure at the time. Callahan invited me to submit a letter documenting "the clearest and most egregious instances of [intellectual] dishonesty on Finkelstein's part." This is part of what I wrote:

> *I would like to point out from the outside that the ugly and false assertions that I will discuss below are not incidental to Finkelstein's purported scholarship; they are his purported scholarship. Finkelstein's entire literary catalogue is one preposterous and discredited ad hominem attack after another. By his own admission, he has conducted no original research, has never been published in a reputable scientific journal, and has made no contributions to our collective historical knowledge . . . although he claims to be a "forensic scholar," he limits his defamations to one ideological group and never applies his so-called "forensic" tools to his own work or to those who share his ideological perspective. . . . That is not forensic scholarship; it is propaganda.*

After discussing his utter lack of any real scholarship, I focused on one particular article he had written about me titled "Should Alan Dershowitz Target Himself for Assassination?"[13] Finkelstein had collaborated with an artist to create a pornographic cartoon of me, masturbating in ecstasy as I watched Israeli soldiers murder Palestinian children. The cartoon aptly represented the content of Finkelstein's article, which accused me of being a "moral pervert." He called me a Nazi, saying that I subscribe to "Nazi ideology," and then he compared me to Nazi propagandist Julius Streicher.

I then proceeded to document a series of made-up quotations used by Finkelstein—quotes that simply didn't exist. These alone should have disqualified him from serious consideration at any university.

In the end, DePaul denied him tenure and fired him. This led Chomsky to escalate his attacks on me, calling me, in his writings and speech, a "maniac," a "supporter of atrocities" and a "passionate opponent of civil rights."

Finkelstein now travels the world—paid in part by Arab sources—attacking Israel, Jews, the United States, DePaul University and me. He visited Lebanon to show solidarity with Hezbollah, the terrorist group that killed hundreds of U.S. soldiers, Jewish children in Argentina and Israeli civilians. As a result of that trip, Israeli authorities prevented him from entering Israel—a decision that I publicly criticized. Lacking the academic imprimatur of a university, his hateful message is fading in the marketplace of ideas, although he still remains popular among left-wing extremists.

The line between extreme anti-Zionism and anti-Semitism often gets blurred, especially when the writer or speaker is Jewish, as Finkelstein and Chomsky are. Their hatred of all things Jewish is as old as Judaism itself. It defies rational, political or moral explanation and demands recourse to psychology. For those of us who are proud of being Jewish, though critical of some aspects of our faith, some of our co-religionists and some Israeli policies, these self-haters are particularly troubling because they give rise to a variation of the argument ad hominem—the fallacy of judging the merit of discourse or an argument by the person who is making it. I call the "self-hating Jew" variant of this fallacy the "argument by ethnic identification." It goes this way: "See, Chomsky is a Jew and if *he* admits that Israel is an Apartheid state, it must be so." It's an absurd argument, but commonly made by Israel-bashers.

Most anti-Zionist Jews try hard to distinguish between hatred of Israel and hatred of the Jewish people. But in the case of Gilad Atzmon—who was not only born Jewish but also Israeli—there is nothing blurry about the line he had crossed.

Atzmon has no academic credentials, but his popularity as a jazz musician has made him a popular anti-Israel speaker on campuses around the world.

In his book *The Wandering Who?* he boasts about "drawing many of my insights from a man who . . . was an anti-Semite as well as a radical misogynist" and a hater of "almost everything that fails to be Aryan masculinity." He declares himself a "proud, self-hating Jew," writes with "contempt" of "the Jew in me," and describes himself as "a strong opponent of . . . Jewishness." His writings, both online and in his book, brim with classic anti-Semitic motifs that are borrowed from Nazi publications.

Throughout his writings, Atzmon argues that Jews "do try to seek to control the world."

Atzmon expanded on this theme in *The Wandering Who?*, repeatedly conflating "the Jews" and "the Zionists." He has made the following claims:

- Calling the credit crunch "The Zio-punch," he says it was not "a Jewish conspiracy" because "it was all in the open."
- Paul Wolfowitz, Rahm Emanuel and other members of "the Jewish elite" remain abroad instead of moving to "Zion" because they "have proved far more effective for the Zionist cause by staying where they are."
- That Jews are evil and a menace to humanity.
- "With Fagin and Shylock in mind Israeli barbarism and organ trafficking seem to be just other events in an endless hellish continuum."
- "The Homo Zionicus quickly became a mass murderer, detached from any recognized form of ethical thinking and engaged in a colossal crime against humanity."
- If Iran and Israel fight a nuclear war that kills tens of millions of people, "some may be bold enough to argue that 'Hitler might have been right after all.'"
- Children should be allowed to question, as he did, "how the teacher could know that these accusations of Jews making Matza out of young Goyim's blood were indeed empty or groundless."

- "The Holocaust religion is probably as old as the Jews themselves."
- The history of Jewish persecution is a myth, and if there was any persecution the Jews brought it on themselves.
- "[I]n order to promote Zionist interests, Israel must generate significant anti-Jewish sentiment. Cruelty against Palestinian civilians is a favorite Israeli means of achieving this aim."
- "Jews may have managed to drop their God, but they have maintained goy-hating and racist ideologies at the heart of their newly emerging secular political identity. This explains why some Talmudic goy-hating elements have been transformed within the Zionist discourse into genocidal practices."
- The "Judaic God" described in Deuteronomy 6:10–12 "is an evil deity, who leads his people to plunder, robbery and theft." Atzmon explains that "Israel and Zionism . . . have instituted the plunder premised by the Hebrew God in the Judaic Holy Scriptures."
- The moral of the Book of Esther is that Jews "had better infiltrate the corridors of power" if they wish to survive.

Finally, Atzmon repeatedly declares that Israel is worse than the Nazis, and he has actually "apologized" to the Nazis for having earlier compared them to Israel:

> Too many of us including me tend to equate Israel to Nazi Germany. Rather often I myself join others and argue that Israelis are the Nazis of our time. I want to take this opportunity to amend my statement Israelis are not the Nazis of our time and the Nazis were not the Israelis of their time. Israel, is in fact far worse than Nazi Germany.

In light of this manifestly unhinged bigotry, it should come as no surprise that even some of the most hardcore anti-Israel activists have shunned Atzmon out of fear that his naked anti-Semitism will discredit their cause. Tony Greenstein, a self-styled "anti-Zionist," denounced *The Wandering Who?* as "a poisonous anti-Semitic tome." Sue Blackwell, who co-wrote the Association of University Teachers' motion to boycott Israeli universities in 2005, removed all links to Atzmon from her website. Socialist Worker, a website that frequently refers to Israeli "apartheid" and publishes articles with titles such as "Israel's Murderous Violence," removed an interview with Atzmon and called the evidence of Atzmon's anti-Semitism "damning." At least ten authors associated with *The Wandering Who?*'s leftist publisher have called on it to distance itself from Atzmon's views, explaining that the "thrust of Atzmon's work is to normalize and legitimize anti-Semitism."

Hardcore neo-Nazis, racists, anti-Semites and Holocaust deniers, on the other hand, have happily counted Atzmon as one of their own. David Duke, America's premier white supremacist, has posted more than a dozen of Atzmon's articles on his website, praising the author for "writ[ing] such fine articles exposing the evil of Zionism and Jewish supremacism." Israel Shamir, a Holocaust denier—who has said that "we must deny the concept of Holocaust without doubt and hesitation," argued that Jews ritually murdered Christian children for their blood, and proclaimed that "the rule of the Elders of Zion is already upon us"—refers to Atzmon as a "good friend" and calls him one of "the shining stars of the battle" against "the Jewish alliance."

But neither Atzmon's well-established reputation for anti-Semitism nor the copious anti-Semitic filth that fills *The Wandering Who?* has deterred Professors John Mearsheimer and Richard Falk from actively endorsing Atzmon's work.[14]

Mearsheimer, the Harrison Distinguished Service Professor of Political Science at the University of Chicago and a member of the American Academy of Arts and Sciences, calls *The Wandering Who?* a "fascinating" book that "should be read widely by Jews and non-Jews alike." Falk, Milbank Professor of International Law and Practice Emeritus at Princeton University and United Nations special rapporteur on "human rights in the Palestinian territories," calls *The Wandering Who?* an "absorbing and moving" book that everyone who "care[s] about real peace" should "not only read, but reflect upon and discuss widely."

Falk's endorsement appears prominently on the cover of Atzmon's book. Mearsheimer's endorsement is featured on its first page. These professors are not merely defending Atzmon's right to publish such a book, they are endorsing its content and urging their colleagues, students and others to read and "reflect upon" the views expressed by Atzmon. One wonders which portions of this bigoted screed Professors Mearsheimer and Falk believe their students and others "should" read and "discuss widely." Mearsheimer has defended his endorsement against attacks by me and others by questioning whether his critics have even read Atzmon's book. Well, I've read every word of it, as well as many of Atzmon's blog posts. No one who has read this material could escape the conclusion that Atzmon freely admits: his writings cross the line from anti-Zionism to crass anti-Semitism.

Yet a number of other prominent academics have defended Atzmon and his endorsers. Brian Leiter, the Llewellyn Professor of Jurisprudence at the University of Chicago Law School, dismissed the reaction to the book and to Mearsheimer's "straightforward" endorsement as "hysterical" and not "advanc[ing] honest intellectual discourse," though he acknowledges not having read Atzmon's book.

On the basis of having perused one brief interview with Atzmon, Leiter was nonetheless prepared to defend him against charges that he is an anti-Semite or a Holocaust denier. He should read the book before leaping to Atzmon's defense.

These endorsements of Atzmon's book are the best evidence yet that academic discourse is beginning to cross a red line, and this crossing must be exposed, rebutted and rejected in the marketplace of ideas and in the academy. Further evidence of this trend appeared recently on Atzmon's website, where he announces that he has been invited to "give a talk on ethics at the Trondheim University" in Norway despite his utter lack of credentials to discuss "ethics." This is the same university whose faculty refused to invite me to speak about the Arab–Israeli conflict when I gave several lectures in Norway in 2011 because Norman Finkelstein had already covered the subject!

I wrote op-eds challenging Professors Mearsheimer, Falk and Leiter to a public debate about why they have endorsed and said such positive things about such a hateful and anti-Semitic book by such a bigoted and dishonest writer. None of them responded.

Efforts by the hard left to demonize Israel and to isolate its Jewish supporters are beginning to spread to high schools, both private and public. The most extreme case occurred in 2012 at the Friends Seminary, a high school in New York City, which invited Atzmon to be a featured performer at a celebration of Martin Luther King.

It is not as if Friends Seminary was unfamiliar with Atzmon's anti-Semitic rants. Atzmon was previously invited to make a guest appearance in a class, and one of his essays was distributed to the students. The essay came from his website, which is replete with anti-Semitic "insights."

When I heard about this bizarre invitation, I wrote the following letter to the school's headmaster:

> *Your school is now legitimating anti-Semitism by inviting a self-described Jew hater, Gilad Atzmon, to participate in events at the school. This sends a powerful message to your students, and to other students around the world, that Atzmon's views are legitimate and an appropriate subject for discussion in academic circles.*
>
> *If you believe these views are appropriately discussed, considered and possibly accepted by your students, then you are doing the right thing by associating your school with the man who expressed them. If not, then you are doing a terrible disservice to your students and to the values for which the Friends School purports to stand.*

I cannot overemphasize how serious this matter is. Legitimating the oldest form of bigotry is a moral and academic sin. I cannot remain silent in the face of complicity with bigotry. Nor should you.

The headmaster did not respond, and Atzmon performed to honor a man—Martin Luther King—who despised anti-Semitism and would have been appalled by Atzmon's hateful words. Students cheered his performance and conversed with him.

I cannot imagine an overtly homophobic, sexist or racist musician being invited by any group in any way associated with Friends even if he was being invited because of his "musical accomplishments." (I hear that David Duke, the white supremacist, plays a mean saxophone. In a post, Atzmon said he would be willing to play alongside Duke. What a duet!)

Atzmon is famous (really, infamous) not because he is a distinguished musician but because he is a notorious anti-Semite whose blogs are featured on neo-Nazi websites all over the world. He never would have been invited but for his well-publicized bigotry.

Friends Seminary is well known for inviting artists whose politics and ideology are consistent with the values of the school. Indeed, the poster advertising his appearance included a description of him as a "writer" and "political activist."

The Friends Seminary, like other elite schools around the country, teaches our future leaders. Many Friends schools around the country have espoused strongly anti-Israel policies for years. The Friends Seminary in New York itself has a rabidly anti-Israel history teacher on its faculty who propagandizes his students against Israel in the classroom and who has a picture of Anne Frank wearing a Palestinian headdress on his website. The school has taken students on trips to the Middle East that present a one-sided perspective. Now they have crossed the line from preaching anti-Zionism to tolerating anti-Semitism. Parents, who complained to me, are afraid to complain to the headmaster out of fear that it would affect their children's college prospects.

The teaching and promoting of anti-Israel extremism that often morphs into anti-Semitism is an increasingly disturbing and dangerous phenomenon on many campuses around the world. Academic freedom requires that schools permit teachers to express bigoted views outside of the classroom.

Students and alumni claimed that anti-Semitic tweets by Columbia professor Hamid Dabashi created a "hostile environment," but because these statements were not made in the classroom, they were regarded as protected free speech. I support this freedom to be bigoted in public as long as the school applies the same standard to all forms of bigotry.

Students in a classroom, on the other hand, are a captive audience who are graded and recommended by teachers. Students, too, have academic freedom, which includes their right to express political views different from those of their teachers without suffering adverse consequences. Yet another Columbia professor reportedly refused to allow a student from Israel to speak in his class unless he first acknowledged that the Israeli army committed war crimes. Such censorship not only created a hostile environment but also clearly violated the student's right of academic freedom. Yet, Columbia did nothing about this professor's misuse of his classroom.

When academic departments—such as Brooklyn College's political science department and many departments at Berkeley and other universities—officially sponsor anti-Israel speakers and events but refuse to sponsor pro-Israel speakers and events, this double standard sends a frightening message to pro-Israel students: that their academic department has an official position different from theirs, and that this difference may influence their evaluations. This, too, raises concern about the academic freedom of students.

Universities, as institutions, must be scrupulously neutral with regard to controversial political issues about which students reasonably disagree. So must academic departments. The issue concerning individual teachers is more complex, requiring distinctions between in-class academic lectures and outside-of-class speeches or writings.

Whatever policies universities adopt with regard to teachers must pass "the shoe on the other foot" test: whatever a left-wing professor is permitted to say, write or do must be the same for a right-wing professor. Whatever the rules are for anti-Israel advocates must be identical for pro-Israel advocates.

Too few schools—colleges, universities or high schools—pass that test today.

One university that did take action against a bigoted professor was the University of Michigan, which disciplined and warned a professor who had agreed to recommend one of his students to a semester-aboard program, but when he found out that this student wanted to spend the semester studying in Israel, he refused to write the recommendation on the ground that it violated his commitment to BDS against Israel.

The battle being waged against the legitimacy of Israel on campuses threatens the future of the nation-state of the Jewish people. Israel has devised defenses—imperfect perhaps, but largely effective—against war, terrorism and even the threat of an Iranian nuclear attack. But neither the Israeli government nor its supporters around the world have come up with effective defenses against the massive propaganda campaign being directed against the crucial bipartisan support that is essential for Israel to maintain its military superiority, its international standing and its legitimacy as the nation-state of the Jewish people. Already, we are seeing erosion in support among the left wing of the Democratic Party.

The election to Congress of several young anti-Israel representatives in the 2018 election is only the latest manifestation of a decade-long trend in diminution of support for Israel among left-wing Democrats.

Congress now includes two Muslim women for the first time, a positive development. Unfortunately, both of these congresswomen, Ilhan Omar from Minnesota and Rashida Tlaib from Michigan, are supporters of BDS, as is the new darling of the hard left, Alexandria Ocasio-Cortez from New York.

On a panel on the Israeli–Palestinian conflict, Somali-born congresswoman Omar, who is now also a member of the Foreign Affairs Committee, said, "I want to talk about the political influence in this country that says it is okay to push for allegiance to a foreign country," essentially accusing American Jews of dual loyalty.

Not surprisingly, David Duke—the neo-Nazi Klansman—came out in support of Omar, calling her "the most important member of Congress" because of her "defiance to ZOG."[15] Those initials stand for "Zionist Occupied Government," which is Duke's description of the U.S. government. The anti-Semitic hard left and neo-Nazi hard right agree when it comes to Zionism and alleged Jewish influence.

After more of Omar's history of anti-Semitic remarks were revealed, House Democrats planned to vote on a resolution condemning anti-Semitism. The resolution was initially intended to be a rebuke of Omar. The text of the resolution, while not directly mentioning Omar, says that "the House of Representatives rejects the perpetuation of anti-Semitic stereotypes in the United States and around the world, including the pernicious myth of dual loyalty and foreign allegiance, especially in the context of support for the United States–Israel alliance." However, when the Black Caucus and Congressional Progressive Caucus questioned the Democratic leadership about why Omar was singled out when other minority groups felt they were under constant attack "in the age of Trump," the Democrats broadened the scope of the resolution and included text to condemn hateful expressions of "intolerance" against African Americans, Native Americans, Muslims, Hindus, Sikhs, immigrants and other people of color.

Contrast this with the reaction by the hard left to those who have suggested changing "Black Lives Matter" to "All Lives Matter." They called broadening the scope "offensive" and "racist."

As Donna Brazile, the former interim chair of the DNC, wrote, "Those who are experiencing the pain and trauma of the black experience in this country don't want their rallying cry to be watered down with a generic feel-good catchphrase." And yet, a "watered down" resolution with "generic feel-good catchphrases" should satisfy American Jews who feel more and more alienated by some leaders of the Democratic Party, who embrace radical identity politics and have a blind spot when it comes to Jewish issues.

Many centrist Democrats could not support Black Lives Matter because its leadership accused Israel of genocide. Others could not support the organizers behind the historic Women's March because its radical leaders called the virulent anti-Semite Louis Farrakhan the "greatest of all time." When Farrakhan was seated next to Bill Clinton at Aretha Franklin's memorial service, I wrote,

> *Liberals need to make unequivocally clear that the Democratic Party tent will never be big enough for anti-Semites and anti-Americans like Farrakhan, just as Republicans need to do the same with sympathizers of the alt-right. There are not "good people" on the side of anti-Semitism, any more than there are "good people" on the side of white supremacy.*
>
> *There is no place for a double standard when it comes to antisemitism. Black antisemitism should not get a pass on account of the oppression suffered by so many African Americans. Neither should "progressive" tolerance of antisemitism of the kind shown by Bernie Sanders backing Jeremy Corbyn, the anti-Semite leader of the British Labour Party who may well become the next prime minister of America's closest ally.*

And yet, many prominent members of the new progressive wing within the Democratic Party, such as Keith Ellison and Maxine Waters, have had close ties to Farrakhan, and too many within the Democratic leadership are unwilling to condemn and oust these anti-Semites from their ranks.[16]

Just as Republicans have a special obligation to condemn anti-Semitism and anti-Muslim attitudes from the far right, so too have

Democrats a special obligation to condemn anti-Semitism on the left, especially as anti-Semitism is on the rise worldwide.

The same is true of many in the media, especially on talk shows and social media that appeal to young viewers, many of whom do not read newspapers and thus get their "information" from these shows and websites. When Congresswoman Rashida Tlaib suggested that her Palestinian ancestors had "g[iven] up their livelihood, their human dignity to provide a safe haven for Jews" who survived the Holocaust, there was understandable criticism of her perversion of history. The Palestinian leadership had, in fact, done everything in its power to deny Jewish victims of the Holocaust "safe Haven." Their leader, Amin al-Husseini, had collaborated with Hitler to prevent Jews from leaving Nazi-occupied Europe and finding safe haven in Palestine. Once Israel was established, Palestinians attacked it in an effort to prevent Holocaust survivors from entering Israel. Yet when Tlaib was interviewed on several talk shows and on social media, she was not confronted with the truthful history of Palestinian opposition to giving safe haven to Holocaust survivors. Instead, she was thrown softball questions and her untruthful responses were greeted with applause from uninformed studio audiences, thus helping to mainstream her anti-Jewish bigotry, and her revisionist and false history.

Not enough is being done to marginalize these anti-Israel Democrats. But in early 2019, a group of prominent present and former Democratic lawmakers—some Jews, some not—was formed to counter what the *New York Times* reported was "alarm" about "the party's drift from the long-standing alignment with Israel" and the "rising skepticism on the left toward the Jewish State."[17] The group calling itself "the Democratic Majority for Israel" includes former Michigan governor (and my former student) Jennifer Granholm, former secretary of housing Henry Cisneros, Congressmen Hakeem Jeffries and Eliot Engel, Democratic operatives Ann Lewis and Mark Mellman and others. They will be supporting "candidates in 2020 who stand unwaveringly" with Israel.

These and other efforts—political, academic, economic, diplomatic, moral—must be deployed in opposition to those who would weaken bipartisan support for Israel. Supporters of Israel should never be reluctant to use U.S. power in the interest of justice. Despite its military strength, Israel remains the underdog in a world dominated by anti-Israel nations, as reflected by the repeated votes of the United Nations. It is in danger of losing the future as greater numbers of young, minority and left-wing people turn against Israel. The anti-Israel forces remain Goliath to Israel's David. The struggle to secure Israel's future must begin on the campuses, but it must not end there. The most powerful weapon in the court of public opinion—truth—must be deployed in every forum where lies are told in an effort to delegitimize the nation-state of the Jewish people. No attempt should be made to censor these lies or those who purvey them. Instead, they must be confronted, debated, corrected and discredited, as I have repeatedly tried to do. I hope to continue to participate in that important effort as long as I have the strength and capacity to speak truth to power. But efforts are underway to try to silence my voice on Israel. An extreme anti-Israel website called Mondoweiss decided to repeat a totally false and thoroughly disproved allegation of sexual misconduct by a woman I had never even met expressly in order to silence me. Here is what it said:

> We have picked up news about the sexual allegations against Dershowitz because Dershowitz is such an outspoken supporter of Israel and the matter has inevitably affected his influence in the foreign policy arena.

It doesn't matter to Israel haters whether the allegations are completely disproved, struck, withdrawn, mistaken and made up—as they were in this case—as long as it negatively impacts my ability to defend Israel. I will continue to fight back against these and other anti-Israel motivated defamations.

Conclusion

Israel—The Next 70 Years

I COMPLETED THE first draft of this memoir 70 years after I first became passionate about the nation-state of the Jewish people, and then began to think about the next 70 years. I decided to travel to Israel for perhaps the 100th time in the last half-century. My pleasure was greatly enhanced by bringing my grandson with me. Lyle, who had recently graduated from college and would soon start medical school, had never been to Israel. Three years earlier I had established this "tradition" by bringing my granddaughter, Lori, to Israel shortly after she graduated. (She, too, is in medical school.) It had been the first trip for her as well.

It was both fascinating and educational for me to see how differently this generation of young people perceives Israel. For them, Israel was not a poor nation, living simply off agriculture and scrounging for weapons with which to defend itself against the mighty armies committed to its destruction that surrounded it. For my grandchildren, Israel is an economic and military superpower, a startup nation whose technological innovations are the envy of the world. Gleaming skyscrapers had replaced the run-down British colonial buildings I witnessed when I first visited Israel. To be sure, my grandchildren knew from having attended college that Israel was also a pariah nation among many on the hard left, especially in academia. They came to Israel with the skepticism that characterizes many millennials raised in secular households and who attended elite colleges. They came to see for themselves and decide for themselves. They knew that their grandfather was a zealous advocate for Israel, though critical of its settlement and occupation policies. They didn't want to be influenced by my ideas, and I know them well enough to understand that any attempt to influence them would backfire.

During my trip with my grandson, we attended the opening of the new U.S. embassy that had just relocated from Tel Aviv to Jerusalem. My grandson had mixed reactions to that event, because it appeared at times like a Republican campaign rally attended primarily by Orthodox Jews, Christian fundamentalists and other assorted right-wingers. Former senator Joe Lieberman and I were the only prominent Democrats seated in places of honor near the front. The event itself was historic, and Lyle understood that he was a witness to both history and controversy. Following the event, we had long and serious conversations about its significance.

That was the only somewhat political event we attended during the 10-day visit. I met with Prime Minister Netanyahu, as I always do when I travel to Israel, but Lyle preferred to wander the streets of Tel Aviv rather than meet my friend Bibi. When I told the prime minister of my grandson's preference, he laughed and said, "Smart kid. I would love to be walking the streets of Tel Aviv myself."

We covered the length and breadth of the tiny country, which Lyle found hard to believe was approximately the size of New Jersey. We were taken inside a terror tunnel built by Hamas under the fence separating Gaza from Israel. We went to a military command center where young female soldiers were each assigned to monitor several hundred yards of the border fence. We discussed with military commanders the options the army has in trying to prevent infiltrators from crossing the border and threatening the Israeli civilians. We both wondered why Israel could not do a better job of avoiding civilian casualties. The commanders explained that they had tried to use sonar devices, teargas, power hoses, rubber bullets and foul-smelling chemicals. None of these nonlethal tactics succeeded in keeping potential terrorists armed with Molotov cocktails, guns and knives from breaking through the fence and attacking nearby civilian targets. Hamas had provided any potential lynch mob with Google Maps coordinates showing the fastest routes from the fence to Jewish kibbutzim, schools and daycare centers. We still wondered whether Israel could do a better job, though we were not as certain that there were viable alternatives.

From the south, we traveled north to the Golan Heights and Israel's border with Syria, Lebanon and Jordan. We flew over the Golan Heights in a helicopter piloted by a former IDF air force officer. At the border fence, we were briefed by the head of the northern command. While we were being briefed, we could see puffs of smoke in the distance and hear the sound of rockets. A few days earlier, these rockets and missiles were aimed at Israel by Iranian forces, but Israel had retaliated and destroyed most of the Iranian rocket launchers. So we were not in danger. But the Iron Dome, which had destroyed the rockets that had crossed into Israel, was visible just yards away from where we were briefed, with its multiple rockets aimed in the direction of Syria in the event that any new missiles approached Israeli territory. We understood why Israel could never turn the Golan Heights over to Syria, who would once again use it as a launching pad for rockets targeting Israeli civilians. It would be as if a nation at war returned a battleship captured from its enemy. (I used this analogy in advocating U.S. recognition of Israel's annexation of the Golan Heights to President Trump.)

We were then taken by my associate Danny Grossman—who had been in both the U.S. and Israeli air forces—to an air force base where Lyle was permitted to "fly" an F15 simulator. He was told he would make a great pilot. When I tried the simulator, I was told to keep my day job. We were then shown a fleet of Israeli drones capable of surveillance as well as bombing. We met with young pilots Lyle's age who flew on missions every day. We were told that there are now more Israeli women flying combat missions in the Israeli air force than there are Saudi women driving cars (although this may now be changing). Lyle had interesting talks with his contemporaries about what it means to risk one's life to protect one's nation and its civilians. Lyle was deeply impressed with the commitment of these pilots, many of whom were active in the peace movement in their spare time. These are warriors who understand the price of war and the benefits of peace.

Lyle loved Jerusalem, especially the juxtaposition of ancient and modern. We went into the tunnels under the Western Wall, and Lyle went through the tunnels in the ancient city of David. We walked through the shuk and along the Via Dolorosa into the Church of the Holy Sepulchre, home to different Christian faiths. We ascended the Temple Mount, where Lyle was forced to put on a "dress" to cover his shorts. We walked up to but not into the two great Muslim holy places: the Al-Aqsa Mosque and the Dome of the Rock. We saw a replica of what the Jewish temple may have looked like when it stood proudly on the Temple Mount.

Lyle is not at all religious, having been raised in a completely secular household. But he was moved by the display of faith evident to anyone who ascends the Temple Mount and then descends to the plaza adjoining the Western Wall. We left notes in the wall, knowing full well that they would never be read. It's a tradition, and traditions have a power of their own regardless of one's belief, disbelief or agnosticism. (I subsequently wrote an op-ed "Confessing" to committing a "war crime" by putting a note in the "unlawfully occupied" Western Wall.)

One of the highlights of our visit was a trip on the back of an ambucycle of United Hatzalah, an Israeli medical rescue organization. By using these ambucycles—high-tech motorcycles that serve as mobile first-responder ambulances—this organization manages to reach anywhere in Israel in about 90 seconds. Its volunteer first-responders speed all over Israel, including the West Bank. Its volunteers include Orthodox Jewish men and women, Christians, secular Jews and Muslims, and everyone else who forms part of the Israeli mosaic. It is an amazing organization, and I have even helped contribute an ambucycle to it. We went to the tech center and watched as accidents showed up on the screen and the nearest volunteers were directed to the victims. It's a perfect marriage of Israel's commitment to high technology and the saving of lives.

Lyle and I ascended Masada, the mountaintop retreat of the remnants of the Jewish community in the first century CE that was destroyed by the Romans. When I first ascended in 1970, it took three hours to hike up the winding road in 100-degree temperature. This time it took five minutes in a funicular. But the impact was still powerful as we saw how the Jews struggled to survive and then chose death over slavery and rape. I bought Lyle a Masada medal with the iconic message that Masada will never fall again—that the nation-state of the Jewish people will never again be put in the position of having to choose between death and slavery.

We visited the Holocaust Museum, which documents an era in which Jews didn't have that choice. Even those who were slaves were murdered. Even those who had converted to Christianity were gassed. Even those who were too young to know they were Jews were subjected to genocide. Lyle was deeply moved by the feeling of helplessness that forced Jews into ghettos and then into extermination camps or death marches. We discussed our own family, many of whom were murdered by the Nazis, including a 17-year-old girl and her 15-year-old brother. I told Lyle the story of my grandfather—his great-great-grandfather—Louis Dershowitz, related briefly in chapter 1, who helped rescue 29 members of our family by securing affidavits, mostly false, from neighbors offering them nonexistent "jobs." They had tried to get visas, but they were rebuffed, like so many other Jews, by the anti-Semitic policies of Roosevelt's State Department. So my grandfather, who lived in the Williamsburg section of Brooklyn, went to neighbors and told them that each of their basements would now become synagogues and they would sign affidavits falsely stating that their "synagogue" needed a rabbi, cantor, sexton, rebetzin, mohel or other religious functionary.

In this way, my grandfather managed to get visas for 28 out of 29 family members who left Czechoslovakia just before the Nazis entered and murdered its Jewish population. But one relative, a teenage girl who was studying the violin in Poland, was left behind. My family wouldn't give up on her, and so my grandfather sent his oldest unmarried son, Milton, into the belly of the beast, Nazi-occupied Poland, to "marry" young Anna. They performed a fake marriage, and they were able to get her out of Poland with his American passport (recall that the United States was not yet at war with Germany). While on the ship returning to America, my uncle actually fell in love with Anna, and they were married shortly after they reached the Statue of Liberty.

Lyle was deeply impressed by the bravery, illegal as it was, of his great-great-grandfather. I could see that Lyle—like his great-great-grandfather, his grandparents and his parents—was determined never to allow an event like the Holocaust to be perpetrated against any group of human beings.

We had fun while in Israel as well. Lyle swam—or rather floated—in the Dead Sea. He rappelled down a 100-foot cliff—as his sister had earlier done—scaring the heck out of his grandfather. We drove through barren deserts, mountain roads, archeological sites and ordinary cities and towns. Lyle was enthralled by the diversity of life in Israel, ranging from the most religious to the most secular, the whitest northern Europeans, blackest Ethiopian Africans, brownest Arabs and swarthiest Persians, as well as multiethnic survivors of Soviet oppression.

Experiencing the difference between religious, traditional, ancient Jerusalem and modern, super-secular, high-tech Tel Aviv is like being in two very different countries. Both of us love architecture, and we admired the Bauhaus district of Tel Aviv as well as the ancient walls and edifices of Jerusalem.

This trip to Israel with my grandson closed a circle for me. This circle began in 1948 with the establishment of the country, my summer in Zionist Hebrew Camp and my support for the new nation-state of the Jewish people. The circle closed with me, as an 80-year-old elder statesman, seeing the love—albeit mixed with skepticism—that my grandson showed toward the same nation 70 years later and nearly 50 years after I first set foot on its soil. This visit coincided with the completion of the first draft of this memoir reflecting on 70 years of passionate, if sometimes critical, support of Israel. It was a fitting end—a trip I will never forget. But Israel's circle of life is never closed. Every year brings new, often unpredictable, challenges. The Talmud says that prophecy ended with the destruction of the Second Temple, and anyone who tries to predict the future is either a knave or a fool. With that caution in mind, I will end this volume by asking what can be done to secure Israel's future, and by suggesting some answers.

The world has benefited in countless ways from the establishment of Israel. I take enormous pride in the indisputable reality that no nation in history, certainly none as tiny as Israel, has contributed more to humankind in so short a period of time as Israel has since its birth only seven decades ago. It has saved countless lives though its medical, pharmaceutical, genetic, agricultural, environmental and other scientific and technological innovations. As the "startup nation," it has contributed disproportionately to the communications revolution. It has revived a dormant language of prayer, turning it into a vibrant spoken and written modern language and literature. It has shown the world how to integrate, though of course not perfectly, immigrants and refugees from Morocco, Algeria, Tunisia, Yemen, Egypt, Iraq, Iran, Syria, Ethiopia, the former Soviet Union and countries in other far-flung corners of the world. It has taught democracies how to fight terrorism while upholding the rule of law. It has prevented Iraq and Syria from developing nuclear arsenals that would have endangered the Middle East and beyond. It has transitioned from a local agrarian subsistence economy into a world-class economic superpower, without reliance on vast natural resources. It has also transitioned its military from a small civilian self-defense force that relied on primitive weapons to one of the world's most powerful and technologically sophisticated armed forces.

Along the way, it has made its share of mistakes, as have all other democracies, especially those facing existential threats.[1] But on balance, Israel has been the most successful new nation that has been born—really reborn—during the past century.[2] Moreover, its "birth certificate" has been more "legitimate" than other nations, which were born of violence, the drawing of colonial maps or coups d'état. Perhaps because so many of Israel's founders were trained in the law, they made sure, like the patriarch Abraham before them, that they secured legal title to the land that became Israel. This legal title was composed of both private and public contracts, treaties, declarations, resolutions and recognitions. Much of the land that the United Nations allocated to a Jewish state in 1947 had already been purchased from absentee landlords at fair market value by the Jewish National Fund and other groups and individuals.

Israel was founded by the pen, though it had to be defended by the sword. Imagine how much more good it could accomplish if its enemies allowed it to turn its swords into plowshares, its nuclear weapons into nuclear medicine.

And yet, despite its lawful birth certificate, and its unparalleled contributions to humankind since its birth, and its successful efforts to defend itself within the rule of law,[3] it is the *only* nation in the world whose legitimacy as a nation is questioned—by other nations, by academicians, by international organizations and even by some "religious" leaders. One powerful nation in particular, Iran, has called for its physical annihilation by military force. This call has been echoed by numerous terrorist organizations, such as Hamas, Hezbollah and ISIS. More than 30 other nations refuse to recognize Israel or establish diplomatic relations with it. Until 1993, this included the Vatican, which only recently changed its view. Several

Protestant denominations, whose leaders routinely demonize the nation-state of the Jewish people, have supported BDS.

Why? Certainly it cannot be because every other nation of the world is more deserving of recognition or diplomatic relations than Israel. Certainly it cannot be because the Palestinians have a more compelling case for statehood than, say, the Kurds. But even if they did, the Palestinians rejected numerous deals that would have accorded them statehood. Even more compelling, recognizing statehood for the Palestinians is not incompatible with recognizing statehood for the Israelis.

Neither is it because Israel receives U.S. aid. So does Egypt, Jordan, the Palestinian Authority, Pakistan and many other nations with horrendous human rights records that are not subjected to the opprobrium to which Israel is regularly subjected.

There is no doubt in my mind that if Israel were not the nation-state of the Jewish people, its actions—indeed is very existence—would not be challenged by the double standards for which it has been judged from even before its birth. In the first place, the Arabs and Muslims would not be as opposed to a non-Jewish state in its midst as they are to a Jewish state. When Lebanon was a hybrid state—divided between Muslim and Christian Arabs—there was far less opposition to the Christian components, one of which was even a Christian president. Even if Lebanon had been divided into two states, one Christian and one Muslim, there would not have been as much opposition to a small Christian state as to a small Jewish one. Nor is it only because both states would have been Arab. Morocco has a substantial non-Arab population, and neither Iran nor Turkey is Arab. According to some Islamic "scholars," even an inch of Muslim land is prohibited from becoming a Jewish state.

Moreover, the world at large, outside of the Muslim Middle East, has always applied a double standard to all matters Jewish. They demand more of a Jewish state than they would of a non-Jewish state. As the bigoted Bishop Tutu acknowledged, Jews are a "peculiar people" who "can't ever hope to be judged by the same standards which are used for other people."[4] Whether this is a theological mandate or simply a cover for anti-Semitism, it is a widespread view among some Christians. How else can the Vatican's long delay in recognizing Israel be explained? The Holy See, which traditionally has more diplomatic relations than most Western countries, refused to recognize the nation-state of the Jewish people until 1993, claiming that the existence of a Jewish state would create a backlash for Christians in Arab countries.

Then there is the role that intersectionality currently plays in the double standard applied to Israel, especially by hard-left academics, students and activists.

Zionism and Jews are accused of being universal oppressors, and the oppressed must stick together to struggle against the oppressors.[5] It's a zero-sum game. So if you are among the oppressed, you can't also be an oppressor. And if you are an oppressor, you cannot be regarded as an ally of the oppressed, even if you are trying to help them. Thus, you cannot be both a Zionist (oppressor) and a feminist (oppressed) or a supporter of gay rights (oppressed) or civil rights (oppressed activist). But if you are a feminist leader of the Women's March or a black supporter of Black Lives Matter, then you get a pass for also supporting an anti-Semite like Louis Farrakhan or the anti-Semitic platform of Black Lives Matter.

It is important not to overstate (or understate) the role that Israel's Jewish character plays in the way it is treated. Criticism of Israel's actions or policies is not anti-Semitic. If it were, the greatest concentration of anti-Semites would be in Tel Aviv! But focusing only on imperfections of the nation-state of the Jewish people is bigotry, pure and simple. As Thomas Friedman has aptly put it:

> *Criticizing Israel is not anti-Semitic, and saying so is vile. But singling out Israel for opprobrium and international sanction— out of all proportion to any other party in the Middle East—is anti-Semitic, and not saying so is dishonest.*

Criticism of Israel is not only *not* anti-Semitic, it is healthy, as long as it doesn't violate my friend Anatoly Sharansky's "three Ds":

The first "D" is the test of demonization. When the Jewish state is being demonized; when Israel's actions are blown out of all sensible proportion; when comparisons are made between Israelis and Nazis and between Palestinian refugee camps and Auschwitz—this is anti-Semitism, not legitimate criticism of Israel.

The second "D" is the test of double standards. When criticism of Israel is applied selectively; when Israel is singled out by the United Nations for human rights abuses while the behavior of known and major abusers, such as China, Iran, Cuba, and Syria, is ignored; when Israel's Magen David Adom, alone among the world's ambulance services, is denied admission to the International Red Cross—this too is anti-Semitism.

The third D is the test of delegitimization: when Israel's fundamental right to exist is denied—alone among all peoples of the world—this, too, is anti-Semitism.

As it begins its eighth decade, Israel remains in a complex situation, its future unpredictable. It has never been stronger—militarily, economically and even diplomatically. But the potential threats it faces from growing anti-Israel sentiment among young left-wingers has rarely been greater. There are also military threats, especially from Iran, which has sworn to wipe Israel off the face of the earth.[6] Its leaders have said that if they were to acquire a nuclear arsenal and bomb Tel Aviv then that would be the end of Israel, because "Israel is a one-bomb state," requiring only a single nuclear bomb to defeat.[7] In 2004, it was reported that the former president of Iran, Hashemi Rafsanjani, a supposed moderate, had "boast[ed] to an American journalist that] if Iran were to develop nuclear weapons and use them to attack Israel, they "would kill as many as five million Jews."

He estimated that even if Israel retaliated by dropping its own nuclear bombs, Iran would probably lose only 15 million people, which he said would be a small "sacrifice" from among the billion Muslims in the world. The journalist said that Rafsanjani seemed pleased with his formulations. He later elaborated on his boast by stating, "The dropping of one atomic bomb would not leave anything in Israel"; however, an Israeli nuclear retaliation would just produce damages in the Muslim world. This "moderate" former present of Iran continued, "It is not irrational to contemplate such an eventuality."[8]

In other worlds, the "not irrational" calculation being contemplated by at least some Iranian leaders is that since Israel is a "one-bomb country," most of whose population (presumably including its 20 percent Arab population) would be killed by one bomb, and since Iran is a far larger country and part of the enormous "Muslim world," the tradeoff might be worth it, especially to an apocalyptic regime that was prepared to sacrifice hundreds of thousands of its citizens—including thousands of child "soldiers"—in a futile war with Iraq. Would not such a regime equally be willing to sacrifice millions of its citizens to achieve its major political and religious imperative, namely the annihilation of the nation-state of the Jewish people, and with it nearly half the world's Jewish population?

For those who believe the United States would never let such a new Holocaust occur, remember the one important lesson Elie Wiesel learned from the Holocaust: "Always believe the threats of your enemies more than the promises of your friends."

Israel lives by that historic reality. Its leaders will almost certainly act to prevent Iran from acquiring nuclear weapons, even if it has to act alone and with great risk to its armed forces. Moreover, the risk would extend to its civilian population as well, since Hezbollah, which is controlled by Iran, has tens of thousands of sophisticated rockets aimed at Israeli cities, towns, airports and military facilities. A war with Iran—even one in which Israel managed to destroy Iran's nuclear capacity—would be catastrophic, but it may be necessary if Iran seeks to develop a nuclear arsenal after the current deal expires.

Containment of a nuclear Iran is not an option Israel can accept. A preventive war, with all the consequences that entails, would be the only option if Israel's intelligence concluded that Iran was close to developing a nuclear arsenal, since Iran already has the capacity to deliver nuclear-tipped rockets to Israeli targets.

Such a cataclysmic confrontation may be unlikely, but it is certainly possible, and Israel is planning for this contingency now.

Were Israel to engage in a preventive war against Iran's nuclear facilities, it would be condemned by the international community, as it has been in the past. It would be condemned—as it always has been—because the world would never see the number of lives saved by such an action, as it will never see the lives saved by Israel's destruction of the nuclear facilities that were being constructed by Iraq and Syria.

While analogies are always imperfect, it may be instructive to imagine how the world would have reacted if Great Britain and France had waged a preventive war against Nazi Germany in the mid-1930s, when the Nazis were building the war machine with which they soon were to conquer much of continental Europe and kill 50 million people, including tens of millions of civilians. Assume that a preventive war directed against the German military would have cost 10,000—or even 100,000—lives. The world would have seen those dead bodies and would have condemned the "aggressors" for the costs in human lives they incurred in order to prevent the possibility that Hitler might carry out the threats he had made in *Mein Kampf* and in his speeches. Had a preventive war stopped Hitler from carrying out those threats, the world would never have seen the lives saved by the preventive war carried out by Britain and France.

History is dumb as to future probabilities or possibilities. It knows only what did happen, not what might have happened if a different course had been followed. Any leaders of Britain and France who had engaged in a preventive war that cost thousands of lives then and saved millions in the future would have been condemned by the verdict of dumb history because the costs would have been visible, but the savings would have been invisible.

The same would be true of any Israeli (or American) leader who engaged in a costly preventive war to avert Iran from securing a nuclear arsenal. The world would see the visible costs but not the invisible benefits. Great statesmen and stateswomen must be prepared to incur condemnation for making bold, lifesaving decisions whose benefits may never become visible to history. I told this to Benjamin Netanyahu during one of our many dinner conversations. He looked at me soberly and said, "I only hope I never have to make that decision."

Another threat faced by Israel, this one in the longer term, is the diminishing support for the nation-state of the Jewish people by young Americans, especially on the left. Until recently, this diminution of support could be seen primarily on the extreme hard left, especially among university faculty, some students and radical activists. This was not terribly concerning, since these fringe groups have little direct impact on American policy. This tactic of seeking universities and corporations to divest from or boycott Israel was failing. Not a single major university or major corporation had divested or boycotted. (When the Hampshire College faculty voted to divest from Israel, I began a campaign among alumni donors to divest—to stop contributing to Hampshire. The president immediately rescinded the faculty vote.) But the tactic succeeded in alienating some on the center left from Israel. It also succeeded in making it "politically incorrect" to be a Zionist. The result has been a diminution of support for Israel among young centrists. This does not always take the form of overt opposition to Israel; more often, it reflects itself in a lack of concern regarding Israel. It is simply easier not to take sides on the Israeli–Palestinian issue, because taking either side incurs a cost in popularity, acceptability and, some believe, even academic standing.

The result has been a hardening of sides: the anti-Israel groups have become more strident and extreme, causing the pro-Israel groups to become more defensive. The large middle of students and others for whom Israel is not a priority has expanded. One reason for this is the shrill demands of "intersectionalists," who say that one cannot be a Zionist and a feminist, gay rights activist, civil rights advocate, environmentalist or other "do-gooder." So those who wish to be accepted as do-gooders by the intersectionalists are coerced or persuaded to abandon their Zionism, or at least make it less visible.

I am proud that my children and grandchildren do not adhere to either extreme. Their support of Israel is critical, nuanced, calibrated and issue-oriented. They may be less passionate than I am and less committed, but they are equally dedicated to justice, fairness and truth. No one could ask for more.

This diminution of support for Israel among current students threatens the bipartisan support for Israel that has long been a staple of American politics. Recent polls suggest a growing disparity between Republicans and Democrats in their support of Israel. This is especially apparent among young Democrats. The electoral victories of three overtly anti-Israel congressional candidates may not be representative of Democratic voters, but it surely is a sign of the changing times.[9]

Today's students and young people are our future leaders, and the current diminution in support for Israel among young Democrats and "progressives" poses dangers to the future of bipartisan support for the nation-state of the Jewish people. These young people did not experience the Holocaust, the difficult birth of Israel, its wars for survival and its heroic actions to defend itself from genocidal threats. What they have seen is the long occupation, the growth in settlement activities, wars of choice, civilian deaths repeatedly shown on television, and a wealthy and powerful Israel confronted by weak Palestinians.

Whenever I speak about Israel—whether in the United States, Israel, Europe, New Zealand, Australia, Qatar or South Africa—I am asked whether I am pessimistic or optimistic about the prospects for peace in the Middle East. I respond by illustrating the difference between an Israeli pessimist and an Israeli optimist. A pessimist says, "Oy, things are so bad, they can't possibly get worse." An optimist replies, "Yes, they can!"

No supporter of Israel, especially a Jew, can ever be a total optimist. There are too many contingencies, too many uncertainties, too many variables, too much history, too much optimism followed by tragedy.

Consider Weimar Germany or socialist France in the 1920s. Life was generally good for the Jews, especially secular and assimilated Jews. To be sure, residual anti-Semitism did exist, but not like in prior decades when German writer Wilhelm Marr had coined the term anti-Semitism as a positive political program, or when the Dreyfus Affair in France, beginning in 1894 and culminating in 1906, uncovered massive anti-Semitism among artists, priests, military leaders and ordinary French citizens. But middle-class and professional Jews—lawyers, professors, politicians, businessmen, doctors, scientists—in the 1920s were overcoming the exclusionary bigotry of the past and rising to the top of their callings.

Then a series of extremely unpredictable contingencies occurred, beginning with the First World War in 1914. No one wanted that war, but an isolated event in an obscure part of the Balkans knocked down a domino that led to an all-out conflict that changed the world forever. Its impact on Jewish life, though unpredictable at the time, was the most profound in two millennia: the destruction of European Jewry and the creation of the modern state of Israel. Neither is likely to have occurred without the First World War.

The defeat of Germany, the humiliation of the Versailles Treaty and massive inflation and unemployment led directly to the rise of Hitler. The destruction of the Ottoman Empire and the defeat of the Turks by the British in Palestine led—at least indirectly—to the Balfour Declaration, the British Mandate over Palestine and the division of that mandate by the United Nations into proposed Jewish and Arab states.

No one during the first quarter of the twentieth century could have predicted (Theodor Herzl came close) these and other unlikely contingencies that led to the Holocaust and the creation of Israel—the two most dramatic events in modern Jewish history. Yet these events occurred. We are now in the first quarter of the twenty-first century. Once again, the future looks bright for the Jewish people and their nation-state. But once again, there are too many contingencies that make optimistic predictions too uncertain to count on. Cautious optimism, coupled with thoughtful preparation for pessimistic outcomes, is the best we can do.

The existence of Israel, with its powerful armed forces that include a nuclear arsenal, makes a repetition of the tragic events of 1939–1945 unlikely. History never repeats itself, because we generally learn its lessons and take steps to prevent precise repetition. But variations on the past are common, as Hitler noted when he said that no one remembers the Turkish genocide of the Armenians.

Jews and supporters of Israel must be prepared for all contingencies, all variations on the past, and all future threats, no matter how unlikely they seem today.

The best way to prepare for an unpredictable contingency is to be ready for the worst while trying to achieve the best. The Jewish people and their nation-state must be strong—materially, morally and psychologically. National strength includes an Israeli armed forces qualitatively superior to all the combined Arab and Muslim armed forces. It also includes political power disproportionate to our numbers. The Israeli lobby in the United States—AIPAC—is accused of being too strong. I think it is not strong enough. Jewish supporters of Israel are accused of being too wealthy and spending too much money to influence American support for Israel. I think they spend too little money to support Israel. Jews are accused of having disproportionate influence in newspapers, television, Hollywood, the news media and other forms of communication. Yet we are losing the communications war. We must do better.

Another tragic lesson of the Holocaust is that Jews and Jewish institutions need disproportionate power to survive. We are small in number, but the hatred against us looms large. Having morality on our side is essential, but it is not sufficient.

The Jews who died in the Holocaust had morality on their side, but it was not enough to protect them against the overwhelming material forces arrayed against them. History has demonstrated that Jews must be prepared to defend themselves—militarily, politically, economically and in every other way. We should try to make and maintain alliances with friends, without ever counting on those friends to come through in the crunch.

Millennia ago, the psalmist wrote, "God will give the Jewish People strength." He then continued, "God will bless the Jewish people with peace."

I interpret that verse to mean that for the Jewish people and their state, strength must precede peace. Without overwhelming strength, they will never experience peace, because they have too many enemies threatening their destruction. The Jews of Europe lacked strength. They relied on governments—some openly hostile, others promising support to prevent the threat of their enemies from materializing. The threats materialized but the promises did not. The lesson must be learned, lest deadly variations on the tragic past become the future.

Back in 1948, no one could have imagined, and certainly could not have accurately predicted, what Israel would be like seven decades in the future. Nor would it have been possible to predict who Israel's most dangerous enemies would be. Early in its history, Israel had good relations with Iran and Turkey and terrible relations with Egypt, the Gulf States and Jordan. Today the situation is somewhat reversed.

Back in 1948, the Democratic Party and the left were the strongest supporters. The Republican Party and the right were far less so. Today the situation is reversed.

Back in 1948, Israel was a socialist, agrarian, Ashkenazi (European heritage), secular society. The right, the religious and the Sephardim were relegated to the margins, both politically and socially. Today the situation is reversed.

Back in 1948, Soviet Jews were the "Jews of Silence," as Elie Wiesel had called them, living under communist repression. Today, they are among Israel's most productive citizens—initiators of the "startup nation."

The future of the Jewish people and its state is promising, but success—indeed survival—is not assured in a world in which enmity toward Jews and their state has been one of the few historical constants. History is not destiny. History is past. Destiny is future. The future is largely, though not exclusively, in our hands. We must determine our destiny, write our future history, and assure the survival of the Jewish people and their nation-state forever.

Acknowledgments

This book could not have been completed without the assistance of my associates and assistants Aaron Voloj and Hannah Dodson, who were primarily responsible for the end notes and research. Thanks to Adam Bellow for his excellent editorial suggestions; to my agent, Karen Gantz, for making it happen; to my assistant Maura Kelley for managing the manuscript; to Alan Rothfeld for proofreading; to other friends and family for their gentle criticisms; and to my wife, Carolyn, for her loving encouragement of everything I do.

Notes

Introduction

1. Patrick Kingsley, "Anti-Semitism Is Back, from the Left, Right, and Islamist Extremes. Why?" *New York Times*, April 4, 2019, https://www.nytimes.com /2019/04/04/world/europe/antisemitism-europe-united-states.html.

2. Brian Klug, "The Myth of the New Anti-Semitism," *The Nation*, June 29, 2015, https://www.thenation.com/article/myth-new-anti-semitism/.

3. "Behold the people, the children of Israel, are more numerous and stronger than we. Come, let us outsmart it lest it become numerous, and it may be that if a war will occur, it, too, may join our enemies . . ." (Exodus 1:9–10). So the pharaoh ordered the Jewish people enslaved and every male baby killed.

4. "There is a certain people scattered abroad and dispersed among the people . . . , and their laws are diverse . . . therefore, it is not for the king's profit to suffer them" (Esther 3:8).

5. Rabbi Lionel Blue, interview, BBC Radio 4.

6. Quoted in Alan Dershowitz, *The Case Against BDS: Why Singling Out Israel for Boycott Is Anti-Semitic and Anti-Peace* (e-book; New York: Post Hill Press, 2018), 57.

7. Alan Dershowitz, *The Case Against Israel's Enemies: Exposing Jimmy Carter and Others Who Stand in the Way of Peace* (e-book; Hoboken, NJ: John Wiley & Sons), 4.

8. "Is BDS Wrong?" Oxford Union debate, November 2015.

9. Dershowitz, *Case Against Israel's Enemies*, 11.

10. C-SPAN, "Cornel West and Alan Dershowitz Mideast Debate," December 1, 2017, https://www.c-span.org/video/?437547-1/cornel-west-alan-dershowitz -mideast-debate.

11. Dershowitz, *Case Against BDS*, 5.

12. Dershowitz, *Case Against BDS*, 5–6.

13. "Activism," *Forward*, November 14, 2003.

Chapter 1

1. Much of the land was bought from distant land speculators in Syria and other locations. "For dozens of years, the Blue Box served as a fundraiser in every Diaspora home and every Jewish institution in Israel and abroad: A cherished, popular means to realize the Zionist vision of establishing a state for the Jewish people." "The Blue Box," Keren Kayemeth LeIsrael Jewish National Fund, http://www.kkl-jnf.org/about-kkl-jnf/the-blue-box/ (accessed February 15, 2019).

2. Land was purchased, primarily, from absentee landlords and real estate speculators at fair or exorbitant prices. See Alan Dershowitz, *The Case for Israel* (New York: John Wiley and Sons, 2003), 25.

3. Ben-Gurion instructed the Jewish refugees never to buy land belonging to local "fellahs or worked by them." Shabtai Teveth, *David Ben-Gurion and the Palestinian Arabs* (New York: Oxford University Press, 1985), 32.

4. There were some Jewish anti-Zionists, even back then. They were primarily aristocratic German Jews who rejected the concept of Judaism as nationalism in addition to religion. There were also some ultraorthodox rabbis and their followers who opposed the secular Jewish state on religious grounds, but both of these groups constituted a small minority within the Jewish community.

5. Dershowitz, *The Case for Israel*, 76.

6. The initial strategy of the Arab armies was the targeting of civilians via "major urban terrorist attacks." The Arab armies also repeatedly and deliberately dropped bombs on civilian population centers near no legitimate military targets. See Dershowitz, *The Case for Israel*, 76.

7. CSPAN, "Cornel West and Alan Dershowitz Mideast Debate," December 1, 2017.

8. See, e.g., Eric Fripp, *Nationality and Statelessness in the International Law and Refugee Status* (Oxford: Hart Publishing, 2016). "Population transfers used to be accepted as a means to settle ethnic conflict."

9. Dershowitz, *The Case for Israel*, 86–87.

10. "To be a colonial country you have to be working on someone's behalf. The Jews who came to Palestine to join their brothers and sisters who had been there for 3000 years came from Russia. . . . The word *colonial* simply doesn't fit an indigenous movement that started with people who lived in countries around the world but who had relatives and coreligionists living in Tzvat," C-SPAN, "Cornel West and Alan Dershowitz Mideast Debate," December 1, 2017.

11. Shibley Telhami, "Americans Are Increasingly Critical of Israel," *Foreign Policy*, December 11, 2018, https://foreignpolicy.com/2018/12/11/americans-are-increasingly-critical-of-israel/.

12. Immanuel Kant, *Anthropology from a Pragmatic Point of View*. Trans. by Victor Lyle Dowdell (Carbondale: Southern Illinois University Press, 1978), paragraph 46.

13. Dershowitz, *The Case for Israel*, 41.

14. "British Palestine Mandate: History & Overview," Jewish Virtual Library, https://www.jewishvirtuallibrary.org/history-and-overview-of-the-british-palestine-mandate (accessed April 13, 2019).

15. Dershowitz, *The Case for Israel*, 65.

16. Several years ago, I wrote to the president of Holy Cross University, urging him to consider changing the name of the University's athletic teams from the "Crusaders," because the actual crusaders were genocidal murderers. I received a curt denial. Dershowitz, *The Case Against Israel's Enemies*, 158.

17. United Nations, "Chapter 2: The Plan of Partition and End of the British Mandate," in *The Question of Palestine and the United Nations*, 2003, https://www.un.org/Depts/dpi/palestine/ch2.pdf.

18. Today there are upward of two million Arabs living in Israel. Bernard Wasserstein, "The Partition of Palestine," Foreign Policy Research Institute, December 9, 2014, https://www.fpri.org/article/2014/12/the-partition-of-palestine/; "Israeli Arabs: Status of Arabs in Israel," Jewish Virtual Library, https://www.jewishvirtuallibrary.org/the-status-of-arabs-in-israel (accessed April 13, 2019).

19. Some Israelis argue that Jordan is the Palestinian state, since it was originally part of the Palestine Mandate and its population is predominantly Palestinian. This doesn't account for the rights of Palestinian Arabs who now live on the West Bank, which Jordan formally ceded to the Palestinian Authority in 1988. United Nations, "Chapter 2: The Plan of Partition and End of the British Mandate."

20. Sari Nusseibeh, "What Next?" *Haaretz*, January 10, 2018, https://www.haaretz.com/1.5346415.

21. Nusseibeh, "What Next?"

22. See Benny Morris, *1948 and After: Israel and the Palestinians* (Oxford: Clarendon Press, 2003); Avi Shlaim, "The War of the Israeli Historians," *Annales* 59, no. 1 (Jan./Feb. 2004): 161–167.

Chapter 2

1. Shortly after the establishment of Israel, hundreds of thousands of Sephardic and Mizrahi Jews left their homes in the Muslim world. Many were forced or pressured to leave. Dershowitz, *The Case for Israel*, 59. 140,000 Holocaust survivors from Europe immigrated to Israel as well. United States Holocaust Memorial Museum, "Jewish Refugees During and After the Holocaust," My

Jewish Learning, February 10, 2017, https://www.myjewishlearning.com
/article/jewish-refugees-during-and-after-the-holocaust/.

2. P. R. Brahmananda, "The Impact on India of Population Transfers in 1947 and After," in *Economics of International Migration*, B. Thomas, ed. (London: Macmillan, 1958).

3. The end of World War II marked the largest population transfers in the history of Europe. Huge numbers of people fled communist regimes while millions of Germans were forced out of Eastern Europe. Bernard Wasserstein, "History: World Wars: European Refugee Movements After World War Two," BBC, February 17, 2011. http://www.bbc.co.uk/history/worldwars/wwtwo/refugees_01 .shtml.

4. In a 2011 interview with Israel's Channel 2 News, Palestinian president Mahmoud Abbas said in reference to the Palestinian rejection of the UN Partition plan, "I know, I know. It was our mistake. It was our mistake. It was an Arab mistake as a whole." Dan Williams, "Abbas Faults Arab Refusal of 1947 U.N. Palestine Plan," Reuters, October 28, 2011, https://www.reuters.com/article /us-palestinians-israel-abbas/abbas-faults-arab-refusal-of-1947-u-n-palestine -plan-idUSTRE79R64320111028.

5. Eliezer Ben Yehuda is largely credited with the revival and modernization of Hebrew in the late nineteenth and early twentieth centuries. He created a modern Hebrew vocabulary and dictionary and was largely responsible for introducing Hebrew into the Israeli school systems. Melissa Weininger, "No. 2882: Eliezer Ben Yehuda," *Engines of Our Ingenuity*, May 10, 2013, https://www.uh .edu/engines/epi2882.htm.

6. Dershowitz, *The Case for Israel*, 156.

7. In response to the question of how many Jews should be admitted to Canada, this official said, "None is too many." Irving Abella and Harold Troper, *None Is Too Many: Canada and the Jews of Europe, 1933–1948* (Toronto: University of Toronto Press, 2012); Ellen Umansky, "Closing Our Doors," *Slate*, March 8, 2017.

8. "West Bank," *Encyclopedia Britannica*, https://www.britannica.com/place /West-Bank (accessed April 13, 2019).

9. "Palestine Liberation Organization," *Encyclopedia Britannica*, https://www .britannica.com/topic/Palestine-Liberation-Organization.Goal of PLO (accessed April 15, 2019).

10. Guy Ziv, "Shimon Peres and the French-Israeli Alliance, 1954–1959," *Journal of Contemporary History* 45, no. 2 (2010): 406–429, http://www.jstor.org/stable /20753593.

11. Alan M. Dershowitz, *Preemption: A Knife That Cuts Both Ways* (New York: W. W. Norton, 2007), chapter 3.

12. Dershowitz, *Preemption*, chapter 3.

13. "As Egyptian President Nasser himself boasted, 'We knew the closing of the Gulf of Aqaba meant war with Israel . . . the objective will be Israel's destruct.'" Dershowitz, *The Case for Israel*, 91–92.

14. Dershowitz, *The Case for Israel*, 91.

15. John R. Crook, "Dean Acheson and International Law," *Proceedings of the Annual Meeting, American Society of International Law* 95 (2001): 118–121, http://www.jstor.org/stable/25659468.

16. "Middle East: Timeline: The Suez Crisis," BBC News, July 19, 2006, http://news.bbc.co.uk/2/hi/middle_east/5194576.stm.

17. John Misachi, "What Was the Suez Crisis?" World Atlas, March 20, 2017, https://www.worldatlas.com/articles/what-was-the-suez-crisis.html.

18. Recently, my cousin Idan Dershowitz, who is a junior fellow at Harvard, wrote a brilliant op-ed in the *New York Times* demonstrating that the prohibition against gay sex in Leviticus may not be as absolute as widely believed. This led some anti-Israel conspiracy theorists to argue that I had put my "son" up to writing a pro-gay article as part of Israel's pinkwashing project.

19. Deborah E. Lipstadt, *The Eichmann Trial* (New York: Schocken, 2011), 179–181.

20. Judy Maltz, "Bobby Kennedy's Little-Known Visit to Israel That Led to His Assassination," *Haaretz*, June 8, 2018, https://www.haaretz.com/us-news/bobby-kennedy-s-israel-visit-that-led-to-his-assassination-1.6153324.

21. Joseph Kennedy Sr. was a staunch isolationist at the outset of World War II and backed Chamberlain's appeasement policy. He also had a strong relationship with Joseph McCarthy and was one of his major financial supporters.

22. Felix Frankfurter met warnings from Polish diplomat Jan Karski about Nazi brutality throughout Poland with disbelief. See Alan Dershowitz, *Chutzpah* (New York: Touchstone, 1991), 279–283.

Chapter 3

1. "Why Do Criminal Attempts Fail? A New Defense," *Yale Law Journal* 70, no. 1 (1960): https://digitalcommons.law.yale.edu/cgi/viewcontent.cgi?article=8810&context=ylj; "Increasing Community Control over Corporate Crime: A Problem in the Law of Sanctions," *Yale Law Journal* 71, no. 35 (1961); Jay Katz, Joseph Goldstein and Alan Dershowitz, *Psychoanalysis, Psychiatry and the Law* (New York: Free Press, 1967).

2. Michael Oren, "The Revelations of 1967: New Research on the Six-Day War and Its Lessons for the Contemporary Middle East," *Israel Studies* 10, no. 2 (2005): 1–14.

3. Simon Dunstan and Peter Dennis, *The Six-Day War, 1967: Jordan and Syria* (London: Osprey Publishing, 2013), 19.

4. Michael B. Oren, *Six Days of War* (London: Penguin, 2003), 132.

5. It is estimated that around 15,000 Palestinians, many of whom were civilians, were killed by Jordan during Black September, when Arafat and the PLO were expelled from Jordan. Rafael Reuveny, "Black September," *Encyclopedia Britannica,* https://www.britannica.com/topic/Black-September-political-organization-Palestine (accessed August 9, 2018).

6. See, e.g., Uri Friedman, "What Obama Meant By '1967 Lines' and Why It Irked Netanyahu," *The Atlantic,* October 30, 2013, https://www.theatlantic.com/international/archive/2011/05/what-obama-meant-1967-lines-why-irked-netanyahu/350925/.

7. See, for example, "About Israel," Israel Ministry of Foreign Affairs, https://mfa.gov.il/MFA/AboutIsrael/Spotlight/Pages/50-years-ago-The-Six-Day-War-and-the-historic-reunification-of-Jerusalem.aspx (accessed April 16, 2019).

8. Dershowitz, *The Case for Israel,* 205.

9. There was a dispute over a small area near Eilat. Both parties agreed to arbitration. Egypt won, and Israel turned over that land. Alan Cowell, "Israel Gives Disputed Resort to Egypt," *New York Times,* March 16, 1989, https://www.nytimes.com/1989/03/16/world/israel-gives-disputed-resort-to-egypt.html.

10. *Security Interests,* April 2002; Arthur Goldberg, "What Resolution 242 Really Said," *American Foreign Policy Interests* (vol. 1, February 1988).

Chapter 4

1. Daniel S. Levy, "Behind the Protests Against the Vietnam War in 1968," *Time,* January 19, 2018, http://time.com/5106608/protest-1968/.

2. Alan Dershowitz, *Taking the Stand* (New York: Crown Press, 2013), 144.

3. Dershowitz, *Taking the Stand,* 144

4. *Rudolph v. Alabama,* 375 U.S. 889 (1963).

5. Evan Mandery, *A Wild Justice: The Death and Resurrection of Capital Punishment in America* (New York: W. W. Norton Company, 2014).

6. Arthur J. Goldberg and Alan M. Dershowitz, "Declaring the Death Penalty Unconstitutional," *Harvard Law Review* 83 (1970).

7. Dershowitz, *Taking the Stand,* 5.

8. *Newsweek,* June 1978.

9. Shimon Peres, *David's Sling: The Arming of Israel* (Great Britain: Weidenfeld and Nicolson, 1970).

10. Marketwired, "Alan Dershowitz Presents a Powerful Case for Israel's Just War on Terrorism in New Book Terror Tunnels," *Yahoo! Finance,* September 15, 2014, https://finance.yahoo.com/news/alan-dershowitz-presents-powerful-case-172030723.html.

Chapter 5

1. Under the U.S. Initial Post-Surrender Policy in Japan, Allied forces were focused on promoting democracy in Japan and de-militarizing the country. In the Allied-occupied West Germany, the U.S. undertook a project of de-Nazification, as well as an economic/aid plan known as the Marshall Plan.

2. Mary G. Gotschall, "Berrigan, Chomsky Discuss Activism During Open Panel," *Harvard Crimson*, April 26, 1976. For Chomsky's assessment of me, see Noam Chomsky and David Barsamian, *Chronicles of Dissent, Interviews of Noam Chomsky by David Barsamian* (Monroe, ME: Common Courage Press, 2002).

3. I then discussed Shahak's charge that Israel was a racist country:

   > Shahak's approach is well illustrated by the content of his interview. He calls Israel "racist" because it designates its residents by their religion. Most countries in the world, of course, do the same thing. Every Arab country draws distinctions between Moslems and non-Moslems. Indeed, even Lebanon, probably the most liberal of Arab countries, explicitly requires certain of its high officials to be Moslems and others to be Christian (Jews—even anti-Zionist Jews like Dr. Shahak—are excluded from attaining these offices). Other Arab countries exclude all non-Moslems from office, and from other important privileges and rights. There are no such exclusions under Israeli law. A Muslim, a Druze, or a Christian could, theoretically, become prime minister of Israel; and many non-Jews do, in fact, hold high office nationally as well as locally. Most countries in the world—and every single Arab country—could learn a great deal from Israel's handling of its minority population.
   >
   > Of course, Israel is a Jewish country. In a world with numerous Moslem, Catholic and Protestant countries, why should there not be one country where Jewish values and culture predominates? As long as there is no discrimination against other minorities, Israel's Jewishness is to be applauded not condemned.

   Alan Dershowitz, "Shahak, Best Proof of Freedom of Speech," *Boston Globe*, April 29, 1973, 5; Noam Chomsky, "In Defense of Shahak," *Boston Globe*, June 5, 1973, 18.

4. Chomsky, "In Defense of Shahak," *Boston Globe*, June 5, 1973.

5. Robert Faurisson, *The "Problem of the Gas Chambers," Or, "The Rumor of Auschwitz"* (Reedy, WV: Liberty Bell Publications, 1979).

6. I did an extensive critique of Faurisson's "findings" in *Chutzpah* (New York: Touchstone, 1991), 174–176.

7. Robert Faurisson and Noam Chomsky, *Memoire en Defense: Contre Ceux Qui Maccusent De Falsifier L'histoire: La Question Des Chambres a Gaz* (Paris: Vieille Taupe, 1980).

8. Alan Dershowitz, "Chomsky Defends Vicious Lie as Free Speech," *Boston Globe*, June 13, 1989.

9. Faurisson and Chomsky, *Memoire en Defense*.

10. The last of our debates can be viewed on YouTube: "Dershowitz vs. Chomsky Debate Israel at Harvard," YouTube, posted January 4, 2012, https://www.youtube.com/watch?v=3ux4JU_sbB0.

11. I tell the story of this case in detail in *The Best Defense* (New York: Vintage, 1982). See also, *U.S. v. Huss*, 482 F2d 38 (2d. Cir. 1973).

12. Telford Taylor, *Courts of Terror: Soviet Criminal Justice and Jewish Emigration* (New York: Knopf, 1976).

13. Dershowitz, *Chutzpah*.

14. David M. Halbfinger, "From Jewish Saint, to Israeli Politician, to Diaspora's Ally," *New York Times*, June 29, 2018, https://www.nytimes.com/2018/06/29/world/middleeast/natan-sharansky-interview.html.

15. I tell the story of my work in this movement more fully in my books *The Best Defense* and *Chuztpah*.

Chapter 6

1. David B. Green, "The Day in Jewish History, 1973: Moshe Dayan Allegedly Suggests Israel Demonstrate Its Nuclear Capacity," *Haaretz*, October 7, 2016.

2. Ralph Blumenthal, "Daniel Berrigan's Speech to Arabs Stirs a Furor over Award," *New York Times*, December 16, 1973.

3. For a discussion of my role in criticizing the Lawyers Guild, see Dershowitz, *Taking the Stand*, 435.

4. It would be 16 years before this bigoted resolution was rescinded.

Chapter 7

1. Quoted in Dershowitz, *Preemption*.

2. Benn, Aluf, "Where First Strikes Are Far From the last Resort," *Washington Post*, November 10, 2002.

3. David Lauterborn, "1983 Beirut Barracks Bombing: The BLT Building Is Gone!" HistoryNet, February 13, 2019, https://www.historynet.com/1983-beirut-bombing-the-blt-building-is-gone.htm.

4. Aharon Barak, Yitzhak Kahan, and Yona Efrat, *The Beirut Massacre: The Complete Kahan Commission Report* (New York: Karz-Cohl Publishing, 1983).

5. Alan M. Dershowitz, "For A P.L.O. Inquiry," *New York Times*, October 17, 1982.

6. Alan M Dershowitz, *Why Terrorism Works: Understanding the Threat, Responding to the Challenge* (Carlton North, Vic.: Scribe, 2003).

7. I was also threatened by a Polish extremist who was angry that I was suing Cardinal Józef Glemp of Poland (see *Chutzpah*). He drove to my house with a baseball bat intending to bash in my head.

Chapter 8

1. I wrote about Vanessa Redgrave in Dershowitz, *Taking the Stand*, 170–176.
2. "Redgrave Is At It Again," *Jewish Telegraph*, November 4, 1980. In more recent years, Redgrave has apparently changed her stance to supporting a two-state solution.
3. Margaretmirren1, "Vanessa Redgrave," YouTube, January 12, 2009 (accessed April 24, 2019. https://www.youtube.com/watch?v=4yKQSMIrGQk).
4. "Redgrave Defends P.L.O. Film," *New York Times*, November 11, 1977 (accessed April 24, 2019. https://www.nytimes.com/1977/11/11/archives/new -jersey-weekly-redgrave-defends-plo-film.html).
5. In recent months, I have defended President Donald Trump's civil liberties, despite accusations that he has denied civil liberties to immigrant families. I have been criticized for this, but I have been doing it since I was a college student, defending the right of communists to speak.
6. The debate can be viewed on YouTube: "Rabbi Kahane Debates Alan Dershowitz Part 1," YouTube, posted May 27, 2015, https://www.youtube.com/watch?v =gAY6vdGV2_4.
7. Paul Hofmann, "Protests from U.S. Jews Stir Controversy in Israel," *New York Times*, June 21, 1979.
8. Hofmann, "Protests from U.S. Stir Controversy in Israel."

Chapter 9

1. Dershowitz, *The Case for Israel*, 72
2. Jonathan A. Greenblatt, "It's Time to Call Out Campus Anti-Semitism by Both the Left and the Right," *Washington Post*, October 26, 2018, https://www .washingtonpost.com/opinions/its-time-to-call-out-campus-anti-semitism -by-both-the-left-and-the-right/2018/10/26/344f0de8-d89b-11e8-a10f -b51546b10756_story.html?utm_term=.5cd6c864a8d4.
3. Haim Shapira, "The Law of Pursuer (Rodef) in Talmudic Sources," Academia .edu, https://www.academia.edu/6228030/The_Law_of_Pursuer_Rodef_in _Talmudic_Sources (accessed April 14, 2019).

Chapter 10

1. Dershowitz, *The Case for Peace*, 36.
2. Elaine Sciolino, "Self-Appointed Israeli and Palestinian Negotiators Offer a Plan for Middle East Peace," *New York Times*, December 2, 2003.

3. Quoted in Dershowitz, *The Case for Peace*, 29.

4. See Dershowitz, *The Case Against Israel's Enemies*, 69.

5. Dershowitz, *The Case for Israel*, 207.

6. Dershowitz, *The Case Against Israel's Enemies*, 39.

7. Stuart E. Eizenstat, *President Carter: The White House Years* (New York: St. Martin's Press, 2018).

8. U.S. Congress, H. Res. 1361, Congress.gov, September 23, 2008, https://www .congress.gov/110/bills/hres1361/BILLS-110hres1361eh.pdf.

9. "Leading International Voices on the 2001 Durban NGO Forum," UN Watch, October 27, 2008, http://blog.unwatch.org/index.php/2008/10/27/leading -international-voices-on-the-2001-durban-ngo-forum/.

10. "Palestinian Campaign for the Academic and Cultural Boycott of Israel," BDS Movement, July 28, 2017, https://bdsmovement.net/pacbi.

11. Dershowitz, *The Case Against BDS*, 8.

12. Maureen Clare Murphy, "Boycotts Work: An Interview with Omar Barghouti," The Electronic Intifada, February 12, 2017, https://electronicintifada.net/content /boycotts-work-interview-omar-barghouti/8263.

13. Dershowitz, *The Case Against Israel's Enemies*, 44–46.

14. Zack Beauchamp, "The Matisyahu Israel Boycott Controversy, Explained," *Vox*, August 19, 2015, https://www.vox.com/2015/8/18/9173239/matisyahu-bds.

15. Maureen Clare Murphy, "Boycotting Israeli Settlement Products: Tactic vs. Strategy," The Electronic Intifada, February 12, 2017, https://electronicintifada .net/content/boycotting-israeli-settlement-products-tactic-vs-strategy/7801.

16. Dershowitz, *The Case for Israel*, 56.

17. Dershowitz, *The Case Against BDS*.

18. Alan Dershowitz, "Ten Reasons Why BDS Is Immoral and Hinders Peace," *Haaretz*, February 12, 2014.

Chapter 11

1. "Kadima," *Encyclopedia Britannica*, https://www.britannica.com/topic/Kadima (accessed April 14, 2019).

2. Charles Krauthammer, "Moral Clarity in Gaza," *Washington Post*, July 17, 2014, https://www.washingtonpost.com/opinions/charles-krauthammer-moral -clarity-in-gaza/2014/07/17/0adabe0c-0de4-11e4-8c9a-923ecc0c7d23_story .html?utm_term=.bc9072b9a0d9.

3. Alan Dershowitz, *Terror Tunnels: The Case for Israel's War Against Hamas* (New York: Rosetta Books, 2014); Alan Dershowitz, *The Case for Moral Clarity: Israel, Hamas and Gaza* (Camera, 2009).

4. "Honorary Doctorate Recipients," Bar Ilan University, https://www1.biu.ac.il /en-about_doctorate (accessed April 14, 2019).

Chapter 12

1. Alex Lockie, "Israel Admits It Took Out a Syrian Reactor in 2007—and It May Have Prevented a Nuclear ISIS," *Business Insider*, March 21, 2018, https://www.businessinsider.com/israel-2007-syria-reactor-strike-prevented-nuclear-isis-2018-.

2. Jack Khoury, Noa Landau, and Ruth Schuster, "Hezbollah Reveals New Details on Kidnapping That Sparked Lebanon War with Israel," *Haaretz*, January 10, 2018, https://www.haaretz.com/israel-news/hezbollah-reveals-new-details-on-kidnapping-that-sparked-lebanon-war-with-israel-1.5418293.

3. As the result of material obtained by Grossman, the *New York Times* presented a much fairer assessment of Hezbollah's use of civilian shields.

4. Alan Dershowitz, "The Case Against the Goldstone Report: A Study in Evidentiary Bias," Harvard Law School, January 27, 2010.

5. Much of that rebuttal appears in my book *The Case Against Israel's Enemies*.

6. See, for example, Steven Erlanger, "A Gaza War Full of Traps and Trickery," *New York Times*, January 10, 2009; Yaakov Katz, "Hamas Used Almost 100 Mosques for Military Purposes," *Jerusalem Post*, March 15, 2010; and "Evidence of the Use of the Civilian Population as Human Shields," Intelligence and Terrorism Information Center at the Israel Intelligence Heritage and Commemoration Center, February 4, 2009.

7. Dershowitz, "The Case Against the Goldstone Report."

8. "Col. Kemp to UN Gaza Session: 'Hamas Seeks Destruction of Israel and Murder of Jews Everywhere,'" UN Watch, May 20, 2018, https://www.unwatch.org/col-kemp-un-gaza-session-hamas-seeks-destruction-israel-murder-jews-everywhere/.

9. "Ehud Olmert Fast Facts," CNN, October 3, 2018, https://www.cnn.com/2013/09/19/world/meast/ehud-olmert-fast-facts/index.html.

10. Josef Federman, "Abbas Admits He Rejected 2008 Peace Offer from Olmert," *Times of Israel*, November 19, 2015, https://www.timesofisrael.com/abbas-admits-he-rejected-2008-peace-offer-from-olmert/.

Chapter 13

1. Alan Dershowitz, "Why I Support Israel and Obama," *Huffington Post*, November 17, 2008.

2. See Dershowitz, *Taking the Stand*, 460.

3. Israel is testing new technologies that could help locate the tunnel routes and exit points. See, for example, Inna Lazareva, "Israel Tests Hi-Tech Tunnel Detection System to Fight Threat from Underground," *Jaffa Telegraph*, July 23, 2014.

4. "Iron Dome: How Israel's Missile Defense System Works," *This Week*, August 1, 2014.

5. "Report: Hamas Planned Rosh Hashanah Attack Through Gaza Tunnels," Jewish Telegraphic Agency, July 28, 2014, citing the newspaper *Maariv* and "security sources."

6. Melanie Lidman, "They Thought It Was Rockets They Had to Be Scared Of," *Times of Israel*, August 6, 2014.

7. Alan M. Dershowitz, "The Case for President's Obama Reelection," *Jerusalem Post*, October 30, 2012.

8. Alan M. Dershowitz, "Obama's Legacy and the Iranian Bomb," *Wall Street Journal*, March 23, 2010, https://www.wsj.com/articles/SB100014240527487 04869304575110042827617582.

9. Cristina Marcos, "House Rejects Obama's Iran Deal," *The Hill*, February 1, 2016. https://thehill.com/blogs/floor-action/house/253370-house-rejects-iran-deal.

10. Alan M. Dershowitz, *The Case Against the Iran Deal: How Can We Now Stop Iran from Getting Nukes?* (New York: Rosetta Press, 2015).

11. Alan M. Dershowitz, "The Consequences of Not Vetoing the Israel Resolution," *Boston Globe*, December 27, 2016.

Chapter 14

1. Jacqueline Thomsen, "Dershowitz to Trump: End Policy Separating Immigrant Families at Border," *The Hill*, June 18, 2018, https://thehill.com/blogs/blog-briefing-room/news/392749-dershowitz-to-trump-end-policy-separating-immigrant-families-at.

2. "Alan Dershowitz Publishes Letter Defending Netanyahu," *Jerusalem Post*, February 28, 2019, https://www.jpost.com/Israel-News/Alan-Dershowitz-publishes-open-letter-to-A-G-defending-Netanyahu-581888.

Chapter 15

1. Florian Eder, "Anti-Semitism in EU Worse over Last 5 Years, Survey," *Politico*, December 10, 2018; "Anti-Semitism in EU Worse over Last 5 years," ADL Global 100, https://global100.adl.org/#map (accessed May 20, 2019).

2. It is impossible to know the precise number of Palestinian civilians killed, because many were "civilians" who engaged in terrorist acts.

3. Josef Federman, "Pro-Palestinian Groups at CUNY Blame 'Zionists' for High Tuition," *Times of Israel*, November 12, 2015, https://www.timesofisrael.com/pro-palestinian-groups-at-cuny-blame-zionists-for-high-tuition/.

4. @HamidDabashi (Hamid Dabashi), "Every dirty treacherous ugly and pernicious act . . ." Twitter, May 8, 2018, 2:02 a.m., https://twitter.com/hamiddabashi/status/993778247799361536?lang=en. These tweets have since been deleted.

5. "War on Nature: How Zionist Colonialism Has Destroyed the Environ-ment in Palestine," *Middle East Monitor*, February 11, 2019, https://www.middleeastmonitor.com/20190211-war-on-nature-how-zionist-colonialism-has-destroyed-the-environment-in-palestine/.

6. Alan M. Dershowitz, "Bishop Tutu Is No Saint When It Comes to Jews," Gate-stone Institute, December 20, 2010.

7. "War on Nature," *Middle East Monitor*.

8. Alan M. Dershowitz, "The Torture Warrant: A Response to Professor Strauss," Heinonline, 2003, https://heinonline.org/HOL/LandingPage?handle=hein.journals/nyls48÷= 17&id=&page=.

9. Alan Dershowitz, "The Newest Abuse Excuse for Violence Against Women," *Huffington Post*, September 19, 2005.

10. Alan Dershowitz, "How Amnesty International Suppresses Free Speech," *Jerusalem Post*, November 11, 2014.

11. See Alan Dershowitz, *The Case for Peace*, "Chapter 16: A Case Study in Intimi-dation."

12. Anthony Julius, "The Poetry of Prejudice," *The Guardian*, June 6, 2003.

13. Norman Finkelstein, "Should Alan Dershowitz Target Himself for Assassination?" Counter Punch, January 26, 2016, https://www.counterpunch.org/2006/08/12/should-alan-dershowitz-target-himself-for-assassination/. For the sources of Finkelstein's quotations, see Dershowitz, *The Case Against Israel's Enemies*.

14. See Alan Dershowitz, "Why Are John Mearsheimer and Richard Falk Endors-ing a Blatantly Anti-Semitic Book?" *New Republic*, November 4, 2011. See also, "No Place for Atzmon at SW.org," SocialistWorker:org (accessed, May 21, 2019); "Mearsheimer Responds to the Latest Smears on Him . . ." Leiter Re-ports: A Philosophy Blog, https://leiterreports.type.pad.com/blog/2011/09/mearsheimer-reponds-to-the-latest-right-wing-smears-on-him.html.

15. Alyssa Fisher, "David Duke Defends Ilhan Omar from Anti-Semitism Accu-sations," *The Forward*, February 11, 2019, https://forward.com/fast-forward/419150/ilhan-omar-david-duke-aipac-zionist-antisemitic-kkk/.

16. I even threatened to leave the Democratic Party if Keith Ellison, the darling of this so-called progressive wing, were elected to head the Democratic Party. He lost in a close vote. See, e.g., Alan Dershowitz, "I Will Leave Democratic Party, If Keith Ellison Is Elected DNC Chairman," *Newsmax*, February 24, 2017.

17. Jonathan Martin, "Prominent Democrats Form Pro-Israel Group to Counter Skepticism on the Left," *New York Times*, January 29, 2019, https://www.nytimes.com/2019/01/28/us/politics/democrats-israel-palestine.html.

Conclusion

1. Dershowitz, *The Case for Israel*, 172.

2. Shoshanna Solomon, "From 1950s Rationing to Modern High-Tech Boom: Israel's Economic Success Story," *Times of Israel*, April 18, 2019, https://www.timesofisrael.com/from-1950s-rationing-to-21st-century-high-tech-boom-an-economic-success-story/.

3. Larry D. Thompson, "Fighting Terrorism, Preserving the Rule of Law," Brookings, July 29, 2016, https://www.brookings.edu/on-the-record/fighting-terrorism-preserving-the-rule-of-law/.

4. Barry Shaw, "Archbishop Tutu, Revisit Israel," *Jerusalem Post*, April 11, 2013.

5. Thus the tolerance for Louis Farrakhan's blatant anti-Semitism, homophobia, antifeminism and overall bigotry and hate by so many on the hard left.

6. Chris McGreal and Ewen MacAskill, "Israel Should Be Wiped Off Map, Says Iran's President," *The Guardian*, October 26, 2005, https://www.theguardian.com/world/2005/oct/27/israel.iran.

7. Jonathan Easley, "GOP Lawmaker Warns Iran Must Be Stopped, Israel Is 'One-Bomb Country,'" *The Hill*, February 3, 2016, https://thehill.com/policy/defense/204311-gop-lawmaker-warns-israel-is-a-one-bomb-country.

8. Dershowitz, *The Case Against the Iran Deal*, 2.

9. John Bresnahan and Andrew Restuccia, "Israel, Anti-Semitism and 2020 Fight on Display as AIPAC Gathers," *Politico*, March 22, 2019, https://www.politico.com/story/2019/03/21/israel-anti-semitism-aipac-2020-1231570.

Index